THE
Ultimate
SLOW COOKER
COOKBOOK

600 Foolproof and Easy Slow Cooker Recipes for Beginners and Advanced Users

TERESA JONES

Disclaimer Notice:
Please note the information contained within this document is for educational and entertainment purposes only. All effort has been executed to present accurate, up to date, reliable, complete information. No warranties of any kind are declared or implied. Readers acknowledge that the author is not engaged in the rendering of legal, financial, medical or professional advice. The content within this book has been derived from various sources. Please consult a licensed professional before attempting any techniques outlined in this book.
By reading this document, the reader agrees that under no circumstances is the author responsible for any losses, direct or indirect, that are incurred as a result of the use of the information contained within this document, including, but not limited to, errors, omissions, or inaccuracies.

Table of Content

Chapter 5 Classic Comfort Foods ·············45

Chapter 6 Soups, Stews, and Chilies ························· 53

Chapter 7 Side Dishes ········· 72

Chapter 8 Vegetarian Mains 87

Chapter 9 Poultry ············ 98

Chapter 10 Red Meat ·········· 116

Chapter 11 Fish and Seafood 137

Chapter 12 Rice, Grains, and Beans · · · · · · · · · · · · · · · · 156

Appendix 1: Measurement Conversion Chart

Reference

Introduction

The ultimate slow cooker companion recipes are here, and you need them! This easy-to-follow cookbook contains 600 flavoursome recipes that have been created exclusively for you and your slow cooker, so, you won't have to spend time adapting conventional recipes that you enjoy making, to work with your new slow cooker. Or, if you already own a slow cooker, you will already know that there is so much more to slow cooking than casseroles and soups, so these recipes will open up a whole new world of flavour!

As its name suggests, a slow cooker will cook any food slowly, using low temperatures. How slow you wish to cook the featured dishes in this book depends on the time settings that you choose. Most slow cook recipes (normally) take between six and ten hours start to finish. The appetizing aromas that will come drifting out of your kitchen to greet you and your family as you walk through the front door will be a lovely welcome home! All you have to do is pre-heat, put your chosen ingredients into your slow cooker, switch it on, set the timer, and off you go, to get on with the other important tasks that fill your busy day.

Recipes for All Tastes and Occasions

From dips to desserts, all of the perfect slow cooker recipes that you will ever need are in here. You can plan and cook for a special event like Christmas, Thanksgiving, or a birthday party. You can create nutritious, exciting meals for everyone for the week ahead. Because there are five hundred recipes, you may never have to use the same recipe twice, unless, of course, it becomes a family favourite! The longer that food simmers, the better the flavour gets. These recipes will ensure that the meals from your slow cooker always delight your palate.

From Novice Home Cook to Master Chef

Cooking with slow cookers doesn't require too many tricky kitchen skills. Using this cook book, you can easily follow the recipes, then just turn on the cooker. Since the 1940s, slow cookers have been created in all sizes, to suit all types of users. The smaller sizes are a great back-up in the kitchen. You can prepare sauces and dips in the small cooker, while you are slow cooking a main course in the larger cooker. The smaller sized cookers are also ideal for single users, or for people who just want to prepare smaller portions. These recipes suit all sizes of slow cooker. You can simply adapt the quantities stated in the individual recipes to suit your own requirements.

Overcooking

It is possible to overcook food in your slow cooker, because some meats, particularly chicken, may become dry if they go too long without enough broth or other liquid. But, actually burning the food is virtually impossible. So, experiment with these beautiful recipes with confidence. Your result may not be absolutely perfect first time, but you will produce something delicious. Guaranteed!

Home Cooked Meals, on Wheels!

If you, and your family are into camping, or you enjoy vacationing in your RV, you can take your trusty slow cooker, and these five hundred fabulous recipes with you! What an efficient, economical and convenient way to provide the quality meals that you enjoy at home while you enjoy the open road and fresh air.

Tasty Recipes that Safely Preserve All the Nutrients

Slow cookers cook between 170 degrees to 300 degrees Fahrenheit, which kills pathogens in food. For instance, meat requires temperatures of over 140 degrees in order to safely eliminate those pathogens, so slow cooking your food is not only an excellent way to preserve the flavour and goodness of the ingredients, it ensures that food is safe to eat. If you use the "keep warm" function, this will enable the food to maintain steady temperatures, and thus prevent the formation of dangerous bacteria, which can thrive in cold food, and which makes re-heating so risky.

It's a Green Machine

Slow cookers are very energy efficient, and they consume only a low amount of electricity. Great for the environment, and great for your pocket! Modern slow cookers can function as multicookers combining several appliance functions into one, therefore, saving you even more money. No need to buy multiple single appliances. Another way that you will save money when you use your slow cooker recipe book, is by buying the cheaper cuts of meat instead of the expensive cuts. These cheaper cuts are often tastier and more nutritious than more costly prime cuts, they just require a longer cooking time. In fact, most of the ingredients used in these slow cooker recipes are often inexpensive. Perfect! Because modern slow cookers can also function as multicookers, combining several appliance functions into one, you aren't using lots of appliances when you cook; which will save you time on the washing. Win-win!

The Six Ps Guide to Perfection

When you are trying out the recipes in this book, especially if you are a novice cook or new to slow cooker use, the Six Ps will be your guide: "Prior Planning and Preparation Prevents Poor Performance!" Changing your plans at the last minute just doesn't work when you are using a slow cooker. I know that it's fun to fling open the 'fridge doors, grab a few random items, and whip up something fast. That method is great for spontaneous "I feel like unleashing my inner chef" moments, and it's fine when you need to eat in a hurry, but it doesn't work with the slow cooker method. So, it's best to check out a recipe in this book that appeals to you, then ensure that you have everything to hand that you will need to get your meal started. Working in this manner may take some getting used to, but, trust me, all the best chefs are always prepared. They make throwing together a fabulous meal look easy, because they have stocked up, done their homework and honed their skills. Practise makes perfect! Using this cook book and your slow cooker means that you will need to know what you are going to cook well in advance of dinner, perhaps even early in the morning. You will have to prepare your ingredients and, if necessary, de-frosted your meat. I like to cook a day ahead anyway, especially when I know I will have a busy work schedule coming up. This book, and this method, works for me, and it will work for you too. It makes serving up really good food, meal after meal, so much easier.

Retire the Can Opener

Many home cooks find that the texture of canned food, particularly vegetables, cooked in a slow cooker is not appetizing. Fresh produce has the structural integrity to be tenderized while slow cooking, so it doesn't turn into mush. So, it's best not to used canned vegetables in recipes as substitutes, especially when the recipe calls for fresh. Frozen produce works, but remember that as it thaws it may make the meal somewhat watery. Stick to fresh. It's best on many levels.

Combining Ingredients

If you combine vegetables and meats in the slow cooker, you may notice that the vegetables (especially potatoes) take longer to cook than the meat. Don't stress, a little extra cooking time won't destroy the quality of the meat at all. If you are concerned, however, you can either precook the vegetables slightly, or put them into the slow cooker well before you add the meat. Chopping them finer helps, as well. The combinations in the recipes in this book are matched beautifully, to give you great results every time.

Nutrients

Because vegetables are sitting in the slow cooker for extended periods of time, they might lose a tiny amount of their nutritional value. But, don't be concerned about this phenomenon, the vitamins and minerals are still present in the broths and sauces of the finished dishes, and, of course, that super-intensified flavour is always a bonus.

Cooking Beans

Raw, dried beans, particularly red kidney beans, contain a toxin called phytohemagglutinin. So, when you are cooking with beans, it is super-important that they are cooked thoroughly, at very high temperatures, before you eat them. This critical rule applies to conventional cooking methods too.

A slow cooker does not get hot enough to destroy the phytohemagglutinin toxin, so, all beans must be boiled before they go into the pot. You can simply use canned or bottled, pre-cooked beans. And this is what I do. It's always more convenient, and it is completely safe.

Tips and Tricks to Use Slow Cooker Successfully

•Pre-heating Your Slow Cooker before you throw in the ingredients will prevent finished food from becoming sloppy. Meat and vegetables will retain their integrity so much better if you simply preheat the pot for twenty minutes before you throw everything in. This step is commonly overlooked, but it's a free tip from an expert. You'll thank me later! Turn pre-heating into a habit.

•Before you get started, let meat come to room temperature before browning and adding any other ingredients. Do this, and the slow cooked meat recipes from this book will always be tender. The natural juices of the meats will distribute more evenly, and, because caramelization is the key to intensifying flavour, your culinary creations will taste even more amazing.

•Only cook with wine that you would want to drink. This makes sense, right? Never, ever use turned or corked wine. Each and every ingredient that you use should be at its best. A long cooking process is not going to make up for bad products. It's like baking a beautiful cake, and using cheap chocolate. It defeats the purpose of the recipe and ultimately detracts from the finished creation.

•The High setting on your slow cooker is for when you want to heat things up. It's best not to cook an entire recipe on "high" for best results. If you want your vegetables to stay whole, please don't be tempted to crank up your slow cooker on the high setting for twelve hours! This works okay with tough-skinned vegetables like squash, but it will obliterate zucchini, peppers, and other soft foods that contain a lot of water.

•Disaster! Did you accidentally add too much liquid? Don't panic! Just transfer the extra juice to a saucepan and reduce it over a medium heat. You can use it later as a sauce or glaze.

•Cooking a day in advance is not only a great time-saver; some recipes will actually taste better on the second day. Here's a little-known fact: in restaurants, the soup of the day is often the soup of yesterday! Many soups, and stews, simply taste better on the second day because the flavours have had more time to develop. Lots of meat dishes will not only taste better the day after they've been made, they'll be even more tender.

•Add dairy products towards the end of the cooking time. Milk, cream, and other dairy items can break down and coagulate if they become overheated. Stir dairy ingredients into the slow cooker in the last 15-30 minutes of cooking, so they have just enough time to heat through without separating.

•Don't keep peeking and stirring! Stop it! Did you know that every time the lid of your slow cooker is opened, the heat escapes, and it takes approximately 20-30 minutes for the slow cooker to come back up to the set temperature? Open the lid as little as possible while cooking. These recipes are specifically designed to be cooked in a slow cooker, so they won't turn out the way they are supposed to if you peek or meddle in the process. Leave it alone. Let your slow cooker do its job.

Now, Let's Get Cooking

Aprons at the ready, let's go! Make some time to try out these recipes this weekend. Sit down, open the book, and find one that really sparks your imagination. It's good to kick off with a dish that you know and love, because you will have a good idea of how it should look and taste. Leave the experiments until you have got the hang of your slow cooker, if this is the first time you have used one. But, even if you are a slow cooker afficionado, it's good to try out something familiar when you are working with a new book. As you cook your way through the recipes (there are five hundred, this might take a while!) it might be fun to make some notes, so that you can tweak and personalize the dishes, or simply rate your results.

The most important aspect of preparing these recipes in your slow cooker is the fun! Cooking is meant to be relaxing and creative, whatever method you use, whatever style of food you enjoy most. So, dust off your chef's hat, sharpen your knives, tie on that apron, and go for it. Just remember: take it slow!

4

Chapter 1 Breakfasts and Brunches

Coconut Almond Granola

Prep time: 5 minutes | Cook time: 5½ to 7½ hours | Makes about 12 cups

Wet Ingredients:
½ cup honey
1 cup canola oil or sunflower seed oil
2 teaspoons pure vanilla extract
1 teaspoon pure almond extract

Dry Ingredients:
6 cups old-fashioned rolled oats
1 cup raw sunflower seeds
1 cup unsweetened shredded coconut
1 cup slivered blanched almonds
1 cup raw wheat germ
1 cup instant nonfat dry milk
½ cup firmly packed light brown sugar

1.Place the wet ingredients in a slow cooker and set it on high. Warm the mixture, uncovered, for 30 minutes to melt the honey, stirring with a whisk to combine well.
2.In a large bowl, combine all the dry ingredients and stir to evenly distribute. Add one-third of the dry ingredients to the warm mixture and stir until evenly moistened with a spatula or wooden spoon. Slowly add the remaining dry ingredients, stirring constantly so that all of it is evenly moistened. Continue to cook on high, uncovered, for exactly 1½ hours, stirring every 30 minutes for even toasting.
3.Turn the cooker to low, cover, and cook the granola until dry and a very light golden color, 4 to 6 hours, stirring every hour or so for even cooking. When done, the granola will slide off a spatula or spoon.
4.Turn off the cooker, remove the lid, and let the granola cool completely at room temperature (it will become crispier as it cools). Serve immediately.

Easy Boston Brown Bread

Prep time: 5 minutes | Cook time: 3 to 4 hours | Serves 6 to 8

¾ cup rye flour
¾ cup whole-wheat flour
¾ cup fine white cornmeal
1¾ teaspoons baking soda
½ teaspoon baking powder
1 teaspoon salt
1⅔ cups buttermilk
½ cup molasses
3 tablespoons butter, melted
¾ cup raisins
2 cups boiling water
Vegetable oil spray

1.Fold four 12 by 8-inch pieces of aluminum foil in half twice to yield rectangles that measure 6 by 4 inches and grease 1 side with vegetable oil spray. Coat inside of four 15-ounce / 425-g cans with oil spray.
2.Whisk rye flour, whole-wheat flour, cornmeal, baking soda, baking powder, and salt together in a large bowl. Whisk buttermilk, molasses, and melted butter together in a second bowl. Stir raisins into buttermilk mixture. Add buttermilk mixture to flour mixture and stir until combined and no dry flour remains. Divide batter evenly among prepared cans and smooth top with back of greased spoon. Wrap tops of cans tightly with prepared foil, greased side facing batter.
3.Line bottom of a slow cooker with parchment paper. Fill the slow cooker with ½ inch boiling water (about 2 cups water) and set cans in the slow cooker. Cover and cook until skewer inserted in the center of loaves comes out clean, 3 to 4 hours on high.
4.Using tongs and sturdy spatula, transfer cans to a wire rack and let cool, uncovered, for 20 minutes. Invert cans and slide loaves onto the rack and let cool completely, about 1 hour. Slice and serve. (Bread can be wrapped tightly in plastic wrap and stored at room temperature for up to 3 days.)

Tofu Shakshuka with Spinach

Prep time: 15 minutes | Cook time: 4 to 5 hours | Serves 6

Shakshuka:

3 tablespoons extra-virgin olive oil
1 large white or red onion, diced
4 cloves garlic, peeled and left whole
2 (28-ounce / 794-g) cans whole plum tomatoes, with their juice
1 (15-ounce / 425-g) can tomato sauce
1 large red bell pepper, deseeded and chopped
1 carrot, grated
½ jalapeño, seeded
2 teaspoons honey
1 teaspoon cracked pepper flakes, such as Aleppo, or a few shakes of hot sauce
½ teaspoon smoked or sweet paprika
½ teaspoon ground turmeric
6 fresh basil leaves, chopped (optional)
Sea salt and freshly ground black pepper, to taste
1 tablespoon unsalted butter
2 (14-ounce / 397-g) packages firm tofu, drained, rinsed, and cut into large cubes
2 cups baby spinach leaves
4 ounces (113 g) feta cheese, cut into small cubes (optional)
2 to 3 tablespoons chopped fresh flat-leaf parsley or cilantro leaves

Yogurt-Tahini Sauce:

½ cup tahini, well stirred
⅓ cup warm water
⅓ cup plain Greek yogurt
¼ cup lemon juice
2 teaspoons ginger juice (grated and squeezed fresh ginger)
Pinch of sea salt

1. In a medium-size skillet, heat the olive oil over medium heat and cook the onion until soft, about 5 minutes. Add the garlic and cook for 1 minute. Transfer the onion and garlic to the slow cooker, along with the tomatoes with their juice (crush the tomatoes with your hands as they go in), tomato sauce, bell pepper, carrot, jalapeño, honey, pepper flakes, paprika, and turmeric. Cover and cook on high for 3 to 4 hours. Add the basil, if using, season to taste with salt and pepper, and add the butter. Use a handheld immersion blender to purée the sauce, you can leave it a bit chunky.

2. While the sauce is cooking, make the yogurt-tahini sauce. Combine all the ingredients in a small bowl and stir well, or pulse in a small food processor until smooth. Cover and refrigerate until ready to serve.

3. Add the tofu cubes to the slow cooker and push them down into the sauce. Add the spinach leaves and stir to collapse them into the hot sauce. Cover and cook on high for 1 hour. Stir in the feta cubes (if using) and sprinkle the parsley or cilantro over the top. Serve the shakshuka in bowls and drizzle with the yogurt-tahini sauce.

Asparagus-Zucchini Frittata

Prep time: 10 minutes | Cook time: 1 hour | Serves 6

3 tablespoons olive oil
2 medium-size shallots, chopped
8 ounces (227 g) asparagus, trimmed and cut into 2-inch pieces on the diagonal
1 medium-size zucchini, sliced ½ inch thick
Nonstick cooking spray
12 large eggs
1 cup grated Parmesan cheese
¼ cup chopped fresh basil or flat-leaf parsley leaves
Sea salt and freshly ground black pepper, to taste

1. In a medium-size skillet, heat the oil over medium-high heat and add the shallots, asparagus, and zucchini. Cook for a few minutes, just so the asparagus begins to be tender and the zucchini browns a bit.

2. Remove from the heat and set aside to cool for 10 minutes.

3. Coat the bottom and 2 inches up the sides of the slow cooker with nonstick cooking spray. Transfer the cooled vegetables to the slow cooker.

4. In a medium-size bowl, whisk together the eggs, Parmesan, and basil. Add some salt and pinch of black pepper. Pour into the slow cooker and stir to mix with the vegetables. Cover and cook on high for 60 to 70 minutes, until the frittata is set and the tip of a knife inserted into the center comes out clean. Do not overcook or else the eggs will become too firm. Cut into 4 sections and lift out with a spatula to plates. Serve immediately.

Cheesy Bacon and Egg Hash

Prep time: 10 minutes | Cook time: 3 to 4 hours | Serves 8 to 10

8 slices thick-cut bacon
2 tablespoons olive oil (if necessary)
8 ounces (227 g) sliced white or cremini mushrooms
Nonstick cooking spray
1 (24- to 30-ounce / 680- to 850-g) bag frozen plain shredded hash brown potatoes, partially thawed
8 ounces (227 g) shredded Cheddar cheese
4 ounces (113 g) shredded or sliced Mozzarella or Monterey Jack cheese
½ cup grated or shredded Parmesan cheese
1 bunch green onions (white part and some of the green), thinly sliced
12 large eggs or 2 large eggs plus 14 large egg whites
1 cup half-and-half
⅓ cup sour cream
3 tablespoons Dijon mustard
¼ teaspoon sea salt
10 grinds freshly ground black or white pepper
Hot sauce, for serving

1. Cook the bacon in a large skillet over medium heat until crisp, about 4 minutes. Remove from the skillet and drain on paper towels. Pour off all but 2 tablespoons of the bacon fat. (Or, if not using bacon, add the olive oil to the skillet.) Add the mushrooms to the skillet and cook until soft, about 4 minutes.
2. Coat the slow cooker with nonstick cooking spray. Using your fingers, layer the hash browns in the bottom and about 1 inch up the sides of the slow cooker. Crumble the bacon and sprinkle it over the hash browns (or overlap Canadian bacon or prosciutto slices), then add the mushrooms, the cheeses, and half of the green onions (reserve the rest of the green onion for garnish).
3. In a medium-size bowl, whisk together the eggs, half-and-half, sour cream, mustard, salt, and pepper and slowly pour the mixture into the slow cooker. Cover and cook on high for 3 to 4 hours, until the eggs are set and a bit brown around the edges. Sprinkle the remaining green onions over the top and remove portions with a nonstick spatula. Serve immediately, with or without hot sauce.

Potato and Beet Hash with Eggs

Prep time: 15 minutes | Cook time: 3½ to 4½ hours | Serves 6

½ onion, finely chopped
2 garlic cloves, minced
1 tablespoon vegetable oil
2 teaspoons minced fresh thyme or ½ teaspoon dried
1 teaspoon paprika
Salt and pepper, to taste
2 pounds (907 g) russet potatoes, peeled and cut into ½-inch pieces
12 ounces (340 g) beets, peeled and cut into ½-inch pieces
½ cup vegetable or chicken broth
¼ cup heavy cream
6 large eggs
2 scallions, thinly sliced
Vegetable oil spray
Hot sauce, for serving

1. Line slow cooker with aluminum foil collar and lightly coat with vegetable oil spray.
2. Microwave onion, garlic, oil, thyme, paprika, and 1 teaspoon of salt in a large bowl, stirring occasionally, until onion is softened, about 3 minutes. Add potatoes and beets and toss to combine, then transfer to prepared slow cooker. Pour broth over vegetables, cover, and cook until vegetables are tender, 3 to 4 hours on high.
3. Discard foil collar. Transfer 2 cups of vegetables to a medium bowl. Add cream and mash with potato masher until smooth. Fold mashed vegetable mixture into remaining vegetables in the slow cooker, then smooth into an even layer.
4. Using back of the spoon, make 6 indentations (about 2½ inches wide) into hash. Crack 1 egg into each indentation and season with salt and pepper. Cover and cook on high until egg whites are just beginning to set but still have some movement when the slow cooker is gently shaken, 20 to 30 minutes.
5. Turn off slow cooker and let eggs sit, covered, for 5 minutes. Sprinkle with scallions and serve with hot sauce.

Ricotta and Spinach Egg Bake

Prep time: 15 minutes | Cook time: 2 to 3 hours | Serves 4

1 onion, finely chopped
1 tablespoon extra-virgin olive oil
3 garlic cloves, minced
10 ounces (283 g) whole-milk ricotta cheese
8 ounces (227 g) frozen chopped spinach, thawed and squeezed dry
4 ounces (113 g) fontina cheese, shredded
4 large eggs, lightly beaten
¼ teaspoon salt
¼ teaspoon pepper
2 plum tomatoes, cored and sliced crosswise ¼ inch thick

1. Microwave onion, oil, and garlic in a large bowl, stirring occasionally, until onion is softened, about 5 minutes. Stir in ricotta, spinach, fontina, eggs, salt, and pepper until well combined. Divide mixture evenly among four greased ramekins and scatter tomatoes over top.
2. Fill a slow cooker with ½ inch boiling water (about 2 cups water) and set ramekins in the slow cooker. Cover and cook until the eggs are set, 2 to 3 hours on low. Using tongs and sturdy spatula, remove ramekins from slow cooker and let cool for 15 minutes before serving.

Slow-Cooker Huevos Rancheros

Prep time: 10 minutes | Cook time: 3½ to 4½ hours | Serves 6

1 onion, chopped
¼ cup extra-virgin olive oil
3 tablespoons chili powder
4 garlic cloves, minced
Salt and pepper, to taste
2 (28-ounce / 794-g) cans fire-roasted diced tomatoes, drained
½ cup canned chopped green chiles
1 tablespoon packed brown sugar
1 tablespoon lime juice
4 ounces (113 g) Pepper Jack cheese, shredded
6 large eggs
½ cup fresh cilantro leaves
3 scallions, thinly sliced
Vegetable oil spray

1. Line slow cooker with aluminum foil collar and lightly coat with vegetable oil spray.
2. Microwave onion, oil, chili powder, garlic, and ½ teaspoon of salt in a bowl, stirring occasionally, until onion is softened, about 5 minutes. Transfer to prepared slow cooker. Stir in tomatoes, green chiles, sugar, and lime juice. Cover and cook until tomato mixture is deeply flavored, 3 to 4 hours on high.
3. Discard foil collar. Smooth tomato mixture into an even layer and sprinkle evenly with cheese. Using back of the spoon, make 6 indentations (about 2½ inches wide) into tomato mixture. Crack 1 egg into each indentation and season with salt and pepper. Cover and cook on high until egg whites are just beginning to set but still have some movement when the slow cooker is gently shaken, 20 to 30 minutes.
4. Turn off slow cooker and let eggs sit, covered, for 5 minutes. Sprinkle with cilantro and scallions. Serve immediately.

Cheese and Ham Breakfast Soufflé

Prep time: 10 minutes | Cook time: 3 to 4 hours | Serves 6

8 slices bread (crusts removed), cubed or torn into squares
2 cups shredded Cheddar, Swiss, or American cheese
1 cup cooked, chopped ham
4 eggs
1 cup light cream or milk
1 cup evaporated milk
¼ teaspoon salt
1 tablespoon parsley
Paprika, to taste
Nonstick cooking spray

1. Lightly grease a slow cooker with nonstick cooking spray. Alternate layers of bread and cheese and ham.
2. Beat together eggs, milk, salt, and parsley in a bowl.
3. Pour over bread in a slow cooker and sprinkle with paprika.
4. Cover and cook on low for 3 to 4 hours. (The longer cooking time yields a firmer, dryer dish.)
5. Serve warm.

Irish Steel Cut Oatmeal

Prep time: 5 minutes | Cook time: 3 to 4 hours | Serves 8

2 tablespoons unsalted butter
2 cups steel-cut oats
8 cups water
1 teaspoon salt

1. Melt butter in a skillet over medium heat. Add oats and toast, stirring constantly, until golden and fragrant, about 2 minutes. Transfer to a slow cooker.
2. Stir water and salt into a slow cooker. Cover and cook until oats are softened and thickened, 3 to 4 hours on high. Stir oatmeal to recombine. Turn off slow cooker and let oatmeal sit for 10 minutes. Serve. (Oatmeal can be refrigerated for up to 4 days. Reheat oatmeal in microwave or in saucepan over medium-low heat; stir often and adjust consistency with hot water as needed.)

Potato and Prosciutto Breakfast Strata

Prep time: 10 minutes | Cook time: 8 hours | Serves 2

1 teaspoon butter, at room temperature, or extra-virgin olive oil
4 eggs
½ cup 2% milk
1 tablespoon minced fresh rosemary
⅛ teaspoon sea salt
Freshly ground black pepper, to taste
2 medium russet potatoes, peeled and thinly sliced
2 ounces (57 g) prosciutto

1. Grease the inside of the slow cooker with the butter.
2. In a small bowl, whisk together the eggs, milk, rosemary, salt, and a few grinds of the black pepper.
3. Layer one-third of the potatoes in the bottom of the slow cooker and top that layer with one-third of the prosciutto. Pour one-third of the egg mixture over the prosciutto. Repeat this layering with the remaining ingredients.
4. Cover and cook on low for 8 hours or overnight. Serve warm.

Western Omelet Bake

Prep time: 15 minutes | Cook time: 8 to 9 hours | Serves 10

1 (32-ounce / 907-g) bag frozen hash brown potatoes
1 pound (454 g) cooked ham, cubed
1 medium onion, diced
1½ cups shredded Cheddar cheese
12 eggs
1 cup milk
1 teaspoon salt
1 teaspoon pepper

1. Layer one-third each of frozen potatoes, ham, onion, and cheese in the bottom of the slow cooker. Repeat 2 times.
2. Beat together eggs, milk, salt, and pepper in a bowl.
3. Pour over mixture in a slow cooker. Cover and cook on low for 8 to 9 hours.
4. Serve with orange juice and fresh fruit, if desired.

Creamy Cheese Grits

Prep time: 5 minutes | Cook time: 2 to 3 hours | Serves 6

3 cups water, plus extra as needed
1 cup whole milk
1 cup old-fashioned grits
Salt and pepper, to taste
8 ounces (227 g) sharp Cheddar cheese, shredded
4 tablespoons butter, softened
4 scallions, thinly sliced
½ teaspoon hot sauce
Vegetable oil spray

1. Lightly coat slow cooker with vegetable oil spray. Whisk water, milk, grits, and 1 teaspoon of salt together in prepared slow cooker. Cover and cook until grits are tender, 2 to 3 hours on high.
2. Whisk Cheddar, butter, scallions, and hot sauce into grits until combined. Season with salt and pepper to taste. Serve. (Grits can be held on warm or low setting for up to 2 hours; adjust consistency with hot water as needed before serving.)

Basic Oatmeal

Prep time: 5 minutes | Cook time: 6 hours | Serves 4

1⅓ cups dry old-fashioned rolled oats
2½ cups plus 1 tablespoon water
Dash of salt

1. Mix together cereal, water, and salt in a slow cooker. Cook on low for 6 hours.
2. Stir and serve.

Fish Congee

Prep time: 10 minutes | Cook time: 4⅓ hours | Serves 6

1½ cups long-grain white rice
1 (1-inch) piece fresh ginger, peeled and grated
3 quarts boiling water
12 ounces (340 g) firm white fish fillets, such as flounder or cod, skin removed, thinly sliced
Coarse salt, to taste
Sliced scallions, for serving

1. Place the rice and ginger into the slow cooker. Add the boiling water and stir. Cover and cook on low until congee reaches consistency of loose porridge, about 4 hours (or on high for 2 hours).
2. Add fish and cook on low until fish falls apart, about 20 minutes more (or on high for 10 minutes). Season to taste with salt and serve with the sliced scallions.

Almond and Date Oatmeal

Prep time: 5 minutes | Cook time: 4 to 6 hours | Serves 8

2 cups dry rolled oats
½ cup dry Grape-Nuts cereal
½ cup slivered almonds
¼ cup chopped dates
4 cups water

1. Combine all ingredients in a slow cooker. Cook on low for 4 to 6 hours.
2. Serve with fat-free milk, if desired.

Cheesy Baked Eggs

Prep time: 10 minutes | Cook time: 4 to 6 hours | Serves 6

3 cups toasted bread cubes
1½ cups shredded cheese
Fried, crumbled bacon or ham chunks (optional)
6 eggs, beaten
3 cups milk
¾ teaspoon salt
¼ teaspoon pepper

1. Combine bread cubes, cheese, and meat (if desired) in a greased slow cooker.
2. Mix together eggs, milk, salt, and pepper in a bowl. Pour over bread and cook on low for 4 to 6 hours.
3. Let cool for 5 minutes before serving.

Sweet Potato and Corn Scramble

Prep time: 10 minutes | Cook time: 8 hours | Serves 2

1 teaspoon butter, at room temperature, or extra-virgin olive oil
4 eggs
½ cup 2% milk
⅛ teaspoon sea salt
½ teaspoon smoked paprika
½ teaspoon ground cumin
Freshly ground black pepper, to taste
1 cup finely diced sweet potato
1 cup frozen corn kernels, thawed
½ cup diced roasted red peppers
2 tablespoons minced onion

1. Grease the inside of the slow cooker with the butter.
2. In a small bowl, whisk together the eggs, milk, salt, paprika, and cumin. Season with the freshly ground black pepper.
3. Put the sweet potato, corn, red peppers, and onion into the slow cooker. Pour in the egg mixture and stir gently.
4. Cover and cook on low for 8 hours or overnight. Serve warm.

Mango Yogurt with Honey and Cardamon

Prep time: 5 minutes | Cook time: 2 hours | Serves 4

4 cups 2% milk
¼ cup plain yogurt
2 mangoes, cut into chunks
1 tablespoon honey
¼ teaspoon ground cardamom

1. Pour the milk into the slow cooker. Cover and cook on low for 2 hours.
2. Turn off the slow cooker and stir in the yogurt. Cover with the lid and wrap the outside of the slow cooker housing with a bath towel to help insulate it. Allow it to rest for 8 hours or overnight.
3. For a thick yogurt, strain the mixture in a medium bowl through a few layers of cheesecloth for 10 to 15 minutes. Discard the whey remaining in the cheesecloth or save it for making smoothies.
4. To serve, stir in the mango chunks, honey, and cardamom.

Maple Cranberry Granola

Prep time: 5 minutes | Cook time: 5½ to 7½ hours | Makes about 10 cups

Wet Ingredients:
¾ cup pure maple syrup
½ cup water
¼ cup firmly packed light brown sugar
¼ cup canola oil or sunflower seed oil
Dry Ingredients:
6 cups old-fashioned rolled oats
1 cup raw sunflower seeds
½ cup raw pumpkin seeds
½ cup raw oat bran

1 cup honey-toasted wheat germ
1½ cups sweetened dried cranberries
½ cup chopped dried apricots
3 tablespoons raw sesame seeds

1. Put the wet ingredients in a slow cooker and set on high. Stir with a whisk to combine well.
2. In a large bowl, combine all the dry ingredients and stir to evenly distribute. Add one-third of the dry ingredients to the warm mixture, stirring until evenly moistened with a spatula or wooden spoon. slowly add the remaining dry ingredients, stirring constantly so that all of it is evenly moistened. Continue to cook on high, uncovered, for exactly 1½ hours, stirring every 30 minutes.
3. Turn the cooker to low, cover, and cook until the granola is dry and a very light golden color, 4 to 6 hours, stirring every hour or so for even cooking. When done, it will slide off a spatula or spoon.
4. While the granola is hot, stir in the wheat germ, dried cranberries, apricots, and sesame seeds. Let cool completely (the mixture will become crispier as it cools). Serve immediately.

Slow-Cooker Egg Casserole with Chorizo

Prep time: 15 minutes | Cook time: 4 to 4½ hours | Serves 8

1 pound (454 g) fresh chorizo or bulk spicy pork sausage
1 medium onion, chopped
1 medium sweet red pepper, chopped
2 jalapeño peppers, deseeded and chopped
1 (30-ounce / 850-g) package frozen shredded hash brown potatoes, thawed
1½ cups shredded Mexican cheese blend
12 large eggs
1 cup 2% milk
½ teaspoon pepper
Chopped avocado, minced fresh cilantro, and lime wedges (optional)

1. In a large skillet, cook chorizo, onion, red pepper, and jalapeños over medium heat until cooked through and vegetables are tender, 7 to 8 minutes, breaking chorizo into crumbles. Drain and let cool slightly.
2. In a greased slow cooker, layer a third of the potatoes, chorizo mixture and cheese blend. Repeat layers twice. In a large bowl, whisk the eggs, milk, and pepper until blended, then pour over top.
3. Cook on low, covered, for 4 to 4½ hours or until the eggs are set and a thermometer reads 160°F (71°C). Uncover and let stand for 10 minutes before serving. If desired, top servings with avocado, cilantro, and lime wedges.

Ham Egg Cheese Casserole

Prep time: 15 minutes | Cook time: 3 to 4 hours | Serves 6

6 large eggs
1 cup biscuit mix
⅔ cup 2% milk
⅓ cup sour cream
2 tablespoons minced fresh parsley
2 garlic cloves, minced
½ teaspoon salt
½ teaspoon pepper
1 cup cubed fully cooked ham
1 cup shredded Swiss cheese
1 small onion, finely chopped
⅓ cup shredded Parmesan cheese

1.In a large bowl, whisk the first eight ingredients until blended. Stir in remaining ingredients. Pour into a greased slow cooker.
2.Cook on low, covered, for 3 to 4 hours or until eggs are set. Cut into wedges and serve.

Cheesy Grits with Collard Greens

Prep time: 10 minutes | Cook time: 3 hours | Serves 8

2 cups white hominy grits (not quick-cooking)
4½ cups hot water, divided
4 cups milk
Coarse salt, to taste
4 ounces (113 g) cotija or feta cheese, crumbled
2 tablespoons extra-virgin olive oil
1 small onion, thinly sliced
6 garlic cloves, thinly sliced
¼ teaspoon red pepper flakes
1 bunch collard greens (about 1 pound / 454 g), tough stems and ribs removed, leaves coarsely chopped
Fried eggs, for serving
Hot sauce, for serving

1.Stir to combine grits with 4 cups of hot water, milk, and 2 teaspoons of salt in the slow cooker. Cover and cook, stirring occasionally, on high until grits are creamy, 3 hours (or on low for 6 hours). Stir in cheese and season with salt.
2.Meanwhile, heat oil in a large skillet over medium heat. Add onion and cook until translucent, about 3 minutes. Add garlic and cook, stirring often, until golden, about 3 minutes. Stir in red pepper flakes and cook until fragrant, about 30 seconds.
3.Stir in collard greens and 1 teaspoon of salt. Reduce heat to medium-low. Add remaining ½ cup of hot water, cover, and steam until greens are just tender and water evaporates, about 10 minutes. (If greens are ready but there is still water in the pan, raise heat to medium-high, and cook, uncovered, until completely evaporated.)
4.Serve grits with greens, fried eggs, and hot sauce.

Sausage Hash Brown Breakfast Casserole

Prep time: 15 minutes | Cook time: 3 hours | Serves 6 to 8

2 tablespoons unsalted butter
2 tablespoons all-purpose flour
¾ cup low-sodium chicken broth
½ cup milk
Coarse salt and freshly ground pepper, to taste
1 pound (454 g) sweet Italian sausage, casings removed
3 sweet peppers, such as Cubanelle, thinly sliced
2 pounds (907 g) russet potatoes, peeled and grated
1 cup grated Cheddar cheese
6 scallions, finely chopped
Fried eggs, for serving
Chopped fresh chives, for garnish

1.Melt butter in a saucepan over medium heat. Whisk in flour and cook for about 1 minute. Add broth and milk and bring to a boil, whisking constantly. Remove from heat and season with salt and pepper. Transfer sauce to a bowl.
2.Heat the saucepan over medium-high heat. Add sausage and cook, breaking up meat with a spoon, until browned, about 5 minutes. Add peppers and continue to cook until peppers are soft, about 5 minutes. Season with salt and pepper. Transfer to a slow cooker, spreading into an even layer.
3.Add potatoes, cheese, and scallions to milk mixture and mix well. Transfer to slow cooker and spread into an even layer. Cover and cook on high until hot and bubbly, about 3 hours (or on low for 6 hours). Serve warm, with fried eggs and topped with chives.

Green Chili Cheddar Crustless Quiche

Prep time: 15 minutes | Cook time: 3 to 4 hours | Serves 6

3 corn tortillas
2 (4-ounce / 113-g) cans whole green chilies
1 (15-ounce / 425-g) can chili con carne
1½ cups shredded Cheddar cheese, divided
4 large eggs
1½ cups 2% milk
1 cup biscuit mix
¼ teaspoon salt
¼ teaspoon pepper
1 teaspoon hot pepper sauce (optional)
1 (4-ounce / 113-g) can chopped green chilies
2 medium tomatoes, sliced
Sour cream (optional)

1. In a greased slow cooker, layer tortillas, whole green chilies, chili con carne and 1 cup of cheese.
2. In a small bowl, whisk the eggs, milk, biscuit mix, salt, pepper, and hot pepper sauce (if desired) until blended, then pour into a slow cooker. Top with chopped green chilies and tomatoes.
3. Cook on low, covered, for 3 to 4 hours or until a thermometer reads 160ºF (71ºC), sprinkling with remaining ½ cup of cheese during the last 30 minutes of cooking.
4. Turn off slow cooker and let stand for 15 minutes before serving. If desired, top with sour cream.

Sausage and Waffle Breakfast Bake

Prep time: 10 minutes | Cook time: 5 to 6 hours | Serves 12

2 pounds (907 g) bulk spicy breakfast pork sausage
1 tablespoon rubbed sage
½ teaspoon fennel seed
1 (12.3-ounce / 349-g) package frozen waffles, cut into bite-sized pieces
8 large eggs
1¼ cups half-and-half
¼ cup maple syrup, plus additional for serving
¼ teaspoon salt
¼ teaspoon pepper
2 cups shredded Cheddar cheese
Cooking spray

1. Fold two 18-inch-long pieces of foil into two 18×4-inch strips. Line the sides around the perimeter of a slow cooker with foil strips. Spray with cooking spray.
2. In a large skillet, cook and crumble sausage over medium heat, about 4 minutes. Drain. Add the sage and fennel seed.
3. Place waffles in the slow cooker and top with sausage. In a bowl, mix eggs, half-and-half, syrup, and seasonings. Pour over the sausage and waffles. Top with cheese. Cook on low, covered, for 5 to 6 hours or until set.
4. Let stand, uncovered, for 15 minutes. Serve with additional maple syrup.

Chapter 2 Appetizers

Simple Spiced Nuts

Prep time: 5 minutes | Cook time: 2 to 3 hours | Serves 10 to 14

1 large egg white
1 tablespoon water
1 teaspoon salt
3 cups whole unblanched almonds, cashews, pecans, or walnuts
¼ cup sugar
2 teaspoons ground cinnamon
1 teaspoon ground ginger
1 teaspoon ground coriander
Vegetable oil spray

1. Lightly coat slow cooker with vegetable oil spray. Whisk egg white, water, and salt together in a large bowl. Add almonds and toss to coat, then drain thoroughly in a fine-mesh strainer.
2. Combine sugar, cinnamon, ginger, and coriander in a separate large bowl. Add almonds and toss to coat. Transfer almond mixture to prepared slow cooker, cover, and cook, stirring every 30 minutes, until almonds are toasted and fragrant, 2 to 3 hours on high.
3. Transfer almond mixture to a rimmed baking sheet and spread into an even layer. Let cool to room temperature, about 20 minutes. Serve immediately. (Almonds can be stored at room temperature for up to 1 week.)

Lemon Artichoke Hearts with Thyme

Prep time: 10 minutes | Cook time: 1 to 2 hours | Serves 8 to 10

3 cups jarred whole baby artichokes packed in water, halved, rinsed, and patted dry
1 cup extra-virgin olive oil
½ cup pitted kalamata olives, halved
3 garlic cloves, peeled and smashed
2 sprigs fresh thyme
¾ teaspoon grated lemon zest plus 2 tablespoons juice

Salt and pepper, to taste
¼ teaspoon red pepper flakes
4 ounces (113 g) feta cheese, cut into ½-inch cubes

1. Combine artichokes, oil, olives, garlic, thyme sprigs, lemon zest and juice, 1 teaspoon salt, and pepper flakes in the slow cooker. Cover and cook until heated through and flavors meld, 1 to 2 hours on low.
2. Discard thyme sprigs. Gently stir in feta and let sit until heated through, about 5 minutes. Season with salt and pepper to taste. Serve warm or at room temperature. (Marinated artichokes can be held on warm or low setting for up to 2 hours.)

Homemade Chile Con Queso

Prep time: 5 minutes | Cook time: 1 to 2 hours | Serves 8 to 10

1 cup chicken or vegetable broth
4 ounces (113 g) cream cheese
1 tablespoon cornstarch
1 tablespoon minced canned chipotle chile in adobo sauce
1 garlic clove, minced
¼ teaspoon pepper
8 ounces (227 g) Monterey Jack cheese, shredded
4 ounces (113 g) American cheese, shredded
1 (10-ounce / 283-g) can Ro-tel Diced Tomatoes & Green Chilies, drained

1. Microwave broth, cream cheese, cornstarch, chipotle, garlic, and pepper in a large bowl, whisking occasionally, until smooth and thickened, about 5 minutes. Stir in Monterey Jack and American cheeses until well combined.
2. Transfer the mixture to slow cooker, cover, and cook until cheese is melted, 1 to 2 hours on low.
3. Whisk dip until smooth, then stir in tomatoes. Serve. (Dip can be held on warm or low setting for up to 2 hours. Adjust consistency with hot water as needed, adding 2 tablespoons at a time.)

Cheesy Beer Fondue

Prep time: 5 minutes | Cook time: 1 to 2 hours | Serves 8 to 10

1 cup mild lager, such as Budweiser
4 ounces (113 g) cream cheese
1 tablespoon cornstarch
1 garlic clove, minced
1 teaspoon dry mustard
¼ teaspoon pepper
8 ounces (227 g) mild Cheddar cheese, shredded
8 ounces (227 g) American cheese, shredded

1. Microwave beer, cream cheese, cornstarch, garlic, mustard, and pepper in a large bowl, whisking occasionally, until smooth and thickened, about 5 minutes. Stir in Cheddar and American cheeses until combined.
2. Transfer the mixture to slow cooker, cover, and cook until cheese is melted, 1 to 2 hours on low.
3. Whisk fondue until smooth. Serve immediately. (Fondue can be held on warm or low setting for up to 2 hours. Adjust consistency with hot water as needed, adding 2 tablespoons at a time.)

Fig and Walnut Baked Brie

Prep time: 10 minutes | Cook time: 1 hour | Serves 8 to 10

1½ pounds (680 g) firm Brie cheese, rind removed and cut into 1-inch pieces
1 cup dried figs, stemmed and halved
1 teaspoon minced fresh thyme
¼ teaspoon pepper
2 tablespoons honey
¼ cup toasted and chopped walnuts
1 tablespoon minced fresh chives
Vegetable oil spray

1. Lightly coat slow cooker with vegetable oil spray. Combine Brie, figs, thyme, and pepper in the prepared slow cooker. Cover and cook until Brie is heated through and begins to soften around edges, about 1 hour on low.
2. Drizzle Brie with honey and sprinkle with walnuts and chives. Serve. (Brie can be held on warm or low setting for up to 2 hours.)

Barbecue Sausage Bites

Prep time: 10 minutes | Cook time: 1 to 2 hours | Serves 8 to 10

1 cup ketchup
½ cup molasses
3 tablespoons cider vinegar
3 tablespoons Dijon mustard
1 tablespoon packed brown sugar
2 teaspoons chili powder
⅛ teaspoon cayenne pepper
3 pounds (1.4 kg) kielbasa sausage, sliced on bias ½ inch thick

1. Combine ketchup, molasses, vinegar, mustard, sugar, chili powder, and cayenne in the slow cooker.
2. Stir in kielbasa, cover, and cook until heated through and flavors meld, 1 to 2 hours on low. Serve. (Kielbasa can be held on warm or low setting for up to 2 hours. Adjust sauce consistency with hot water as needed, adding 2 tablespoons at a time.)

Garlic Shrimp

Prep time: 15 minutes | Cook time: 50 minutes | Serves 8 to 10

¾ cup extra-virgin olive oil
6 garlic cloves, thinly sliced
1 teaspoon smoked paprika
1 teaspoon salt
¼ teaspoon pepper
¼ teaspoon red pepper flakes
2 pounds (907 g) large shrimp, peeled and deveined
1 tablespoon minced fresh parsley

1. Combine oil, garlic, paprika, salt, pepper, and pepper flakes in the slow cooker. Cover and cook until flavors meld, about 30 minutes on high.
2. Stir in shrimp, cover, and cook on high until opaque throughout, about 20 minutes, stirring halfway through cooking. Transfer shrimp and oil mixture to a serving dish. Sprinkle with parsley and serve.

Swedish Meatballs with Dill

Prep time: 10 minutes | Cook time: 4½ to 5½ hours | Serves 10 to 12

6 tablespoons unsalted butter, divided
2 onions, finely chopped
4 slices caraway-rye bread, crusts removed and torn into 1-inch pieces
3½ cups beef broth, divided
1 cup sour cream, divided
2 large egg yolks
½ teaspoon ground allspice
¼ teaspoon ground nutmeg
Salt and pepper, to taste
1 pound (454 g) 90% lean ground beef
1 pound (454 g) ground pork
½ cup all-purpose flour
2 tablespoons soy sauce
2 teaspoons minced fresh dill, plus extra for serving
Vegetable oil spray

1.Preheat the oven to 475ºF (245ºC). Set wire rack in aluminum foil-lined rimmed baking sheet and coat with vegetable oil spray. Set aside.
2.Melt 1 tablespoon of butter in a skillet over medium heat. Add onions and cook until softened, about 8 minutes. Transfer the onions to a large bowl. Add bread, ¼ cup of broth, ¼ cup of sour cream, egg yolks, allspice, nutmeg, ½ teaspoon salt, and ¼ teaspoon pepper and mash with fork until smooth. Add ground beef and pork and knead with hands until well combined.
3.Pinch off and roll meat mixture into tablespoon-size meatballs (about 60 meatballs) and arrange on the prepared rack. Bake in the preheated oven until lightly browned, about 15 minutes. Transfer meatballs to slow cooker.
4.Melt remaining 5 tablespoons of butter in the same skillet over medium heat. Add flour and cook, whisking often, until beginning to brown, about 3 minutes. slowly whisk in remaining 3¼ cups of broth, smoothing out any lumps, and bring to simmer, then transfer to a slow cooker. Cover and cook until meatballs are tender and sauce is slightly thickened, 4 to 5 hours on low.
5.Using a large spoon, skim excess fat from surface of sauce. Whisk ½ cup sauce, soy sauce, dill, and remaining ¾ cup of sour cream together in a small bowl (to temper), then gently stir mixture back into slow cooker. Season with salt and pepper to taste. Sprinkle with extra dill and serve. (Meatballs can be held on warm or low setting for up to 2 hours. Adjust sauce consistency with hot water as needed, adding 2 tablespoons at a time.)

Turkey Meatballs with Garlic and Pesto

Prep time: 10 minutes | Cook time: 4 to 5 hours | Serves 12 to 14

4 cups lightly packed fresh basil leaves
4 garlic cloves, minced
⅓ cup extra-virgin olive oil
2 ounces (57 g) Parmesan cheese, grated (1 cup)
1⅓ cups panko bread crumbs
2 large egg yolks
Salt and pepper, to taste
2 pounds (907 g) ground turkey
1 (28-ounce / 794-g) can crushed tomatoes
Vegetable oil spray

1.Preheat the oven to 475ºF (245ºC). Set a wire rack in aluminum foil-lined rimmed baking sheet and coat with vegetable oil spray. Set aside.
2.Process basil and garlic in a food processor until finely ground, about 30 seconds, scraping down sides of bowl as needed. With processor running, slowly add oil and process until smooth, about 30 seconds. Measure out and reserve 2 tablespoons of pesto for serving. Transfer remaining pesto to a large bowl.
3.Stir Parmesan, panko, egg yolks, ½ teaspoon salt, and ¼ teaspoon pepper into remaining pesto. Add ground turkey and knead with hands until well combined. Pinch off and roll turkey mixture into tablespoon-size meatballs (about 60 meatballs) and arrange on the prepared rack. Bake in the preheated oven until no longer pink, about 10 minutes. Transfer meatballs to slow cooker.
4.Gently stir tomatoes and ½ teaspoon salt into a slow cooker, cover, and cook until meatballs are tender, 4 to 5 hours on low.
5.Using a large spoon, skim excess fat from surface of sauce. Stir reserved pesto into meatballs and season with salt and pepper to taste. Serve. (Meatballs can be held on warm or low setting for up to 2 hours. Adjust sauce consistency with hot water as needed, adding 2 tablespoons at a time.)

Cheesy Pepperoni Pizza Dip

Prep time: 15 minutes | Cook time: 2½ hours | Makes 5 cups

4 cups shredded Cheddar cheese
4 cups shredded part-skim Mozzarella cheese
1 cup mayonnaise
1 (6-ounce / 170-g) jar sliced mushrooms, drained
2 (2¼-ounce / 64-g) cans sliced ripe olives, drained
1 (3½-ounce / 99-g) package pepperoni slices, quartered
1 tablespoon dried minced onion
Assorted crackers, for serving

1. In a slow cooker, combine the cheeses, mayonnaise, mushrooms, olives, pepperoni and onion.
2. Cover and cook for 1½ hours on low, then stir. Cover and cook for 1 hour more or until heated through. Serve with assorted crackers.

Veggie Loaded Dip

Prep time: 25 minutes | Cook time: 1 to 2 hours | Makes 5 cups

¾ cup finely chopped fresh broccoli
½ cup finely chopped cauliflower
½ cup finely chopped fresh carrot
½ cup finely chopped red onion
½ cup finely chopped celery
2 garlic cloves, minced
4 tablespoons olive oil, divided
1 (14-ounce / 397-g) can water-packed artichoke hearts, rinsed, drained and chopped
1 (6½-ounce / 184-g) package spreadable garlic and herb cream cheese
1 (1.4-ounce / 40-g) package vegetable recipe mix (Knorr)
1 teaspoon garlic powder
½ teaspoon white pepper
⅛ to ¼ teaspoon cayenne pepper
¼ cup vegetable broth
¼ cup half-and-half
3 cups (12 ounces / 340 g) shredded Italian cheese blend
½ cup minced fresh basil
1 (9-ounce / 255-g) package fresh spinach, finely chopped
Assorted crackers or baked pita chips, for serving

1. In a large skillet, sauté the broccoli, cauliflower, carrot, onion, celery and garlic in 2 tablespoons of oil until tender. Stir in the artichokes, cream cheese, vegetable recipe mix, garlic powder, white pepper, and cayenne. Set aside.
2. In a slow cooker, combine the broth, half-and-half, and remaining 2 tablespoons of oil. Stir in the broccoli mixture, Italian cheese blend, and basil. Fold in spinach. Cover and cook on low for 1 to 2 hours or until cheese is melted and spinach is tender. Serve with crackers.

Spanish Tortilla with Peas

Prep time: 15 minutes | Cook time: 3 to 4 hours | Serves 8

2 pounds (907 g) russet potatoes, peeled, quartered lengthwise, and sliced ⅛ inch thick
2 onions, finely chopped
1 red bell pepper, stemmed, deseeded, and cut into ½-inch pieces
¼ cup extra-virgin olive oil
6 garlic cloves, minced
1 tablespoon minced fresh oregano or 1 teaspoon dried
¼ teaspoon red pepper flakes
1 cup frozen peas
12 large eggs
1 teaspoon salt
½ teaspoon pepper
Vegetable oil spray

1. Line slow cooker with aluminum foil collar, then line with foil liner and lightly coat with vegetable oil spray.
2. Microwave potatoes, onions, bell pepper, oil, garlic, oregano, and pepper flakes in a large covered bowl, stirring occasionally, until potatoes are nearly tender, about 9 minutes. Stir in peas, then transfer potato mixture to prepared slow cooker.
3. Whisk eggs, salt, and pepper together in another bowl, then pour mixture evenly over potato mixture. Gently press potato mixture into egg mixture. Cover and cook until center of tortilla is just set, 3 to 4 hours on low.
4. Turn slow cooker off and let tortilla rest, covered, until fully set, about 20 minutes. Using foil liner, transfer tortilla to a serving platter and serve.

Beef and Green Olive Dip

Prep time: 15 minutes | Cook time: 3 to 4 hours | Makes 8 cups

1 pound (454 g) ground beef
1 medium sweet red pepper, chopped
1 small onion, chopped
1 (16-ounce / 454-g) can refried beans
1 (16-ounce / 454-g) jar mild salsa
2 cups (8 ounces / 227 g) shredded part-skim Mozzarella cheese
2 cups (8 ounces / 227 g) shredded Cheddar cheese
1 (5¾-ounce / 163-g) jar sliced green olives with pimientos, drained
Tortilla chips, for serving

1. In a large skillet, cook the beef, pepper and onion over medium heat until meat is no longer pink, about 6 to 8 minutes. Drain.
2. Transfer the beef mixture to a greased slow cooker. Stir in the beans, salsa, cheeses and olives. Cover and cook on low for 3 to 4 hours or until cheese is melted, stirring occasionally. Serve with chips.

Creamy Garlic Onion Dip

Prep time: 15 minutes | Cook time: 4 to 5 hours | Makes 5 cups

4 cups finely chopped sweet onions
¼ cup butter, cubed
¼ cup white wine or chicken broth
6 garlic cloves, minced
1 bay leaf
2 cups (8 ounces / 227 g) shredded Gruyere or Swiss cheese
1 (8-ounce / 227-g) package cream cheese, softened
¼ cup sour cream
Assorted crackers or breadsticks, for serving

1. In a slow cooker, combine the sweet onions, butter, wine, garlic and bay leaf. Cover and cook on low for 4 to 5 hours or until onions are tender and golden brown.
2. Discard bay leaf. Stir in the Gruyere cheese, cream cheese and sour cream. Cover and cook for 1 hour longer or until the cheese is melted. Serve warm with crackers.

Creamy Crab Dip

Prep time: 20 minutes | Cook time: 1½ to 2½ hours | Makes 2⅓ cups

1 (8-ounce / 227-g) package cream cheese, softened
2 green onions, chopped
¼ cup chopped sweet red pepper
2 tablespoons minced fresh parsley
2 tablespoons mayonnaise
1 tablespoon Dijon mustard
1 teaspoon Worcestershire sauce
¼ teaspoon salt
¼ teaspoon pepper
2 (6-ounce / 170-g) cans lump crab meat, drained
2 tablespoons capers, drained
Dash hot pepper sauce
Assorted crackers, for serving

1. In a slow cooker, combine the first nine ingredients. Add crab and stir well.
2. Cover and cook on low for 1 to 2 hours. Stir in capers and pepper sauce and cook for 30 minutes longer to allow the flavors to blend. Serve with crackers.

Creamy Beef and Cheese Dip

Prep time: 15 minutes | Cook time: 2 hours | Makes about 6 cups

1 pound (454 g) ground beef
1 onion, chopped
1 (2-pound / 907-g) box Velveeta cheese, cubed
1 (10¾-ounce / 305-g) can cream of mushroom soup
1 (14½-ounce / 411-g) can diced tomatoes with green chilies

1. Brown beef and onion in a skillet over medium heat, about 6 to 8 minutes. Drain meat mixture and place in a slow cooker.
2. Add all remaining ingredients into a slow cooker and combine.
3. Cover and cook on low for 2 hours, or until cheese is melted, stirring occasionally.
4. Serve over baked potatoes or with tortilla chips, if desired.

Glazed Hawaiian Kielbasa Bites

Prep time: 15 minutes | Cook time: 2½ to 3½ hours | Serves 12

2 pounds (907 g) smoked kielbasa or Polish sausage, cut into 1-inch pieces
1 (20-ounce / 567-g) can unsweetened pineapple chunks, undrained
½ cup ketchup
2 tablespoons brown sugar
2 tablespoons yellow mustard
1 tablespoon cider vinegar
¾ cup lemon-lime soda
2 tablespoons cornstarch
2 tablespoons cold water

1. Place sausage in a slow cooker. Drain pineapple, reserving ¾ cup juice; set pineapple aside. In a small bowl, whisk the ketchup, brown sugar, mustard, and vinegar. Stir in soda and reserved pineapple juice. Pour over sausage and stir to coat. Cover and cook on low for 2 to 3 hours or until heated through.
2. Stir in pineapple. In a separate bowl, combine cornstarch and water until smooth. Whisk into a slow cooker. Cover and cook for 30 minutes more, or until sauce is thickened. Serve with toothpicks.

Meaty Chili Cheese Dip

Prep time: 20 minutes | Cook time: 4½ to 5½ hours | Makes 8 cups

1 pound (454 g) 90% lean ground beef
1 medium onion, chopped
1 (16-ounce / 454-g) can kidney beans, rinsed and drained
1 (15-ounce / 425-g) can black beans, rinsed and drained
1 (14½-ounce / 411-g) can diced tomatoes in sauce, undrained
1 cup frozen corn, thawed
¾ cup water
1 (2¼-ounce / 64-g) can sliced ripe olives, drained
3 teaspoons chili powder
½ teaspoon dried oregano
½ teaspoon chipotle hot pepper sauce
¼ teaspoon garlic powder
¼ teaspoon ground cumin

1 (16-ounce / 454-g) package reduced-fat process cheese (Velveeta), cubed
Corn chips or tortilla chips, for serving

1. In a large skillet, cook the beef and onion over medium heat for 6 to 8 minutes, or until the beef is no longer pink, and the onion is tender, breaking up beef into crumbles. Drain and transfer to a slow cooker.
2. Stir in beans, tomatoes, corn, water, olives, chili powder, oregano, pepper sauce, garlic powder, and cumin. Cook on low, covered, for 4 to 5 hours or until heated through.
3. Stir in cheese. Cook on low, covered, for 30 minutes longer or until cheese is melted. Serve with corn chips.

Turkey Teriyaki Sandwiches

Prep time: 20 minutes | Cook time: 5¾ to 6¾ hours | Serves 20

2 boneless skinless turkey breast halves (2 pounds / 907 g each)
⅔ cup packed brown sugar
⅔ cup reduced-sodium soy sauce
¼ cup cider vinegar
3 garlic cloves, minced
1 tablespoon minced fresh ginger
½ teaspoon pepper
2 tablespoons cornstarch
2 tablespoons cold water
20 Hawaiian sweet rolls
2 tablespoons butter, melted

1. Place turkey in a slow cooker. In a small bowl, combine the brown sugar, soy sauce, vinegar, garlic, ginger, and pepper. Pour over turkey and stir to coat. Cover and cook on low for 5 to 6 hours or until meat is tender.
2. Remove turkey from the slow cooker. In another bowl, mix cornstarch and cold water until smooth. Gradually stir the mixture into cooking liquid. When cool enough to handle, shred meat with two forks and return meat to a slow cooker. Cook on high, covered, for 30 to 35 minutes or until sauce is thickened.
3. Preheat the oven to 325°F (163°C). Split rolls and brush cut sides with butter, then place on a baking sheet, cut side up. Bake for 8 to 10 minutes or until toasted and golden brown. Spoon ⅓ cup turkey mixture on roll bottoms. Replace tops and serve.

Lemony Chicken Wings

Prep time: 15 minutes | Cook time: 6 to 8 hours | Makes about 4 dozen

5 pounds (2.3 kg) chicken wings (about 25 wings)
1 (12-ounce / 340-g) bottle chili sauce
¼ cup lemon juice
¼ cup molasses
2 tablespoons Worcestershire sauce
6 garlic cloves, minced
1 tablespoon chili powder
1 tablespoon salsa
1 teaspoon garlic salt
3 drops hot pepper sauce

1.Cut chicken wings into three sections, discarding wing tips. Place the wings in a slow cooker.
2.In a small bowl, combine the remaining ingredients. Pour over chicken and stir to coat. Cover and cook on low for 6 to 8 hours or until chicken is tender. Serve warm.

slow Cooker Chex Mix

Prep time: 5 minutes | Cook time: 1 to 1½ hours | Makes about 3 quarts

4 cups Wheat Chex
4 cups Cheerios
3 cups pretzel sticks
1 (12-ounce / 340-g) can salted peanuts
¼ cup butter, melted
2 to 3 tablespoons grated Parmesan cheese
1 teaspoon celery salt
½ to ¾ teaspoon seasoned salt

1.In a slow cooker, combine cereals, pretzels, and peanuts. Combine the butter, cheese, celery salt, and seasoned salt in a bowl. Drizzle over cereal mixture and mix well.
2.Cover and cook on low for 1 to 1½ hours, stirring every 20 minutes. Serve warm or at room temperature.

Sweet and Spicy Peanuts

Prep time: 10 minutes | Cook time: 1½ hours | Makes 4 cups

3 cups salted peanuts
½ cup sugar
⅓ cup packed brown sugar
2 tablespoons hot water
2 tablespoons butter, melted
1 tablespoon Sriracha Asian hot chili sauce or hot pepper sauce
1 teaspoon chili powder

1.Place peanuts in a greased slow cooker. In a small bowl, combine the sugars, water, butter, hot sauce, and chili powder. Pour over peanuts and stir to coat. Cover and cook on high for 1½ hours, stirring once.
2.Spread on waxed paper to cool. Serve warm.

BBQ Party Starters

Prep time: 15 minutes | Cook time: 2¼ to 3¼ hours | Serves 16

1 pound (454 g) ground beef
¼ cup finely chopped onion
1 (16-ounce / 454-g) package miniature hot dogs, drained
1 (12-ounce / 340-g) jar apricot preserves
1 cup barbecue sauce
1 (20-ounce / 567-g) can pineapple chunks, drained

1.In a large bowl, combine beef and onion, mixing lightly but thoroughly. Shape into 1-inch balls. In a large skillet over medium heat, cook the meatballs in two batches until cooked through, turning occasionally.
2.Using a slotted spoon, transfer the meatballs to a slow cooker. Add the miniature hot dogs, apricot preserves, and barbecue sauce, stirring well. Cover and cook on high for 2 to 3 hours or until heated through.
3.Stir in the pineapple chunks. Cook, covered, for 15 to 20 minutes longer or until heated through. Serve warm.

Tomato Salsa

Prep time: 15 minutes | Cook time: 2½ to 3 hours | Makes about 2 cups

10 plum tomatoes
2 garlic cloves
1 small onion, cut into wedges
2 jalapeño peppers
¼ cup cilantro leaves
½ teaspoon salt (optional)

1.Core tomatoes and cut a small slit in two tomatoes, then insert a garlic clove into each slit. Place tomatoes and onion in a slow cooker.
2.Cut stems off jalapeños and remove seeds if a milder salsa is desired. Place jalapeños in the slow cooker.
3.Cover and cook on high for 2½ to 3 hours or until vegetables are softened (some may brown slightly). Allow to cool for 10 minutes.
4.In a blender, combine the tomato mixture, cilantro, and salt (if desired). Process until blended. Refrigerate until ready to serve.

Grape Jelly Meatballs

Prep time: 10 minutes | Cook time: 4 to 5 hours | Makes about 10½ dozen

1 cup grape juice
1 cup apple jelly
1 cup ketchup
1 (8-ounce / 227-g) can tomato sauce
1 (64-ounce / 1.8-kg) package frozen fully cooked Italian meatballs

1.In a small saucepan, combine the juice, jelly, ketchup, and tomato sauce. Cook and stir over medium heat until jelly is melted.
2.Place the meatballs in a slow cooker. Pour the sauce over the top and gently stir to coat. Cover and cook on low for 4 to 5 hours or until heated through. Serve warm.

Sweet and Spicy Chicken Wings

Prep time: 15 minutes | Cook time: 5 to 6 hours | Makes about 2½ dozen

3 pounds (1.4 kg) chicken wings
1½ cups ketchup
1 cup packed brown sugar
1 small onion, finely chopped
¼ cup finely chopped sweet red pepper
2 tablespoons chili powder
2 tablespoons Worcestershire sauce
1½ teaspoons crushed red pepper flakes
1 teaspoon ground mustard
1 teaspoon dried basil
1 teaspoon dried thyme
1 teaspoon pepper

1.Cut wings into three sections, discarding wing tip sections. Place the chicken in a slow cooker.
2.In a small bowl, combine the remaining ingredients. Pour over chicken and stir until coated. Cover and cook on low for 5 to 6 hours or until chicken juices run clear. Serve warm.

Cranberry Swedish Meatballs

Prep time: 10 minutes | Cook time: 3 to 4 hours | Makes about 5 dozen

2 envelopes brown gravy mix
1 (32-ounce / 907-g) package frozen fully cooked Swedish meatballs
⅔ cup jellied cranberry sauce
2 teaspoons Dijon mustard
¼ cup heavy whipping cream

1.Prepare the gravy mix according to the package directions. In a slow cooker, combine the meatballs, cranberry sauce, mustard, and gravy. Cover and cook on low for 3 to 4 hours or until heated through, adding cream during the last 30 minutes of cooking. Serve warm.

Cheese Pulled Pork Crostini

Prep time: 30 minutes | Cook time: 6 to 8 hours | Makes 32 appetizers

1 boneless pork shoulder butt roast (about 2 pounds / 907 g)
½ cup lime juice
2 envelopes mesquite marinade mix
¼ cup sugar
¼ cup olive oil
Salsa:
1 cup frozen corn, thawed
1 cup canned black beans, rinsed and drained
1 small tomato, finely chopped
2 tablespoons finely chopped deseeded jalapeño pepper
2 tablespoons lime juice
2 tablespoons olive oil
1½ teaspoons ground cumin
1 teaspoon chili powder
½ teaspoon salt
¼ teaspoon crushed red pepper flakes

Sauce:
1 (4-ounce / 113-g) can chopped green chilies
⅓ cup apricot preserves
⅛ teaspoon salt
Crostini:
32 slices French bread baguette (¼ inch thick)
¼ cup olive oil
⅔ cup crumbled queso fresco or feta cheese
Lime wedges, for serving (optional)

1. Place roast in a slow cooker. In a small bowl, whisk lime juice, marinade mix, sugar, and oil until blended. Pour over roast and stir until well coated. Cook on low, covered, for 6 to 8 hours or until meat is tender.
2. For salsa, in a small bowl, combine corn, beans, tomato, and jalapeño. Stir in lime juice, oil, and seasonings. Set aside.
3. In a small saucepan, combine sauce ingredients. Cook and stir over low heat until blended. Set aside.
4. For crostini, preheat broiler. Brush bread slices on both sides with oil and place on baking sheets. Broil for 1 to 2 minutes on each side or until golden brown.
5. Remove roast from the slow cooker and let cool slightly. Shred pork with two forks. To serve, layer toasts with salsa, pork, and cheese. Top with sauce. If desired, serve with lime wedges.

Barbecued Smokies

Prep time: 5 minutes | Cook time: 5 to 6 hours | Serves 8

1 (1-pound / 454-g) package miniature smoked sausages
1 (28-ounce / 794-g) bottle barbecue sauce
1¼ cups water
3 tablespoons Worcestershire sauce
3 tablespoons steak sauce
½ teaspoon pepper

1. In a slow cooker, combine all ingredients. Cover and cook on low for 5 to 6 hours or until heated through. Serve warm.

Simple Pizza Bites

Prep time: 10 minutes | Cook time: 1 hour | Serves 8

1 pound (454 g) ground beef
1 pound (454 g) bulk Italian sausage
1 pound (454 g) Velveeta cheese, cubed
4 teaspoons pizza seasoning
½ teaspoon Worcestershire sauce

1. In a large nonstick skillet, brown beef and sausage until crumbly. Drain and place in a slow cooker.
2. Add remaining ingredients to the slow cooker and stir to combine. Cover and cook on low for 1 hour. Serve warm.

Chapter 3 Stocks and Sauces

Chicken Stock

Prep time: 20 minutes | Cook time: 8 hours | Makes 4 to 5 quarts

2 to 3 pounds (907 g to 1.4 kg) chicken bones
2 carrots, chopped
2 onions, quartered
3 celery stalks, chopped
1 leek, split lengthwise, rinsed well, and chopped
1 head garlic, cut in half
1 dried bay leaf
1 tablespoon black peppercorns
3 thyme sprigs
5 flat-leaf parsley sprigs
3 to 4 quarts boiling water

1.Place all ingredients except boiling water in a slow cooker. Add the boiling water (it should cover the ingredients by 3 inches). Cover and cook on low for 8 hours.
2.Remove from heat and strain stock through a fine-mesh sieve (discard solids). Let stock cool completely. (Stock can be refrigerated in an airtight container for up to 1 week, or frozen for up to 6 months.)

Beef Stock

Prep time: 20 minutes | Cook time: 9 hours | Makes 4 to 5 quarts

3½ pounds (1.6 kg) beef bones, such as shanks, necks, knuckles, and shins
1 tablespoon olive oil
2 onions, quartered
2 carrots, chopped
2 celery stalks, chopped
1 head garlic, halved
3 thyme sprigs
5 flat-leaf parsley sprigs
1 dried bay leaf
6 white mushrooms
2 leeks, split lengthwise, rinsed, and roughly chopped
2 plum tomatoes, chopped

4 to 5 quarts boiling water

1.Preheat the oven to 400ºF (205ºC).
2.Combine beef bones and oil in a large bowl, tossing to combine. Arrange on a rimmed baking sheet and roast for about 30 minutes. Add onions, carrots, celery, garlic, thyme, parsley, bay leaf, mushrooms, leeks, and tomatoes to the baking sheet, and roast until bones are deeply browned, about 30 minutes.
3.Using a slotted spoon, transfer bones and vegetable mixture to a slow cooker. Add the boiling water. Cover and cook on low for 8 hours.
4.Remove from heat and strain stock through a fine-mesh sieve (discard solids). Let stock cool completely. (Stock can be refrigerated in an airtight container for up to 1 week, or frozen for up to 6 months.)

Fish Stock

Prep time: 15 minutes | Cook time: 8 hours | Makes 4 to 5 quarts

2 pounds (907 g) fish bones (from non-oily, firm fish, such as snapper, sole, and bass), rinsed
1 onion, quartered
2 celery stalks, chopped
2 leeks, split lengthwise, rinsed well, and chopped
1 carrot, chopped
2 garlic cloves
3 thyme sprigs
5 flat-leaf parsley sprigs
4 quarts boiling water

1.Place all ingredients, except boiling water, in a slow cooker. Add the boiling water (it should cover the ingredients by 3 inches). Cover and cook on low for 8 hours.
2.Remove from heat and strain stock through a fine-mesh sieve (discard solids). Let stock cool completely. (Stock can be refrigerated in an airtight container for up to 1 week, or frozen for up to 6 months.)

Vegetable Stock

Prep time: 20 minutes | Cook time: 8½ hours | Makes 4 to 5 quarts

3 onions, quartered
5 celery stalks, chopped
3 carrots, chopped
1 head garlic, halved
1 fennel bulb, chopped
5 white mushrooms
2 leeks, split, rinsed well, and chopped
2 tablespoons olive oil
4 quarts boiling water
1 dried bay leaf
1 teaspoon black peppercorns
3 thyme sprigs
5 flat-leaf parsley sprigs

1.Preheat the oven to 425ºF (220ºC).
2.Combine onions, celery, carrots, garlic, fennel, mushrooms, and leeks in a large bowl, tossing with oil. Spread in a single layer on a rimmed baking sheet and roast until golden, tossing halfway through, about 30 minutes.
3.Transfer vegetables to a slow cooker. Add the boiling water, bay leaf, peppercorns, thyme, and parsley. Cover and cook on low for 8 hours. Remove from heat and strain stock through a fine-mesh sieve (discard solids). Let stock cool completely. (Stock can be refrigerated in an airtight container for up to 1 week, or frozen for up to 6 months.)

Vegan Garlic Pasta Sauce

Prep time: 20 minutes | Cook time: 4 hours | Makes 8 cups

2 tablespoon extra-virgin olive oil
2 cloves garlic, minced
½ teaspoon red pepper flakes
1 large onion, coarsely chopped
2 portobello mushrooms, coarsely chopped
1 medium red bell pepper, deseeded and coarsely chopped
1 medium yellow bell pepper, deseeded and coarsely chopped
1 tablespoon dried oregano
2 teaspoons dried basil
Salt, to taste
2 tablespoons balsamic vinegar

2 (32-ounce / 907-g) cans crushed plum tomatoes
Freshly ground black pepper, to taste

1.Heat the oil in a large sauté pan over medium-high heat. Add the garlic and red pepper flakes, and sauté until the garlic is fragrant, about 1 minute. Add the onion and sauté until the onion begins to soften, another 2 minutes. Add the remaining vegetables, the oregano, basil, and 2 teaspoons of salt and sauté until the vegetables give off some liquid, about 5 minutes.
2.Using a slotted spoon, transfer the vegetables to a slow cooker. Stir in the vinegar and tomatoes. Cover and cook on high for 4 hours or on low for 8 hours. Season with salt and pepper.
3.Serve immediately or refrigerate until ready to serve.

BBQ Sauce

Prep time: 10 minutes | Cook time: 3 hours | Makes 4 cups

2 tablespoons safflower or canola oil
1 onion, finely chopped
3 garlic cloves, minced
Coarse salt and freshly ground pepper, to taste
1¼ teaspoons chili powder
1 (28-ounce / 794-g) can whole peeled tomatoes, puréed with their juices
¾ cup water, plus more as needed
¼ cup packed dark brown sugar
¼ cup ketchup
2 tablespoons apple cider vinegar

1.Heat oil in a saucepan over medium-high heat. Add onion, garlic, 1 teaspoon of salt, and ½ teaspoon of pepper, and cook until onion is translucent, about 5 minutes. Stir in chili powder and cook until fragrant, about 1 minute. Transfer onion mixture to a slow cooker. Add tomatoes, water, brown sugar, and ketchup. Cover and cook on high for 3 hours (or on low for 6 hours). Let cool slightly.
2.Transfer sauce to a blender and purée. Stir in vinegar and season with salt and pepper. Serve immediately or refrigerate in an airtight container for up to 2 weeks.

Citrus and Chili Ketchup

Prep time: 10 minutes | Cook time: 3 to 4 hours | Makes 1 quart

1 (28-ounce / 794-g) can diced tomatoes
1 onion, quartered
3 garlic cloves, smashed
6 tablespoons dark brown sugar
¼ cup apple cider vinegar
1 cup water
2 teaspoons dry mustard
Pinch ground nutmeg
¼ teaspoon ground allspice
Pinch chili powder
½ teaspoon finely grated orange zest plus ⅓ cup fresh orange juice
2 tablespoons brewed espresso
1 dried bay leaf
1 fresh habañero chile
Coarse salt and freshly ground pepper, to taste

1.Purée tomatoes, onion, garlic, and brown sugar in a food processor. Transfer mixture to a slow cooker. Add vinegar, water, mustard, nutmeg, allspice, chili powder, orange zest and juice, espresso, bay leaf, and chile. Cook, uncovered, on high until thickened, 3 to 4 hours.
2.Remove chile. Purée half or whole chile (depending on desired heat) with 1 cup of tomato mixture in the food processor. Return ketchup to slow cooker and stir until well blended. Season with salt and pepper. Let cool completely before serving.

Easy Marinara Sauce

Prep time: 10 minutes | Cook time: 4 to 5 hours | Makes about 5 cups

⅓ cup olive oil, divided
1 medium-size yellow onion, finely chopped
1 clove garlic, minced
2 (28-ounce / 794-g) cans whole plum tomatoes, with their juice, or 3 pounds (1.4 kg) ripe plum tomatoes, seeds squeezed out, and cut into chunks
3 ounces (85 g) tomato paste
Pinch of sugar
Salt and freshly ground black pepper, to taste

1.In a medium-size skillet over medium heat, heat

3 tablespoons of oil, then cook the onion and garlic, stirring, until softened, about 5 minutes.
2.Transfer to the slow cooker, add the remaining olive oil, tomatoes, tomato paste, and sugar, and stir to combine. Cover and cook on low for 4 to 5 hours.
3.Season the sauce with salt and pepper. If using canned tomatoes, use a handheld immersion blender to purée the sauce right in the slow cooker; if using fresh, purée with the fine disk of a food mill to remove the tomato skins. If not serving the sauce with hot pasta immediately, return it to the cooker where it will stay warm on low for a few hours. The sauce will keep, refrigerated, for up to a week or frozen for 2 months.

Basil Tomato Sauce

Prep time: 15 minutes | Cook time: 2½ to 3 hours | Makes about 5 cups

2 tablespoons unsalted butter
2 tablespoons olive oil
1 medium-size yellow onion, finely chopped
1 to 2 cloves garlic, minced
2 (28-ounce / 794-g) cans whole plum tomatoes, drained (if packed in purée, don't drain) and coarsely chopped
2 tablespoons dry red or white wine
Pinch of sugar
¼ cup shredded fresh basil, divided
Pinch of dried thyme or oregano
Salt and freshly ground black pepper, to taste
2 tablespoons chopped fresh flat-leaf parsley

1.In a medium-size skillet over medium heat, melt the butter in the olive oil. Cook the onion, stirring, until softened, about 5 minutes. Add the garlic and cook, stirring, for 2 minutes.
2.Transfer to the slow cooker. Add the tomatoes, wine, sugar, 2 tablespoons of the basil, and thyme and stir to combine. Cover and simmer on high for 2 to 2½ hours.
3.Season the sauce with salt and pepper and stir in the remaining 2 tablespoons of basil and the parsley. Cover and cook on low for 20 to 30 minutes longer. Serve the sauce hot. It will keep, refrigerated, for up to a week and frozen for 2 months.

Italian Beef Sauce

Prep time: 20 minutes | Cook time: 6 to 8 hours | Makes 8 to 9 cups

½ cup olive oil
2 medium-size yellow onions, chopped
2 medium-size carrots, finely chopped
2 ribs celery, finely chopped
1 pound (454 g) lean ground beef
Salt and freshly ground black pepper, to taste
1½ cups dry red wine, such as Chianti
2 (28-ounce / 794-g) cans whole plum tomatoes, with their juice; or 2 pounds (907 g) fresh ripe plum tomatoes, peeled, deseeded, and cut into chunks
1 (6-ounce / 170-g) can tomato paste
½ cup beef broth

1.Heat the oil in a large skillet over medium heat. Cook the onions, carrots, and celery, stirring occasionally, until just browned, 10 to 15 minutes. Add the beef and cook until no longer pink. Season with salt and pepper.
2.Transfer to the slow cooker. Add the wine to the skillet over high heat and cook, scraping up any browned bits stuck to the bottom, until it reduces to half its volume. Pour into the slow cooker and add the tomatoes, tomato paste, and broth. Cover and cook on low for 6 to 8 hours. Serve the sauce hot. It will keep in the refrigerator for up to 4 days and in the freezer for a month.

Salsa Mexicana

Prep time: 20 minutes | Cook time: 5 to 6 hours | Makes about 3 cups

3 tablespoons olive oil
1 large yellow banana chile, peeled, deseeded, and chopped
2 small white onions, chopped
2 cloves garlic, chopped
1 (28-ounce / 794-g) can tomato purée
2 tablespoons tomato paste
1½ cups chicken broth
2 tablespoons chopped fresh cilantro
1 tablespoon chili powder, or more to taste
½ teaspoon ground cumin
½ teaspoon dried Mexican oregano or marjoram
Salt, to taste

1.In a medium-size skillet over medium heat, heat the oil, then cook the chile, onions, and garlic, stirring, until softened, about 5 minutes. Transfer to the slow cooker and add the tomato purée and paste, broth, cilantro, chili powder, cumin, and oregano. Stir to combine, then cover and simmer on low for 5 to 6 hours.
2.Use a handheld immersion blender to partially purée the sauce right in the slow cooker or transfer to a blender to purée. Season with salt. The sauce will keep, refrigerated, for 5 to 7 days and frozen for up to a month.

Classic Bolognese Sauce

Prep time: 15 minutes | Cook time: 6 to 7 hours | Makes 10 cups

1 tablespoon unsalted butter
2 tablespoons olive oil
1 large sweet onion, such as Vidalia, finely chopped
1 cup finely diced carrot
1 cup finely diced celery
1 clove garlic, minced
1 pound (454 g) lean ground pork
8 ounces (227 g) ground veal
8 ounces (227 g) lean ground beef
⅛ teaspoon ground nutmeg
⅛ teaspoon ground cinnamon
1 cup whole milk
1 cup dry white wine or vermouth
3 (32-ounce / 907-g) cans crushed plum tomatoes
Salt and freshly ground black pepper, to taste

1.Melt the butter in the oil in a large skillet over medium heat. Add the onion, carrot, celery, and garlic and sauté until the vegetables are softened. Add the meats and sauté until no longer pink, breaking up any large chunks with a wooden spoon.
2.Spoon off any fat or water from the pan until the pan is dry. Add the nutmeg and cinnamon and sauté for another 2 minutes to allow the flavors to blend. Stir in the milk and boil until the milk has just about evaporated.
3.Transfer the contents of the skillet to a slow cooker. Add the wine and tomatoes and stir to blend. Cover and cook the sauce on high for 6 to 7 hours. Season with salt and pepper.
4.Serve immediately or refrigerate until ready to serve.

Garlic Fresh Tomato Sauce

Prep time: 10 minutes | Cook time: 5 hours | Makes about 3 cups

2 pounds (907 g) ripe plum tomatoes, peeled cored, halved, and seeded
4 garlic cloves, smashed and peeled
¼ cup extra-virgin olive oil
4 to 5 basil sprigs
1 teaspoon coarse salt, plus more to taste
¼ teaspoon freshly ground pepper
Pinch sugar
½ cup boiling water

1.Add tomatoes, garlic, oil, basil, salt, pepper, and sugar to a slow cooker. Stir to combine. Add the boiling water. Cover and cook on high until sauce thickens slightly, 1 hour. Reduce heat to low and cook for 4 hours more.
2.For a thicker sauce, continue cooking on low for 2 hours, or until desired thickness is reached. Serve sauce immediately, or let cool to room temperature and refrigerate in an airtight container for up to 3 days.

Shallot and Red Wine Sauce

Prep time: 5 minutes | Cook time: 5 hours | Makes about 10 cups

½ cup (¼ stick) unsalted butter, melted
½ cup finely chopped shallots
2 teaspoons dried thyme
2 cups full-bodied red wine
8 cups beef broth
½ teaspoon freshly ground black pepper

¼ cup all-purpose flour

1.Combine ¼ cup of the butter, shallots, thyme, red wine, broth, and pepper in a slow cooker. Cook, uncovered, on high for 4 hours, until the mixture is reduced by one-third.
2.Stir the remaining melted butter and flour together, then whisk into the sauce. Cover and cook for an additional 45 minutes, until the sauce is thickened.
3.Serve immediately or refrigerate until ready to serve.

Berry Sauce

Prep time: 10 minutes | Cook time: 4 hours | Makes about 10 cups

2 pints fresh blackberries
2 pints fresh strawberries, hulled, cut into quarters if large
2 pints fresh blueberries, picked over for stems
1 to 1½ cups sugar (depending on the sweetness of the berries)
2 tablespoons fresh lemon juice
Grated zest of 1 lemon
2 tablespoons cornstarch

1.Mix all the ingredients together in a slow cooker. Cover and cook on low for 4 hours, stirring twice during the cooking time.
2.Allow the sauce to cool before removing from the cooker. Store in airtight containers in the refrigerator for up to 1 week or in the freezer for up to 3 months.

Chapter 4 Desserts

Cinnamon Brandied Peaches

Prep time: 10 minutes | Cook time: 2 hours | Serves 8

½ cup brandy
½ cup (1 stick) unsalted butter, melted
1½ cups firmly packed light brown sugar
2 (4-inch) cinnamon sticks
4 whole cloves
½ cup peach nectar
8 large peaches, peeled, halved, and pitted

1. Combine the brandy, butter, sugar, cinnamon sticks, cloves, and nectar in a slow cooker and stir to dissolve the sugar. Add the peaches to the slow cooker and turn to coat them with the syrup.
2. Cover and cook on high for 2 hours. Allow the peaches to cool slightly. Using a slotted spoon, remove the spices from the sauce.
3. Serve the peaches with the sauce poured over.

Caramel Peach Cobbler

Prep time: 10 minutes | Cook time: 2 to 2½ hours | Serves 8

2½ cups firmly packed dark brown sugar, divided
¼ teaspoon ground ginger
½ teaspoon ground cinnamon
2 tablespoons cornstarch
2 tablespoons bourbon
8 large ripe peaches, peeled, pitted, and cut into wedges
¾ cup (1½ sticks) unsalted butter, divided
1 cup all-purpose flour
¼ teaspoon freshly grated nutmeg
1 cup chopped pecans
Nonstick cooking spray
Vanilla ice cream, for serving

1. Coat the insert of a slow cooker with nonstick cooking spray. Add 1½ cups of the sugar, ginger, cinnamon, cornstarch, and bourbon to the slow cooker and stir until blended. Add the peaches and stir to coat them with the sugar.

2. Melt ¼ cup of the butter and add it to the slow cooker, stirring to blend. Stir together the flour, remaining 1 cup of sugar, and nutmeg in a mixing bowl.
3. Add the remaining ½ cup butter to the mixing bowl and cut it in, using a blending fork or pastry blender, until the mixture resembles coarse crumbs.
4. Sprinkle over the top of the peaches and spread the pecans evenly over the crumble. Cover and cook on high for 2 to 2½ hours, until a skewer inserted into the crumble comes out clean. Uncover the cooker and allow to cool for 30 minutes.
5. Serve with vanilla ice cream.

Baked Apples with Raisins and Walnuts

Prep time: 10 minutes | Cook time: 2½ to 3 hours | Serves 8

8 medium apples
½ cup golden raisins
½ cup finely chopped walnuts
1 cup firmly packed light brown sugar
1 teaspoon ground cinnamon
2 tablespoons dark rum
4 tablespoons (½ stick) unsalted butter, melted
1½ cups apple juice or apple cider
Unsweetened whipped cream, for garnish
Cinnamon sugar, for garnish

1. Core the apples and place them in a slow cooker. Stir together the raisins, walnuts, sugar, cinnamon, rum, and butter in a mixing bowl and fill the apples with the mixture. Pour the apple juice into the bottom of the slow cooker. Cover and cook on low for 2½ to 3 hours on high, until the apples are tender.
2. Remove the apples using a spatula to catch any filling that may fall out of the bottom of the apple.
3. Serve the apples with some of thesomesome sauce from the bottom of the slow cooker and a dollop of whipped cream, sprinkled with cinnamon sugar.

Apple-Cranberry Cobbler

Prep time: 15 minutes | Cook time: 2½ hours | Serves 8

6 large Golden Delicious apples, peeled, cored, and coarsely chopped
1 (12-ounce / 340-g) package fresh cranberries, washed and picked over (discard any white cranberries)
2½ cups sugar, divided
1 tablespoons cornstarch
1 teaspoon ground cinnamon
1 teaspoon cloves
⅛ teaspoon ground ginger
1½ cups (3 sticks) unsalted butter, melted
2 cups unbleached all-purpose flour
¼ cup maple syrup
2 large eggs, beaten
Nonstick cooking spray
Vanilla ice cream, for serving

1. Coat the insert of a slow cooker with nonstick cooking spray. Add the apples, cranberries, 1 cup of the sugar, the cornstarch, cinnamon, cloves, and ginger to the slow cooker and stir to combine.
2. Stir together the butter, flour, remaining 1½ cups sugar, maple syrup, and eggs in a mixing bowl and spread the batter over the apple mixture. Cover and cook on high for 2½ hours, until a skewer inserted into the center of the batter comes out clean. Uncover and cool for 30 minutes.
3. Serve the cobbler warm with vanilla ice cream.

Strawberry Rhubarb Crisp

Prep time: 20 minutes | Cook time: 2½ hours | Serves 8

4 cups strawberries, hulled and cut into quarters
4 stalks bright red rhubarb, cut into ½-inch slices
1½ cups granulated sugar
1 teaspoon ground cinnamon
Grated zest of 1 orange
1 tablespoon cornstarch
⅔ cup old-fashioned rolled oats
¾ cup firmly packed light brown sugar
½ cup finely chopped white chocolate
1 cup all-purpose flour
½ cup (1 stick) unsalted butter, chilled and cut

into ½-inch pieces
Nonstick cooking spray
Vanilla ice cream, for serving

1. Coat the insert of a slow cooker with nonstick cooking spray. Stir the berries, rhubarb, granulated sugar, cinnamon, zest, and cornstarch together in the insert. Set aside while making the crumble.
2. Stir together the oats, brown sugar, chocolate, and flour in a mixing bowl. Add the butter and cut the butter into the dry ingredients, using a blending fork or pastry blender, until the mixture forms coarse crumbs about the size of peas.
3. Sprinkle the crumble over the fruit. Cover and cook on low for 2½ hours, until the crumble is set, and the fruit is bubbling. Uncover the slow cooker and allow to cool for 30 minutes.
4. Serve warm with vanilla ice cream.

Red Wine Poached Pears

Prep time: 10 minutes | Cook time: 2 to 2½ hours | Serves 6 to 8

1 cup full-bodied red wine
1 cup ruby port
1½ cups firmly packed light brown sugar
1 (4-inch) cinnamon stick
6 large firm red pears, halved and cored
6 ounces (170 g) Stilton cheese, at room temperature

1. Combine the wine, port, brown sugar, and cinnamon stick in the insert of a slow cooker. Add the pears to the slow cooker, arranging them in layers, and spoon some of thesomesomesome sauce over the pears.
2. Cover and cook on high for 2 to 2½ hours, until the pears are softened. Uncover the slow cooker and allow the pears to cool to room temperature. Carefully remove them from the cooker and arrange them on a platter. Strain the sauce through a fine-mesh sieve and boil for 5 to 10 minutes until the sauce becomes syrupy.
3. Spoon the syrup over the pears on the platter and scoop a bit of Stilton into the center of each pear. Serve at room temperature.

Spiced Pear and Almond Crumble

Prep time: 10 minutes | Cook time: 2½ hours | Serves 8

1 cup firmly packed light brown sugar
¼ cup amaretto liqueur
¾ cup (1½ sticks) unsalted butter, melted
8 large firm pears, peeled, cored and coarsely chopped
½ cup granulated sugar
½ cup all-purpose flour
¾ teaspoon ground cinnamon
¼ teaspoon freshly grated nutmeg
⅔ cup sliced almonds
Nonstick cooking spray
Whipped cream, for serving

1.Coat the insert of a slow cooker with nonstick cooking spray. Add the brown sugar, amaretto, and ½ cup of the butter to the slow cooker and stir until blended. Add the pears and turn the pears to coat with the syrup.
2.Stir together the granulated sugar, flour, cinnamon, nutmeg, and almonds in a small bowl. Drizzle the remaining ¼ cup butter into the flour mixture and stir with a fork until the mixture begins to form crumbs. Sprinkle over the top of the pears. Cover and cook on high for 2½ hours, until a skewer inserted into the crumble comes out clean. Uncover and allow to cool for 30 minutes.
3.Serve the crumble warm with a dollop of whipped cream.

Lemony Blueberry Pudding Cake

Prep time: 5 minutes | Cook time: 2½ hours | Serves 6

1 cup fresh blueberries
4 large eggs, separated
Grated zest of 1 lemon
⅓ cup fresh lemon juice
4 tablespoons (½ stick) butter, at room temperature
1⅔ cups milk
1 cup sugar
⅓ cup all-purpose flour
⅛ teaspoon salt
Nonstick cooking spray

1.Coat the insert of a slow cooker with nonstick cooking spray. Spread the blueberries over the bottom of the slow cooker. Beat the egg whites in a large mixing bowl until soft peaks form and set aside.
2.Whisk the egg yolks in another mixing bowl. Add the zest and juice, butter, and milk and whisk until blended. Stir together the sugar, flour, and salt in another bowl and add to the egg yolk mixture. Beat until smooth, then fold into the reserved egg whites.
3.Transfer the batter to the slow cooker. Cover and cook on high for 2½ hours.
4.Allow the cake to cool slightly before serving.

Chocolate Upside-Down Fudge Cake

Prep time: 5 minutes | Cook time: 2 hours | Serves 4 to 6

½ cup milk
3 tablespoons unsalted butter, melted
1 teaspoon vanilla bean paste
1 cup granulated sugar
1 cup all-purpose flour
½ cup cocoa powder (make sure to use natural cocoa powder and not Dutch process), divided
2 teaspoons baking powder
¾ cup firmly packed light brown sugar
1¾ cups boiling water
Nonstick cooking spray
Vanilla ice cream or unsweetened whipped cream, for serving

1.Coat the insert of a slow cooker with nonstick cooking spray. Stir together the milk, butter, and vanilla bean paste in a mixing bowl. Gradually stir in the granulated sugar, flour, ¼ cup of the cocoa powder, and baking powder. Spread the batter in the slow cooker.
2.Mix together the brown sugar and remaining ¼ cup cocoa powder in a small bowl and sprinkle evenly over the batter. Pour in the boiling water (do not stir). Cover and cook on high for 2 hours, until a skewer inserted into the center comes out clean. Uncover and allow to cool for about 20 minutes.
3.Serve in bowls with vanilla ice cream.

Pecan and Butterscotch Bread Pudding

Prep time: 15 minutes | Cook time: 3 to 4 hours | Serves 8

9 cups cubed day-old white bread (about 8 slices)
½ cup chopped pecans
½ cup butterscotch chips
4 eggs
2 cups half-and-half
½ cup packed brown sugar
½ cup butter, melted
1 teaspoon vanilla extract
Whipped cream and butterscotch ice cream topping, for serving

1.Place bread, pecans, and butterscotch chips in a greased slow cooker. In a large bowl, whisk eggs, half-and-half, brown sugar, melted butter, and vanilla until blended. Pour over bread mixture, stirring gently to combine.
2.Cook, covered, on low for 3 to 4 hours or until a knife inserted in center comes out clean. Serve warm with whipped cream and butterscotch topping.

Rocky Road Chocolate Cake

Prep time: 20 minutes | Cook time: 3 to 4 hours | Serves 16

1 package German chocolate cake mix (regular size)
1 (3.9-ounce / 111-g) package instant chocolate pudding mix
1 cup sour cream
⅓ cup butter, melted
3 eggs
1 teaspoon vanilla extract
3¼ cups 2% milk, divided
1 (3.4-ounce / 96-g) package cook-and-serve chocolate pudding mix
1½ cups miniature marshmallows
1 cup semisweet chocolate chips
½ cup chopped pecans, toasted
Vanilla ice cream (optional)

1.In a large bowl, combine the first six ingredients. Add 1¼ cups milk. Beat on low speed 30 seconds. Beat on medium 2 minutes. Transfer to a greased slow cooker. Sprinkle cook-and-serve pudding mix over batter.
2.In a small saucepan, heat remaining milk until bubbles form around sides of pan. Gradually pour over dry pudding mix.
3.Cook, covered, on high for 3 to 4 hours or until a toothpick inserted in cake portion comes out with moist crumbs.
4.Turn off the slow cooker. Sprinkle marshmallows, chocolate chips, and pecans over cake. Let stand, covered, for 5 minutes or until marshmallows begin to melt. Serve warm. If desired, top with ice cream.

Amaretto Cherries with Dumplings

Prep time: 15 minutes | Cook time: 7¾ hours | Serves 6

2 (14½-ounce / 411-g) cans pitted tart cherries
¾ cup sugar
¼ cup cornstarch
⅛ teaspoon salt
¼ cup amaretto or ½ teaspoon almond extract
Dumplings:
1 cup all-purpose flour
¼ cup sugar
1 teaspoon baking powder
½ teaspoon grated lemon peel
⅛ teaspoon salt
⅓ cup 2% milk
3 tablespoons butter, melted
Vanilla ice cream (optional)

1.Drain cherries, reserving ¼ cup juice. Place cherries in a slow cooker.
2.In a small bowl, mix the sugar, cornstarch and salt. Stir in reserved juice until smooth. Stir into cherries. Cook, covered, on high for 7 hours. Drizzle amaretto over cherry mixture.
3.For dumplings, in a small bowl, whisk flour, sugar, baking powder, lemon peel, and salt. In another bowl, whisk milk and melted butter. Add to flour mixture, stirring just until moistened.
4.Drop by tablespoonfuls on top of hot cherry mixture. Cook, covered, for 45 minutes or until a toothpick inserted in center of dumplings comes out clean. If desired, serve warm with ice cream.

Spiced Rice Pudding with Cherries

Prep time: 10 minutes | Cook time: 2 to 3 hours | Serves 12

4 cups cooked long grain rice
1 (12-ounce / 340-g) can evaporated milk
1 cup 2% milk
⅓ cup sugar
¼ cup water
¾ cup dried cherries
3 tablespoons butter, softened
2 teaspoons vanilla extract
½ teaspoon ground cinnamon
¼ teaspoon ground nutmeg
Cooking spray

1.In a large bowl, combine the rice, evaporated milk, milk, sugar, and water. Stir in the remaining ingredients. Transfer to a slow cooker coated with cooking spray.
2.Cover and cook on low for 2 to 3 hours or until mixture is thickened. Stir lightly and serve.

Apple Pie Oatmeal

Prep time: 10 minutes | Cook time: 4 to 5 hours | Serves 6

1 cup quick-cooking oats
½ cup all-purpose flour
⅓ cup packed brown sugar
2 teaspoons baking powder
1½ teaspoons apple pie spice
¼ teaspoon salt
3 eggs
1⅔ cups 2% milk, divided
1½ teaspoons vanilla extract
3 medium apples, peeled and finely chopped
Vanilla ice cream (optional)

1.In a large bowl, whisk oats, flour, brown sugar, baking powder, pie spice and salt. In a small bowl, whisk eggs, 1 cup milk and vanilla until blended. Add to oat mixture, stirring just until moistened. Fold in apples.
2.Transfer to a greased slow cooker. Cook, covered, on low for 4 to 5 hours or until apples are tender and top is set.
3.Stir in remaining milk. Serve warm or cold with ice cream if desired.

Pear and Cherry Buckle

Prep time: 10 minutes | Cook time: 3 to 4 hours | Serves 6

2 (15-ounce / 425-g) cans sliced pears, drained
1 (21-ounce / 595-g) can cherry pie filling
¼ teaspoon almond extract
1 package yellow cake mix (regular size)
¼ cup old-fashioned oats
¼ cup sliced almonds
1 tablespoon brown sugar
½ cup butter, melted
Vanilla ice cream (optional)

1.In a greased slow cooker, combine pears and pie filling, then stir in extract. In a large bowl, combine cake mix, oats, almonds, and brown sugar. Stir in melted butter. Sprinkle over fruit.
2.Cook, covered, on low for 3 to 4 hours or until topping is golden brown. If desired, serve with ice cream.

Coconut Bananas Foster

Prep time: 10 minutes | Cook time: 2 hours | Serves 5

5 medium firm bananas
1 cup packed brown sugar
¼ cup butter, melted
¼ cup rum
1 teaspoon vanilla extract
½ teaspoon ground cinnamon
⅓ cup chopped walnuts
⅓ cup flaked coconut
Vanilla ice cream or sliced pound cake, for serving

1.Cut bananas in half lengthwise, then widthwise. Layer in the bottom of a slow cooker. Combine the brown sugar, butter, rum, vanilla, and cinnamon, then pour over bananas. Cover and cook on low for 1½ hours or until heated through.
2.Sprinkle with walnuts and coconut and cook for 30 minutes longer. Serve with ice cream or pound cake.

Slow-Cooker Blueberry Grunt

Prep time: 20 minutes | Cook time: 2½ to 3½ hours | Serves 6

4 cups fresh or frozen blueberries
¾ cup sugar
½ cup water
1 teaspoon almond extract
Dumplings:
2 cups all-purpose flour
4 teaspoons baking powder
1 teaspoon sugar
½ teaspoon salt
1 tablespoon cold butter
1 tablespoon shortening
¾ cup 2% milk
Vanilla ice cream (optional)

1. Place blueberries, sugar, water, and extract in a slow cooker, stirring to combine. Cook, covered, on high for 2 to 3 hours or until bubbly.
2. For dumplings, in a small bowl, whisk flour, baking powder, sugar, and salt. Cut in butter and shortening until crumbly. Add milk and stir just until a soft dough forms.
3. Drop dough by tablespoonfuls on top of hot blueberry mixture. Cook, covered, for 30 minutes longer or until a toothpick inserted in center of dumplings comes out clean. If desired, serve warm with ice cream.

Chocolate Cherry Pudding Cake

Prep time: 20 minutes | Cook time: 2 to 2½ hours | Serves 8

½ cup reduced-fat sour cream
2 tablespoons canola oil
1 tablespoon butter, melted
2 teaspoons vanilla extract
1 cup all-purpose flour
¼ cup sugar
¼ cup packed brown sugar
3 tablespoons baking cocoa
2 teaspoon baking powder
½ teaspoon ground cinnamon
⅛ teaspoon salt
1 cup fresh or frozen pitted dark sweet cherries, thawed
1 cup fresh or frozen pitted tart cherries, thawed
⅓ cup 60% cacao bittersweet chocolate baking chips
Cooking spray
Pudding:
½ cup packed brown sugar
2 tablespoons baking cocoa
1¼ cups hot water

1. In a large bowl, beat the sour cream, oil, butter, and vanilla until blended. Combine the flour, sugars, cocoa, baking powder, cinnamon, and salt. Add to sour cream mixture and stir just until combined. Stir in cherries and chips. Pour into a slow cooker coated with cooking spray.
2. In a small bowl, combine brown sugar and cocoa. Stir in hot water until blended. Pour over the batter (do not stir). Cover and cook on high for 2 to 2½ hours or until set. Let stand for 15 minutes. Serve warm.

Old-Fashioned Pearl Tapioca Pudding

Prep time: 10 minutes | Cook time: 4½ to 5½ hours | Serves 18

8 cups 2% milk
1 cup pearl tapioca
1 cup plus 2 tablespoons sugar
⅛ teaspoon salt
4 eggs
1½ teaspoons vanilla extract
Sliced fresh strawberries and whipped cream (optional)

1. In a slow cooker, combine the milk, tapioca, sugar, and salt. Cover and cook on low for 4 to 5 hours.
2. In a large bowl, beat the eggs. Stir in a small amount of hot tapioca mixture. Return all to the slow cooker, stirring to combine. Cover and cook for 30 minutes longer or until a thermometer reads 160ºF (71ºC). Stir in vanilla.
3. Serve with strawberries and whipped cream if desired.

Raisin Bread Pudding with Bourbon Sauce

Prep time: 20 minutes | Cook time: 3 hours | Serves 6

3 eggs
1¼ cups 2% milk
½ cup sugar
3 teaspoons vanilla extract
½ teaspoon ground cinnamon
¼ teaspoon ground nutmeg
⅛ teaspoon salt
4½ cups cubed day-old brioche or egg bread
1¼ cups raisins
Bourbon Sauce:
¼ cup butter, cubed
½ cup sugar
¼ cup light corn syrup
3 tablespoons bourbon

1.In a large bowl, whisk the first seven ingredients. Stir in bread and raisins. Transfer to a greased slow cooker. Cover and cook on low for 3 hours.
2.Meanwhile, in a small saucepan over medium heat, heat the butter. Stir in sugar and corn syrup, then bring to a boil. Reduce heat, cook and stir until sugar is dissolved.
3.Remove from the heat and stir in bourbon. Serve warm with bread pudding.

Ginger and Pink Grapefruit Cheesecake

Prep time: 15 minutes | Cook time: 2 hours | Serves 6

¾ cup graham cracker crumbs
1 tablespoon plus ⅔ cup sugar, divided
1 teaspoon grated grapefruit peel
¼ teaspoon ground ginger
2½ tablespoons butter, melted
2 (8-ounce / 227-g) packages cream cheese, softened
½ cup sour cream
2 tablespoons pink grapefruit juice
2 eggs, lightly beaten

1.Place a greased springform pan on a double thickness of heavy-duty foil. Wrap foil securely around pan. Pour 1 inch water in a slow cooker. Layer two 24-inch pieces of aluminum foil. Starting with a long side, fold up foil to create a 1-inch-wide strip; roll into a coil. Place in a slow cooker to form a rack for the cheesecake.
2.In a small bowl, mix cracker crumbs, 1 tablespoon sugar, peel, and ginger. Stir in butter. Press onto bottom and about 1 inch up sides of prepared pan.
3.In a large bowl, beat cream cheese and remaining sugar until smooth. Beat in sour cream and grapefruit juice. Add eggs and beat on low speed just until combined.
4.Pour into crust. Place springform pan on top of coil. Cover slow cooker with a double layer of paper towels and place lid securely over towels. Cook on high, covered, for 2 hours. Do not remove lid. Turn off the slow cooker and let cheesecake stand, covered, in slow cooker for 1 hour. The center of the cheesecake will be just set and the top will appear dull.
5.Remove springform pan from slow cooker and remove foil from pan. Cool cheesecake on a wire rack for 1 hour before serving.

Apple Cinnamon Brown Betty

Prep time: 15 minutes | Cook time: 2 to 3 hours | Serves 6

5 medium tart apples, cubed
2 tablespoons lemon juice
1 cup packed brown sugar
1 teaspoon ground cinnamon
¼ teaspoon ground nutmeg
6 tablespoons butter, melted
6 cups cubed day-old cinnamon-raisin bread (about 10 slices)
Sweetened whipped cream (optional)

1.In a large bowl, toss apples with lemon juice. In a small bowl, mix brown sugar, cinnamon, and nutmeg. Add to apple mixture and toss to coat. In a separate large bowl, drizzle butter over bread cubes and toss to coat.
2.Place 2 cups bread cubes in a greased slow cooker. Layer with half of the apple mixture and 2 cups bread cubes. Repeat layers. Cook on low, covered, for 2 to 3 hours or until apples are tender. Stir before serving. If desired, top with whipped cream.

Molten Chocolate Mocha Cake

Prep time: 10 minutes | Cook time: 2½ to 3 hours | Serves 4

4 eggs
1½ cups sugar
½ cup butter, melted
3 teaspoons vanilla extract
1 cup all-purpose flour
½ cup baking cocoa
1 tablespoon instant coffee granules
¼ teaspoon salt
Fresh raspberries or sliced fresh strawberries and vanilla ice cream (optional)

1. In a large bowl, beat eggs, sugar, butter, and vanilla until blended. In another bowl, whisk flour, cocoa, coffee granules, and salt. Gradually beat into egg mixture.
2. Transfer to a greased slow cooker. Cook, covered, on low for 2½ to 3 hours or until a toothpick comes out with moist crumbs. If desired, serve warm cake with berries and ice cream.

Chocolate Peanut Cluster

Prep time: 10 minutes | Cook time: 1½ hours | Makes about 11 dozen

4 ounces (113 g) German sweet chocolate, chopped
1 (12-ounce / 340-g) package semisweet chocolate chips
4 (10- to 12-ounce / 283- to 340-g) packages white baking chips
2 (16-ounce / 454-g) jars lightly salted dry roasted peanuts

1. In a slow cooker, layer ingredients in order listed (do not stir). Cover and cook on low for 1½ hours. Stir to combine. (If chocolate is not melted, cover and cook for 15 minutes longer; stir. Repeat in 15-minute increments until chocolate is melted.)
2. Drop mixture by rounded tablespoonfuls onto waxed paper. Let stand until set. Serve immediately or store in an airtight container at room temperature.

Baked Cinnamon Apples

Prep time: 10 minutes | Cook time: 3 to 4 hours | Serves 7

6 large tart apples
2 tablespoons lemon juice
½ cup packed brown sugar
½ cup sugar
2 tablespoons all-purpose flour
1 teaspoon ground cinnamon
¼ teaspoon ground nutmeg
6 tablespoons butter, melted
Vanilla ice cream, for serving

1. Peel, core and cut each apple into eight wedges. Transfer the wedges to a slow cooker. Drizzle with lemon juice.
2. Combine the sugars, flour, cinnamon, and nutmeg in a bowl. Sprinkle the mixture over apples and drizzle with butter.
3. Cover and cook on low for 3 to 4 hours or until apples are tender. Serve in dessert dishes with ice cream.

Fallen Chocolate Soufflé Cake

Prep time: 5 minutes | Cook time: 6 hours | Serves 10 to 12

1 (18¼-ounce / 517-g) package chocolate cake mix
½ cup vegetable oil
2 cups sour cream
4 eggs, beaten
1 (3-ounce / 85-g) box instant chocolate pudding mix
1 cup chocolate chips (optional)

1. Combine all ingredients in a greased slow cooker.
2. Cover and cook on low for 6 hours. (Do not lift the lid until the end of the cooking time!)
3. Insert a toothpick into the center of cake to see if it comes out clean. If it does, the soufflé is finished. If it doesn't, continue cooking for another 15 minutes. Check again. Repeat until it's finished cooking.
4. Serve warm.

Creamy Pumpkin Pie Pudding

Prep time: 10 minutes | Cook time: 3 hours | Serves 8

1 (15-ounce / 425-g) can pumpkin
1 (12-ounce / 340-g) can evaporated skim milk
¾ cup Splenda
½ cup low-fat buttermilk baking mix
2 eggs, beaten, or 6 egg whites
2 teaspoons pumpkin pie spice
1 teaspoon lemon zest
Cooking spray

1. Combine all ingredients in a slow cooker sprayed with cooking spray. Stir until lumps disappear.
2. Cover and cook on low for 3 hours.
3. Serve warm or cold.

Black and Blue Berry Cobbler

Prep time: 20 minutes | Cook time: 2 to 2½ hours | Serves 6

1 cup flour
¾ cup sugar
1 teaspoon baking powder
¼ teaspoon salt
¼ teaspoon ground cinnamon
¼ teaspoon ground nutmeg
2 eggs, beaten
2 tablespoons milk
2 tablespoons vegetable oil
Berry:
2 cups fresh or frozen blueberries
2 cups fresh or frozen blackberries
¾ cup water
1 teaspoon grated orange peel
¾ cup sugar

1. Combine flour, sugar, baking powder, salt, cinnamon, and nutmeg in a bowl.
2. Whisk eggs, milk, and oil in a separate bowl. Stir into dry ingredients until moistened.
3. Spread the batter evenly over bottom of a greased slow cooker.
4. In a saucepan, combine berries, water, orange peel, and sugar. Bring to a boil. Remove from heat and pour over batter in the slow cooker.
5. Cover and cook on high for 2 to 2½ hours, or until a toothpick inserted into batter comes out clean.
6. Turn off the cooker. Uncover and let stand for 30 minutes before serving.

Spiced Applesauce Cake

Prep time: 10 minutes | Cook time: 3 to 4 hours | Serves 6

1 cup all-purpose flour
½ teaspoon baking soda
¼ teaspoon ground cinnamon
¼ teaspoon salt
Pinch ground nutmeg
Pinch ground cloves
½ cup granulated sugar
½ cup unsweetened applesauce
1 large egg
½ teaspoon vanilla extract
6 tablespoons unsalted butter, melted
Confectioners' sugar, for dusting

1. Fill a slow cooker with ½ inch water (about 2 cups) and place aluminum foil rack in bottom. Grease a springform pan and line with parchment paper.
2. Whisk flour, baking soda, cinnamon, salt, nutmeg, and cloves together in a bowl. In a large bowl, whisk granulated sugar, applesauce, egg, and vanilla until smooth, then slowly whisk in melted butter until well combined. Stir in flour mixture until just incorporated.
3. Scrape batter into prepared pan and smooth top. Gently tap pan on the counter to release air bubbles. Set pan on prepared rack, cover, and cook until toothpick inserted in center comes out clean, 3 to 4 hours on high.
4. Let cake cool in pan on wire rack for 10 minutes. Run a small knife around edge of cake, then remove sides of pan. Remove cake from pan bottom, discarding parchment, and let cool completely on a rack, 1 to 2 hours. Transfer to a serving dish and dust with confectioners' sugar. Serve.

Simple Pineapple Tapioca

Prep time: 10 minutes | Cook time: 3 hours | Serves 4 to 6

2½ cups water
2½ cups pineapple juice
½ cup dry small pearl tapioca
¾ to 1 cup sugar
1 (15-ounce / 425-g) can crushed pineapple, undrained

1. Mix first four ingredients together in a slow cooker.
2. Cover and cook on high for 3 hours.
3. Stir in crushed pineapple. Chill for several hours before serving.

Cherry and Hazelnut Stuffed Apples

Prep time: 10 minutes | Cook time: 4 to 5 hours | Serves 6

7 large Granny Smith apples

8 tablespoons unsalted butter, softened
¼ cup packed brown sugar
⅓ cup dried cherries, chopped
⅓ cup hazelnuts, toasted, skinned, and chopped
3 tablespoons old-fashioned rolled oats
1 teaspoon grated orange zest
½ teaspoon pepper
Pinch salt
Vegetable oil spray
⅓ cup maple syrup

1. Peel and core 1 apple and cut into ¼-inch pieces. Combine apple pieces, 5 tablespoons butter, sugar, cherries, hazelnuts, oats, orange zest, pepper, and salt in a bowl. Set aside.
2. Shave thin slice off bottom (blossom end) of remaining 6 apples to allow them to sit flat. Cut top ½ inch off stem end of apples and reserve. Peel apples and use melon baller or small measuring spoon to cut 1½-inch diameter opening from core, being careful not to cut through bottom of apple. Spoon filling inside apples, mounding excess filling over cavities. Top with reserved apple caps.

3. Lightly coat slow cooker with vegetable oil spray. Arrange stuffed apples in a prepared slow cooker. Drizzle with maple syrup, cover, and cook until skewer inserted into apples meets little resistance, 4 to 5 hours on low.
4. Using tongs and sturdy spatula, transfer apples to a serving dish. Whisk remaining 3 tablespoons butter into cooking liquid, 1 tablespoon at a time, until incorporated. Spoon sauce over apples and serve.

Raisin Rice Pudding

Prep time: 10 minutes | Cook time: 2 hours | Serves 6

2½ cups rice, cooked
1½ cups evaporated milk or scalded milk
⅔ cup brown or white sugar
1 tablespoon butter, softened
2 teaspoons vanilla
½ to 1 teaspoon nutmeg
1 eggs, beaten
½ to 1 cup raisins

1. Mix together all ingredients in a bowl. Pour into lightly greased slow cooker.
2. Cover and cook on high for 2 hours, or on low for 4 to 6 hours. Stir after first hour.
3. Serve warm or cold.

Chocolate Fondue

Prep time: 5 minutes | Cook time: 1 to 3 hours | Serves 6

1 (8 squares) package semisweet chocolate
1 (4-ounce / 113-g) package sweet cooking chocolate
¾ cup sweetened condensed milk
¼ cup sugar
2 tablespoons kirsch

1. Break both chocolates into pieces and place in a slow cooker. Set cooker to high and stir chocolate constantly until it melts.
2. Turn cooker to low and stir in milk and sugar. Stir until thoroughly blended.
3. Stir in kirsch. Cover and cook on low until fondue comes to a very gentle simmer, about 1 to 3 hours. Serve warm.

Fruity Cake with Walnuts

Prep time: 10 minutes | Cook time: 3 to 5 hours | Serves 10 to 12

1 or 2 (21-ounce / 595-g) cans apple, blueberry, or peach pie filling
1 (18¼-ounce / 517-g) package yellow cake mix
1 stick (½ cup) butter, melted
⅓ cup chopped walnuts
Nonstick cooking spray

1. Spray the insert of the slow cooker with nonstick cooking spray.
2. Place pie filling in a slow cooker.
3. In a mixing bowl, combine dry cake mix and butter. Spoon over filling.
4. Drop walnuts over top.
5. Cover and cook on low for 3 to 5 hours, or until a toothpick inserted into the center of topping comes out clean. Serve warm.

Chocolate Chip Graham Cracker Cookies

Prep time: 10 minutes | Cook time: 1½ hours | Makes 4 dozen

1 (12-ounce / 340-g) package semi-sweet chocolate chips
2 (1-ounce / 28-g) squares unsweetened baking chocolate, shaved
2 (14-ounce / 397-g) cans sweetened condensed milk
3¾ cups crushed graham cracker crumbs, divided
1 cup finely chopped walnuts

1. Place chocolate in a slow cooker.
2. Cover and cook on high for 1 hour, stirring every 15 minutes. Continue to cook on low, stirring every 15 minutes, or until chocolate is melted (about 30 minutes).
3. Stir milk into melted chocolate.
4. Add 3 cups of graham cracker crumbs, 1 cup at a time, stirring after each addition.
5. Stir in nuts. Mixture should be thick but not stiff.
6. Stir in remaining ¾ cup of graham cracker crumbs to reach consistency of cookie dough.
7. Drop by heaping teaspoonfuls onto lightly greased cookie sheets. Keep remaining mixture warm by covering and turning the slow cooker to Warm.
8. Bake in oven at 325ºF (163ºC) for 7 to 9 minutes, or until tops of cookies begin to crack. Remove from oven and cool for 10 minutes before serving.

Fudgy Brownies

Prep time: 10 minutes | Cook time: 3 to 4 hours | Serves 6

½ cup all-purpose flour
½ teaspoon baking powder
⅛ teaspoon salt
2 ounces (57 g) unsweetened chocolate, chopped
5 tablespoons unsalted butter
⅔ cup packed brown sugar
1 large egg plus 1 large yolk, room temperature
½ teaspoon vanilla extract
⅓ cup toasted and chopped walnuts (optional)

1. Fill a slow cooker with ½ inch water (about 2 cups) and place aluminum foil rack in bottom. Grease a springform pan and line with parchment paper.
2. Whisk flour, baking powder, and salt together in a bowl. In a large bowl, microwave chocolate and butter at 50 percent power, stirring occasionally, until melted, 1 to 2 minutes; let cool slightly. Whisk sugar, egg and yolk, and vanilla into cooled chocolate mixture until well combined. Stir in flour mixture until just incorporated.
3. Scrape batter into prepared pan, smooth top, and sprinkle with walnuts, if using. Set pan on prepared rack, cover, and cook until toothpick inserted into center comes out with few moist crumbs attached, 3 to 4 hours on high.
4. Let brownies cool completely in pan on the wire rack, 1 to 2 hours. Cut into wedges and serve.

Cinnamon Applesauce

Prep time: 10 minutes | Cook time: 8 to 10 hours | Serves 8 to 10

8 apples, peeled, cored, and cut into chunks or slices (6 cups)
1 teaspoon cinnamon
½ cup water
½ to 1 cup sugar

1. Combine all ingredients in a slow cooker.
2. Cook on low for 8 to 10 hours, or on high 3 to 4 hours. Serve warm.

Stewed Dried Apricots

Prep time: 5 minutes | Cook time: 3 to 4 hours | Serves 6

1 (12-ounce / 340-g) package dried apricots
1 strip lemon or orange zest

1. Put the apricots and citrus zest in the slow cooker and add water to cover. Cover and cook on low until plump and tender, 3 to 4 hours.
2. Turn off the cooker, remove the lid, and let the apricots cool. Serve.

Strawberry Rhubarb Compote

Prep time: 10 minutes | Cook time: 3 to 4 hours | Serves 6

¼ cup water or orange juice
1 cup sugar
1 pound (454 g) fresh rhubarb, trimmed of leaves and cut into 1½-inch chunks (about 4 cups)
2 teaspoons fresh lemon juice
2 pints fresh strawberries, hulled and cut in half

1. Combine the water, sugar, and rhubarb in the slow cooker. Cover and cook on low until soft, 3 to 4 hours.
2. Mash the rhubarb a bit with a fork or the back of a large spoon. Add the lemon juice and strawberries and stir once to distribute.
3. Turn off the cooker and let the fruit cool a bit. Serve warm or at room temperature. Or transfer to a storage container, refrigerate, and serve chilled, ladled into dessert bowls. The compote will keep, tightly covered, for 4 days in the refrigerator.

Lemon Blueberry Cornmeal Cake

Prep time: 10 minutes | Cook time: 2 to 3 hours | Serves 6

1 cup all-purpose flour
¼ cup cornmeal
½ teaspoon baking powder
½ teaspoon baking soda
Salt, to taste
½ cup plain yogurt
⅓ cup granulated sugar
1 large egg
2 teaspoons grated lemon zest plus 4 teaspoons juice
½ teaspoon vanilla extract
4 tablespoons unsalted butter, melted
5 ounces (142 g) blueberries
¾ cup confectioners' sugar
Cooking spray

1. Fill a slow cooker with ½ inch water (about 2 cups) and place aluminum foil rack in bottom. Make foil sling for 8½ by 4½-inch loaf pan by folding 2 long sheets of foil; first sheet should be 8½ inches wide and second sheet should be 4½ inches wide. Lay sheets of foil in a pan perpendicular to each other, with extra foil hanging over edges of pan. Push foil into corners and up sides of pan, smoothing foil flush to pan. Lightly grease foil with cooking spray.
2. Whisk flour, cornmeal, baking powder, baking soda, and ½ teaspoon of salt together in a bowl. In a large bowl, whisk yogurt, granulated sugar, egg, lemon zest, and vanilla until smooth, then slowly whisk in melted butter until well combined. Stir in flour mixture until just incorporated. Gently fold in blueberries.
3. Scrape batter into prepared pan and smooth top. Gently tap pan on the counter to release air bubbles. Set pan on prepared rack, cover, and cook until toothpick inserted in center comes out clean, 2 to 3 hours on high.
4. Let cake cool in pan on wire rack for 10 minutes. Using foil overhang, lift cake out of pan and transfer to rack, discarding foil. Let cake cool completely, 1 to 2 hours.
5. Whisk confectioners' sugar, pinch salt, and lemon juice in a small bowl until smooth. Flip cake over onto a serving dish. Drizzle top and sides with glaze and let glaze set before serving, about 25 minutes.

Chocolate Snack Cake

Prep time: 10 minutes | Cook time: 1 to 2 hours | Serves 6

½ cup all-purpose flour
½ teaspoon salt
½ teaspoon baking soda
⅛ teaspoon baking powder
1½ ounces (43 g) unsweetened chocolate, chopped
3 tablespoons unsweetened cocoa powder
3 tablespoons unsalted butter, cut into 3 pieces
¼ teaspoon instant espresso powder
¼ cup boiling water
½ cup packed light brown sugar
¼ cup sour cream
1 large egg
½ teaspoon vanilla extract
Confectioners' sugar, for dusting

1. Fill a slow cooker with ½ inch water (about 2 cups) and place aluminum foil rack in bottom. Grease a springform pan and line with parchment paper.
2. Whisk flour, salt, baking soda, and baking powder together in a bowl. In a large bowl, combine chocolate, cocoa, butter, and espresso powder. Pour boiling water over chocolate mixture, cover, and let sit until chocolate and butter are melted, 3 to 5 minutes. Whisk mixture until smooth and let cool slightly. Whisk brown sugar, sour cream, egg, and vanilla into cooled chocolate mixture until well combined. Stir in flour mixture until just incorporated.
3. Scrape batter into prepared pan and smooth top. Gently tap pan on the counter to release air bubbles. Set pan on prepared rack, cover, and cook until toothpick inserted in center comes out with few moist crumbs attached, 1 to 2 hours on high.
4. Let cake cool in pan on wire rack for 10 minutes. Run a small knife around edge of cake, then remove sides of pan. Remove cake from pan bottom, discarding parchment, and let cool completely on a rack, 1 to 2 hours. Transfer to a serving dish and dust with confectioners' sugar. Serve.

Carrot Cake with Cream Cheese Frosting

Prep time: 15 minutes | Cook time: 3 to 4 hours | Serves 6

Cake:
¾ cup plus 2 tablespoons all-purpose flour
½ teaspoon baking powder
½ teaspoon baking soda
½ teaspoon ground cinnamon
Pinch ground cloves
Pinch salt
½ cup packed brown sugar
1 large egg
7 tablespoons vegetable oil
¾ cup shredded carrots

Frosting:
4 ounces (113 g) cream cheese, softened
2 tablespoons unsalted butter, softened
1 teaspoon vanilla extract
Pinch salt
½ cup confectioner's sugar

1. For the cake: Fill a slow cooker with ½ inch water (about 2 cups) and place aluminum foil rack in bottom. Grease a springform pan and line with parchment paper.
2. Whisk flour, baking powder, baking soda, cinnamon, cloves, and salt together in a bowl. In a large bowl, whisk sugar and egg until smooth, then slowly whisk in oil until well combined. Stir in flour mixture until just incorporated. Gently fold in carrots.
3. Scrape batter into prepared pan and smooth top. Gently tap pan on the counter to release air bubbles. Set pan on prepared rack, cover, and cook until toothpick inserted in center comes out clean, 3 to 4 hours on high.
4. Let cake cool in pan on wire rack for 10 minutes. Run a small knife around edge of cake, then remove sides of pan. Remove cake from pan bottom, discarding parchment, and let cool completely on a rack, 1 to 2 hours. Transfer cake to a serving dish.
5. For the frosting: Using a handheld mixer set at medium-high speed, beat cream cheese, butter, vanilla, and salt in a medium bowl until smooth, 1 to 2 minutes, scraping down sides of bowl as needed. Reduce speed to medium-low, gradually add sugar, and beat until smooth, 2 to 3 minutes. Increase speed to medium-high and beat until frosting is pale and fluffy, 2 to 3 minutes. Spread frosting evenly over top of cake. Serve.

Creamy Cheesecake

Prep time: 10 minutes | Cook time: 1½ to 2½ hours | Serves 8

6 whole graham crackers, broken into 1-inch pieces
2 tablespoons unsalted butter, melted
⅔ cup plus 1 tablespoon sugar, divided
½ teaspoon ground cinnamon
Salt, to taste
18 ounces (510 g) cream cheese, softened
1 teaspoon vanilla extract
¼ cup sour cream
2 large eggs

1. Pulse graham crackers in a food processor to fine crumbs, about 20 pulses. Add melted butter, 1 tablespoon sugar, cinnamon, and pinch salt and pulse to combine, about 4 pulses. Sprinkle crumbs into a springform pan and press into an even layer using the bottom of the dry measuring cup. Wipe out processor bowl.
2. Process cream cheese, vanilla, ¼ teaspoon salt, and remaining ⅔ cup sugar in the processor until combined, about 15 seconds, scraping down sides of bowl as needed. Add sour cream and eggs and process until just incorporated, about 15 seconds; do not over mix. Pour filling into prepared pan and smooth top.
3. Fill a slow cooker with ½ inch water (about 2 cups) and place aluminum foil rack in bottom. Set pan on prepared rack, cover, and cook until cheesecake registers 150ºF (66ºC), 1½ to 2½ hours on high. Turn off slow cooker and let cheesecake sit, covered, for 1 hour.
4. Transfer cheesecake to a wire rack. Run a small knife around edge of cake and gently blot away condensation using paper towels. Let cheesecake cool in pan to room temperature, about 1 hour. Cover with plastic wrap and refrigerate until well chilled, at least for 3 hours or up to 3 days.
5. About 30 minutes before serving, run a small knife around edge of cheesecake, then remove sides of pan. Invert cheesecake onto sheet of parchment paper, then turn cheesecake right side up onto a serving dish. Serve.

Pumpkin Spice Cheesecake

Prep time: 10 minutes | Cook time: 1½ to 2½ hours | Serves 8

6 whole graham crackers, broken into 1-inch pieces
2 tablespoons unsalted butter, melted
⅔ cup plus 1 tablespoon sugar, divided
1½ teaspoons ground cinnamon, divided
Salt, to taste
1 cup canned unsweetened pumpkin purée
12 ounces (340 g) cream cheese, softened
½ teaspoon ground ginger
⅛ teaspoon ground cloves
¼ cup sour cream
2 large eggs

1. Pulse graham crackers in a food processor to fine crumbs, about 20 pulses. Add melted butter, 1 tablespoon sugar, ½ teaspoon cinnamon, and pinch salt and pulse to combine, about 4 pulses. Sprinkle crumbs into a springform pan and press into an even layer using the bottom of the dry measuring cup. Wipe out processor bowl.
2. Spread pumpkin purée over baking sheet lined with several layers of paper towels and press dry with additional towels. Transfer purée to the processor bowl (purée will separate easily from towels). Add cream cheese, ginger, cloves, ½ teaspoon salt, remaining ⅔ cup sugar, and remaining 1 teaspoon cinnamon and process until combined, about 15 seconds, scraping down sides of bowl as needed. Add sour cream and eggs and process until just incorporated, about 15 seconds; do not over mix. Pour filling into prepared pan and smooth top.
3. Fill a slow cooker with ½ inch water (about 2 cups) and place aluminum foil rack in bottom. Set pan on prepared rack, cover, and cook until cheesecake registers 150ºF (66ºC), 1½ to 2½ hours on high. Turn off slow cooker and let cheesecake sit, covered, for 1 hour.
4. Transfer cheesecake to a wire rack. Run a small knife around edge of cake and gently blot away condensation using paper towels. Let cheesecake cool in pan to room temperature, about 1 hour. Cover with plastic wrap and refrigerate until well chilled, at least for 3 hours or up to 3 days.
5. About 30 minutes before serving, run a small knife around edge of cheesecake, then remove sides of pan. Invert cheesecake onto sheet of parchment paper, then turn cheesecake right side up onto a serving dish. Serve.

Ultimate Chocolate Cheesecake

Prep time: 5 minutes | Cook time: 1½ to 2½ hours | Serves 8

8 chocolate sandwich cookies
2 tablespoons unsalted butter, melted
4 ounces (113 g) semisweet chocolate, chopped
18 ounces (510 g) cream cheese, softened
⅔ cup sugar
¼ teaspoon salt
¼ cup sour cream
2 large eggs
2 tablespoons unsweetened cocoa powder
1 teaspoon vanilla extract

1.Pulse cookies in a food processor to fine crumbs, about 20 pulses. Add melted butter and pulse to combine, about 4 pulses. Sprinkle crumbs into a springform pan and press into an even layer using the bottom of the dry measuring cup. Wipe out processor bowl.
2.Microwave chocolate in a bowl at 50 percent power, stirring occasionally, until melted, 1 to 2 minutes. Let cool slightly. Process cream cheese, sugar, and salt in the processor until combined, about 15 seconds, scraping down sides of bowl as needed. Add cooled chocolate, sour cream, eggs, cocoa, and vanilla and process until just incorporated, about 15 seconds; do not over mix. Pour filling into prepared pan and smooth top.
3.Fill a slow cooker with ½ inch water (about 2 cups) and place aluminum foil rack in bottom. Set pan on prepared rack, cover, and cook until cheesecake registers 150°F (66°C), 1½ to 2½ hours on high. Turn off slow cooker and let cheesecake sit, covered, for 1 hour.
4.Transfer cheesecake to a wire rack. Run a small knife around edge of cake and gently blot away condensation using paper towels. Let cheesecake cool in pan to room temperature, about 1 hour. Cover with plastic wrap and refrigerate until well chilled, at least for 3 hours or up to 3 days.
5.About 30 minutes before serving, run a small knife around edge of cheesecake, then remove sides of pan. Invert cheesecake onto sheet of parchment paper, then turn cheesecake right side up onto a serving dish. Serve.

Coconut Key Lime Pie

Prep time: 10 minutes | Cook time: 1 to 2 hours | Serves 8

6 whole graham crackers, broken into 1-inch pieces
2 tablespoons unsalted butter, melted
1 tablespoon sugar
Salt, to taste
1 (14-ounce / 397-g) can sweetened condensed milk
1 tablespoon grated lime zest plus ½ cup juice (4 limes)
2 ounces (57 g) cream cheese, softened
1 large egg yolk, room temperature
¼ cup sweetened shredded coconut, toasted

1.Pulse graham crackers in a food processor to fine crumbs, about 20 pulses. Add melted butter, sugar, and pinch salt and pulse to combine, about 4 pulses. Sprinkle crumbs into a springform pan and press into an even layer using the bottom of the dry measuring cup. Wipe out processor bowl.
2.Process condensed milk, lime zest and juice, and cream cheese in the processor until combined, about 15 seconds, scraping down sides of bowl as needed. Add egg yolk and process until just incorporated, about 5 seconds. Pour filling into prepared pan and smooth top.
3.Fill a slow cooker with ½ inch water (about 2 cups) and place aluminum foil rack in bottom. Set pan on prepared rack, cover, and cook until pie registers 150°F (66°C), 1 to 2 hours on high. Turn slow cooker off and let pie sit, covered, for 1 hour.
4.Transfer pie to a wire rack. Run a small knife around edge of pie and gently blot away condensation using paper towels. Let pie cool in pan to room temperature, about 1 hour. Cover with plastic wrap and refrigerate until well chilled, at least for 3 hours or up to 3 days.
5.About 30 minutes before serving, run a small knife around edge of pie, then remove sides of pan. Invert pie onto sheet of parchment paper, then turn pie right side up onto a serving dish. Press coconut gently against sides of pie to adhere, wiping away excess coconut. Serve.

Ginger Peach Crumble

Prep time: 15 minutes | Cook time: 3 to 4 hours | Serves 8 to 10

Filling:
4 pounds (1.8 kg) frozen sliced peaches, thawed and drained (7 cups)
¾ cup granulated sugar
3 tablespoons chopped crystallized ginger
4 teaspoons instant tapioca
1 teaspoon lemon juice
1 teaspoon vanilla extract

Topping:
1 cup all-purpose flour
¼ cup granulated sugar
¼ cup packed light brown sugar
2 teaspoons vanilla extract
¾ teaspoon ground ginger
⅛ teaspoon salt
8 tablespoons unsalted butter, cut into 6 pieces and softened
½ cup sliced almonds, divided

1. For the filling: Combine all ingredients in a slow cooker. Cover and cook until peaches are tender and sauce is thickened, 3 to 4 hours on low or 2 to 3 hours on high.
2. For the topping: Preheat the oven to 350°F (180°C). Pulse flour, granulated sugar, brown sugar, vanilla, ginger, and salt in a food processor until combined, about 5 pulses. Sprinkle butter and ¼ cup almonds over top and process until mixture clumps together into large crumbly balls, about 30 seconds. Sprinkle remaining ¼ cup almonds over top and pulse to incorporate, about 2 pulses.
3. Spread topping evenly over parchment paper-lined rimmed baking sheet and pinch it between your fingers into small pea-size pieces (with some smaller loose bits). Bake until golden brown, about 18 minutes, rotating sheet halfway through baking. Let cool slightly. (Topping can be stored in an airtight container for up to 1 day.)
4. Turn off slow cooker and let peach filling cool for 20 minutes. Gently stir peaches to coat with sauce. Sprinkle individual portions of filling with crumbles before serving.

Apple Crisp with Oat Topping

Prep time: 15 minutes | Cook time: 3 to 4 hours | Serves 6 to 8

Filling:
1½ pounds (680 g) Granny Smith apples, peeled, cored, and cut into ½-inch-thick wedges
1½ pounds (680 g) Golden Delicious apples, peeled, cored, and cut into ½-inch-thick wedges
½ cup apple cider
2 tablespoons packed light brown sugar
4 teaspoons instant tapioca
2 teaspoons lemon juice
¼ teaspoon ground cinnamon

Topping:
½ cup sliced almonds
½ cup all-purpose flour
¼ cup packed light brown sugar
¼ teaspoon ground cinnamon
¼ teaspoon salt
⅛ teaspoon ground nutmeg
5 tablespoons unsalted butter, melted
¾ cup old-fashioned rolled oats
2 tablespoons honey

1. For the filling: Combine all ingredients in a slow cooker. Cover and cook until apples are tender and sauce is thickened, 3 to 4 hours on low or 2 to 3 hours on high.
2. For the topping: Preheat the oven to 400°F (205°C). Pulse almonds, flour, sugar, cinnamon, salt, and nutmeg in a food processor until nuts are finely chopped, about 10 pulses. Drizzle melted butter over top and pulse until mixture resembles crumbly wet sand, about 5 pulses. Add oats and honey and pulse until evenly incorporated, about 3 pulses.
3. Spread topping evenly over parchment paper-lined rimmed baking sheet and pinch it between your fingers into small pea-size pieces (with some smaller loose bits). Bake until golden brown, 8 to 12 minutes, rotating sheet halfway through baking. Let cool slightly. (Topping can be stored in airtight container for up to 1 day.)
4. Turn off slow cooker and let apple filling cool for 20 minutes. Gently stir apples to coat with sauce. Sprinkle individual portions of filling with crumbles before serving.

Vanilla Creme Brûlée

Prep time: 5 minutes | Cook time: 2 to 3 hours | Serves 4

2 cups heavy cream
5 large egg yolks
⅓ cup granulated sugar
1 teaspoon vanilla extract
Pinch salt
4 teaspoons turbinado or Demerara sugar

1.Whisk cream, egg yolks, granulated sugar, vanilla, and salt in a bowl until sugar has dissolved. Strain custard through a fine-mesh strainer into a 4-cup liquid measuring cup. Divide custard evenly among four 6-ounce / 170-g ramekins. Fill a slow cooker with ½ inch water (about 2 cups) and set ramekins in a slow cooker. Cover and cook until centers are just barely set and register 185°F (85°C), 2 to 3 hours on low.
2.Using tongs and sturdy spatula, transfer ramekins to a wire rack and let cool to room temperature, about 2 hours. Cover with plastic wrap and refrigerate until well chilled, at least for 4 hours or up to 2 days.
3.To serve, gently blot away condensation using paper towels. Sprinkle each ramekin with 1 teaspoon turbinado sugar. Tilt and tap each ramekin to distribute sugar evenly, then dump out excess sugar and wipe rims of ramekins clean. Ignite torch and caramelize sugar. Refrigerate ramekins, uncovered, to re-chill custard before serving, 30 to 45 minutes.

Fruit Compote

Prep time: 10 minutes | Cook time: 3 to 4 hours | Serves 6

2 pounds (907 g) frozen sliced peaches, cut into 1-inch pieces
⅓ cup sugar
2 tablespoons instant tapioca
1 teaspoon lemon juice
1 teaspoon vanilla extract
⅛ teaspoon salt
10 ounces (283 g) raspberries
¼ cup chopped fresh mint
2 pints vanilla ice cream or frozen yogurt

1.Combine peaches, sugar, tapioca, lemon juice, vanilla, and salt in a slow cooker. Cover and cook until peaches are tender and sauce is thickened, 3 to 4 hours on low or 2 to 3 hours on high. (Compote can be held on warm or low setting for up to 2 hours.)
2.Stir raspberries into compote and let sit until heated through, about 5 minutes. Stir in mint. Portion ice cream into individual bowls and spoon compote over top. Serve.

Chapter 5 Classic Comfort Foods

Slow-Cooker Chicken Enchiladas

Prep time: 25 minutes | Cook time: 4⅓ to 5⅓ hours | Serves 4 to 6

1 onion, finely chopped
¼ cup vegetable oil, divided
3 tablespoons chili powder
3 garlic cloves, minced
2 teaspoons ground coriander
2 teaspoons ground cumin
1 (15-ounce / 425-g) can tomato sauce, divided
2 teaspoons sugar
1 pound (454 g) boneless, skinless chicken thighs, trimmed
Salt and pepper, to taste
8 ounces (227 g) Monterey Jack cheese, shredded (2 cups)
½ cup minced fresh cilantro
¼ cup jarred jalapeños, chopped
1 tablespoon lime juice
12 (6-inch) corn tortillas

1. Microwave onion, 2 tablespoons of oil, chili powder, garlic, coriander, and cumin in a bowl, stirring occasionally, until onions are softened, about 5 minutes; transfer to a slow cooker. Stir in tomato sauce and sugar. Season chicken with pepper and nestle into a slow cooker. Cover and cook until chicken is tender, 4 to 5 hours on low.
2. Transfer chicken to a cutting board, let cool slightly, then shred into bite-size pieces using 2 forks. Combine chicken, ¾ cup of sauce, 1½ cups of Monterey Jack, cilantro, jalapeños, and lime juice in a large bowl. Season with salt and pepper to taste.
3. Preheat the oven to 450°F (235°C). Spread ¾ cup of sauce over bottom of a baking dish. Brush both sides of tortillas with remaining 2 tablespoons of oil. Stack tortillas, wrap in damp dish towel, and place on a plate. Microwave until warm and pliable, about 1 minute.
4. Working with 1 warm tortilla at a time, spread ⅓ cup chicken filling across center of tortilla. Roll tortilla tightly around filling and place seam-side down in the baking dish. Arrange enchiladas in 2 columns across the width of dish.
5. Pour remaining sauce over enchiladas to cover completely and sprinkle with remaining ½ cup of Monterey Jack. Cover dish tightly with greased aluminum foil. Bake until enchiladas are heated through and cheese is melted, 15 to 20 minutes. Let cool for 5 minutes before serving.

Italian Meatball Stew

Prep time: 20 minutes | Cook time: 8½ to 10½ hours | Serves 8

2 (12-ounce / 340-g) packages frozen fully cooked Italian meatballs
5 medium potatoes, peeled and cubed
1 pound (454 g) fresh baby carrots
1 medium onion, halved and sliced
1 (4½-ounce / 128-g) jar sliced mushrooms, drained
2 (8-ounce / 227-g) cans tomato sauce
1 (10½-ounce / 298-g) can condensed beef broth, undiluted
¾ cup water
¾ cup dry red wine or beef broth
½ teaspoon garlic powder
¼ teaspoon pepper
2 tablespoons all-purpose flour
½ cup cold water

1. Place the meatballs, potatoes, carrots, onion, and mushrooms in a slow cooker. In a large bowl, combine the tomato sauce, broth, water, wine, garlic powder and pepper; pour over top. Cover and cook on low for 8 to 10 hours or until vegetables are tender.
2. Combine flour and water until smooth, then gradually stir into stew. Cover and cook on high for 30 minutes or until thickened. Serve.

Parmesan Chicken Pot Pie

Prep time: 25 minutes | Cook time: 4 to 5 hours | Serves 6

2 pounds (907 g) boneless, skinless chicken thighs, trimmed
Salt and pepper, to taste
¼ cup extra-virgin olive oil, divided
8 ounces (227 g) cremini mushrooms, trimmed and sliced ¼ inch thick
4 carrots, peeled, halved lengthwise, and sliced ½ inch thick
1 onion, finely chopped
½ cup all-purpose flour
2 teaspoons minced fresh thyme or ½ teaspoon dried
1 teaspoon tomato paste
2½ cups chicken broth, plus extra as needed
1 tablespoon soy sauce
1 (9½ by 9-inch) sheet puff pastry, thawed
1 ounce (28 g) Parmesan cheese, grated (½ cup)
1 cup frozen peas, thawed
¼ cup heavy cream
¼ cup chopped fresh parsley

1. Pat chicken dry with paper towels and season with salt and pepper.
2. Heat 1 tablespoon of oil in a skillet over medium-high heat until just smoking. Brown half of chicken, about 4 minutes per side. Transfer to a slow cooker. Repeat with 1 tablespoon of oil and remaining chicken. Transfer to a slow cooker.
3. Heat 1 tablespoon of oil the skillet over medium heat until shimmering. Add mushrooms, carrots, onion, and ½ teaspoon of salt and cook until vegetables are softened and lightly browned, 8 to 10 minutes. Stir in flour, thyme, and tomato paste and cook until fragrant, about 1 minute. slowly stir in 1½ cups of broth, scraping up any browned bits and smoothing out any lumps. Transfer to a slow cooker.
4. Stir remaining 1 cup of broth and soy sauce into a slow cooker. Cover and cook until chicken is tender, 4 to 5 hours on low.
5. Preheat the oven to 400ºF (205ºC). Roll puff pastry into 12 by 9-inch rectangle on a lightly floured surface. Using a paring knife, cut pastry in half lengthwise, then into thirds widthwise to create 6 pieces. Cut four 1-inch slits in each piece and arrange upside down on parchment paper-lined baking sheet. Brush pieces with remaining 1 tablespoon of oil, sprinkle with Parmesan and ¼ teaspoon of pepper, and bake until puffed and lightly browned, 10 to 15 minutes, rotating sheet halfway through baking. Let pastry cool on the sheet.
6. Transfer chicken to a cutting board, let cool slightly, then pull apart into large chunks using 2 forks. Stir chicken, peas, and cream into filling and let sit until heated through, about 5 minutes. Adjust consistency with extra hot broth as needed. Stir in parsley and season with salt and pepper to taste. Top individual portions with pastry before serving.

Caramelized Onion Pot Roast

Prep time: 15 minutes | Cook time: 8 to 10 hours | Serves 4

1 cup water
1 cup beer or beef broth
½ cup beef broth
¼ cup packed brown sugar
3 tablespoons Dijon mustard
2 tablespoons cider vinegar
1 boneless beef chuck roast (4 pounds / 1.8 kg), trimmed
1 teaspoon onion salt
1 teaspoon coarsely ground pepper
1 tablespoon olive oil
3 large sweet onions, halved and sliced
2 tablespoons cornstarch
2 tablespoons cold water

1. In a large bowl, combine the first six ingredients; set aside. Sprinkle roast with onion salt and pepper. In a large skillet, brown meat in oil on all sides. Place onions and roast in a slow cooker; pour beer mixture over top. Cover and cook on low for 8 to 10 hours or until meat is tender.
2. Remove roast and onions and keep warm. Skim fat from cooking juices; transfer 2 cups to a small saucepan. Bring liquid to a boil. Combine cornstarch and water until smooth, then gradually stir into the pan. Bring to a boil, cook and stir for 2 minutes or until thickened. Serve the gravy with the roast and onions.

Chicken and Dumplings

Prep time: 25 minutes | Cook time: 4½ to 5½ hours | Serves 8

Filling:
3 pounds (1.4 kg) boneless, skinless chicken thighs, trimmed
Salt and pepper, to taste
3 tablespoons vegetable oil, divided
2 onions, finely chopped
2 celery ribs, sliced ¼ inch thick
2 carrots, peeled and cut into ¼-inch pieces
¼ cup all-purpose flour
4 garlic cloves, minced
1 tablespoon tomato paste
1 tablespoon minced fresh thyme or 1 teaspoon dried
4 cups chicken broth, plus extra as needed
½ cup dry white wine
2 bay leaves
1 cup frozen peas, thawed
Dumplings:
1¾ cups all-purpose flour
1 tablespoon baking powder
1 teaspoon salt
1 cup whole milk
4 tablespoons unsalted butter, melted

1. For the filling: Pat chicken dry with paper towels and season with salt and pepper. Heat 1 tablespoon of oil in a skillet over medium-high heat until just smoking. Brown half of chicken, about 4 minutes per side. Transfer to a slow cooker. Repeat with 1 tablespoon of oil and remaining chicken. Transfer to a slow cooker.
2. Heat remaining 1 tablespoon of oil in the skillet over medium heat until shimmering. Add onions, celery, and carrots and cook until softened and lightly browned, 8 to 10 minutes. Stir in flour, garlic, tomato paste, and thyme and cook until fragrant, about 1 minute. slowly stir in 1 cup of broth and wine, scraping up any browned bits and smoothing out any lumps. Transfer to a slow cooker.
3. Stir remaining 3 cups of broth and bay leaves into a slow cooker. Cover and cook until chicken is tender, 4 to 5 hours on low.
4. Discard bay leaves. Transfer chicken to a cutting board, let cool slightly, then pull apart into large chunks using 2 forks. Stir chicken and peas into filling. Adjust consistency with extra hot broth as needed.
5. For the dumplings: Whisk flour, baking powder,

and salt together in a large bowl. Stir in milk and melted butter until just incorporated. Using greased ¼-cup measure, drop 8 dumplings around perimeter of filling. Cover and cook on high until dumplings have doubled in size, 30 to 40 minutes. Serve.

Farmhouse Chicken Casserole with Carrots

Prep time: 20 minutes | Cook time: 4 to 5 hours | Serves 6

1 pound (454 g) red potatoes, unpeeled and cut into ½-inch pieces
3 carrots, peeled, halved lengthwise, and sliced ½ inch thick
3 tablespoons extra-virgin olive oil, divided
¼ cup chicken broth, plus extra as needed
2 tablespoons instant tapioca
2 pounds (907 g) boneless, skinless chicken thighs, trimmed
Salt and pepper, to taste
1 (12-inch) baguette, cut into ½-inch pieces
1 (5.2-ounce / 147-g) package Boursin Garlic and Fine Herbs cheese, crumbled
½ cup frozen peas, thawed

1. Microwave potatoes, carrots, and 1 tablespoon of oil in a covered bowl, stirring occasionally, until vegetables are softened, about 5 minutes; transfer to a slow cooker. Stir in broth and tapioca. Season chicken with salt and pepper and nestle into a slow cooker. Cover and cook until chicken is tender, 4 to 5 hours on low.
2. Preheat the oven to 450°F (235°C). Arrange bread in a single layer on rimmed baking sheet and bake until browned and crisp, about 10 minutes, stirring halfway through baking. Toss croutons with remaining 2 tablespoons of oil, and season with salt and pepper to taste. Set aside for serving.
3. Transfer chicken to a cutting board, let cool slightly, then pull apart into large chunks using 2 forks. Stir Boursin into filling until well combined. Stir in chicken and peas and let sit until heated through, about 5 minutes. Adjust consistency with extra hot broth as needed. Season with salt and pepper to taste. Top individual portions with croutons and serve.

Hearty Paella

Prep time: 30 minutes | Cook time: 2 to 3 hours | Serves 6 to 8

1 onion, finely chopped
2 tablespoons extra-virgin olive oil
6 garlic cloves, minced
2 tablespoons tomato paste
1 teaspoon smoked paprika
¼ teaspoon cayenne pepper
Pinch saffron threads, crumbled
Salt and pepper, to taste
2 cups long-grain white rice, rinsed
1 (8-ounce / 227-g) bottle clam juice
⅔ cup water
⅓ cup dry sherry
1½ pounds (680 g) boneless, skinless chicken thighs, trimmed and halved
8 ounces (227 g) Spanish-style chorizo sausage, cut into ½-inch pieces
1 pound (454 g) extra-large shrimp (21 to 25 per pound), peeled, deveined, and tails removed
½ cup frozen peas, thawed
½ cup jarred roasted red peppers, rinsed, patted dry, and thinly sliced
2 tablespoons chopped fresh parsley
Vegetable oil spray
Lemon wedges, for serving

1. Line slow cooker with aluminum foil collar and lightly coat with vegetable oil spray.
2. Microwave onion, oil, garlic, tomato paste, paprika, cayenne, saffron, and 1 teaspoon of salt in a bowl, stirring occasionally, until onion is softened, about 5 minutes. Transfer to prepared slow cooker. Stir in rice.
3. Microwave clam juice, water, and sherry in the bowl until steaming, about 5 minutes. Transfer to a slow cooker. Season chicken with salt and pepper and arrange in an even layer on top of rice. Scatter chorizo over chicken. Gently press 16 by 12-inch sheet of parchment paper onto surface of chorizo, folding down edges as needed. Cover and cook until liquid is absorbed and rice is just tender, 2 to 3 hours on high.
4. Discard parchment and foil collar. Season shrimp with salt and pepper and scatter on top of paella. Cover and cook on high until shrimp is opaque throughout, 20 to 30 minutes.
5. Sprinkle peas and red peppers over shrimp, cover, and let sit until heated through, about 5 minutes. Sprinkle with parsley and serve with lemon wedges.

Pork and White Bean Stew

Prep time: 25 minutes | Cook time: 6 to 8 hours | Serves 6 to 8

1 (14½-ounce / 411-g) can whole peeled tomatoes
2 (15-ounce / 425-g) cans cannellini beans, rinsed
2 onions, finely chopped
2 slices bacon, finely chopped
3 tablespoons tomato paste
3 tablespoons minced fresh oregano
6 garlic cloves, minced
Salt and pepper, to taste
¼ cup dry white wine
8 ounces (227 g) parsnips, peeled and cut into ½-inch pieces
4 carrots, peeled and cut into ½-inch pieces
1½ pounds (680 g) boneless country-style pork ribs, trimmed and cut into 1½-inch pieces
1 (12-inch) baguette, cut into ½-inch pieces
2 tablespoons extra-virgin olive oil, plus extra for drizzling

1. Process tomatoes and their juice and half of beans in blender until smooth, about 30 seconds. Transfer to a slow cooker.
2. Microwave onions, bacon, tomato paste, 1 tablespoon oregano, garlic, and ½ teaspoon salt in bowl, stirring occasionally, until onions are softened, about 5 minutes; transfer to a slow cooker. Stir in remaining beans, wine, parsnips, and carrots. Season pork with salt and pepper and stir into a slow cooker. Cover and cook until pork is tender, 6 to 8 hours on low or 4 to 6 hours on high.
3. Preheat the oven to 450°F (235°C). Arrange bread in a single layer on a rimmed baking sheet and bake until browned and crisp, about 10 minutes, stirring halfway through baking. Toss croutons with oil and remaining 2 tablespoons oregano, and season with salt and pepper to taste. Set aside for serving.
4. Adjust consistency of filling as needed with hot water. Season with salt and pepper to taste. Top individual portions with croutons and drizzle with extra oil. Serve.

Turkey Mushroom Meatloaf

Prep time: 20 minutes | Cook time: 2 to 3 hours | Serves 6 to 8

1 shallot, minced
2 garlic cloves, minced
1 tablespoon vegetable oil
1 teaspoon minced fresh thyme or ¼ teaspoon dried
¼ teaspoon cayenne pepper
2 slices hearty white sandwich bread, torn into 1-inch pieces
⅓ cup whole milk
1 large egg
2 tablespoons Worcestershire sauce
1 teaspoon salt
¾ teaspoon pepper
4 ounces (113 g) white mushrooms, trimmed
2 pounds (907 g) ground turkey
Vegetable oil spray
½ cup ketchup
2 tablespoons cider vinegar
2 tablespoons packed brown sugar
1 teaspoon hot sauce

1. Stir shallot, garlic, oil, thyme, and cayenne together in large bowl and microwave until fragrant, about 1 minute.
2. Process bread, milk, egg, Worcestershire, salt, and pepper in food processor to smooth paste, about 30 seconds, scraping down sides of bowl as needed. Add mushrooms and pulse until coarsely chopped, about 10 pulses. Transfer to bowl with shallot mixture. Add ground turkey and knead with hands until well combined.
3. Fold sheet of aluminum foil into 12 by 9-inch sling and lightly coat with vegetable oil spray. Shape turkey mixture into firm 9 by 5-inch loaf across the center of foil sling using wet hands. Using sling, transfer meatloaf to prepared slow cooker.
4. Combine ketchup, vinegar, sugar, and hot sauce in a bowl. Brush meatloaf with half of ketchup mixture. Cover and cook until meatloaf registers 160ºF (71ºC), 2 to 3 hours on low.
5. Adjust oven rack 6 inches from broiler element and heat broiler. Using sling, transfer meatloaf to a rimmed baking sheet, allowing juices to drain back into slow cooker; remove any albumin from meatloaf. Press edges of foil flat. Brush meatloaf with remaining ketchup mixture. Broil until bubbling and spotty brown, 3 to 5 minutes. Let meatloaf cool for 15 minutes before serving.

Chili Mac and Cheese

Prep time: 25 minutes | Cook time: 1 to 2 hours | Serves 6 to 8

1 slice hearty white sandwich bread, torn into 1-inch pieces
2 tablespoons whole milk
Salt and pepper, to taste
1 pound (454 g) 85% lean ground beef
3 tablespoons vegetable oil
2 onions, finely chopped
3 tablespoons chili powder
6 garlic cloves, minced
4 teaspoons ground cumin
1 pound (454 g) elbow macaroni or small shells
1 (28-ounce / 794-g) can crushed tomatoes
2½ cups water, plus extra as needed
1 (15-ounce / 425-g) can tomato sauce
8 ounces (227 g) Pepper Jack cheese, shredded (2 cups)
Vegetable oil spray

1. Line slow cooker with aluminum foil collar and lightly coat with vegetable oil spray. Mash bread, milk, ¼ teaspoon salt, and ¼ teaspoon pepper into paste in a large bowl using a fork. Add ground beef and knead with hands until well combined.
2. Heat oil in a Dutch oven over medium heat until shimmering. Add beef mixture and cook, breaking up meat into rough 1-inch pieces with wooden spoon, until no longer pink, about 5 minutes. Add onions, ½ teaspoon salt, and ¼ teaspoon pepper and cook until onions are softened, about 5 minutes. Stir in chili powder, garlic, and cumin and cook until fragrant, about 1 minute.
3. Reduce heat to medium-low. Add macaroni and cook, stirring occasionally, until edges are translucent, about 4 minutes. Off heat, stir in tomatoes, water, and tomato sauce, scraping up any browned bits. Stir in 1 cup pepper Jack. Transfer mixture to prepared slow cooker, cover, and cook until macaroni is tender, 1 to 2 hours on high.
4. Discard foil collar. Gently stir macaroni to recombine. Adjust consistency with extra hot water as needed. Season with salt and pepper to taste. Sprinkle with remaining 1 cup pepper Jack, cover, and let sit until melted, about 20 minutes. Serve.

Baked Ziti with Sausage

Prep time: 15 minutes | Cook time: 2⅓ to 3⅓ hours | Serves 6 to 8

2 tablespoons extra-virgin olive oil
1 pound (454 g) hot or sweet Italian sausage, casings removed
1 onion, finely chopped
Salt and pepper, to taste
3 garlic cloves, minced
2 teaspoons minced fresh oregano or ½ teaspoon dried
8 ounces (227 g) ziti
1 (28-ounce / 794-g) can crushed tomatoes
1 (15-ounce / 425-g) can tomato sauce
8 ounces (227 g) whole-milk ricotta cheese
4 ounces (113 g) Mozzarella cheese, shredded (1 cup)
2 tablespoons shredded fresh basil
Vegetable oil spray

1.Line slow cooker with aluminum foil collar and lightly coat with vegetable oil spray. Heat oil in a Dutch oven over medium-high heat until just smoking. Cook sausage, breaking up pieces with wooden spoon, until well browned, 6 to 8 minutes. Stir in onion, ½ teaspoon salt, and ½ teaspoon pepper and cook until onion is softened and lightly browned, 5 to 7 minutes. Stir in garlic and oregano and cook until fragrant, about 1 minute.

2.Reduce heat to medium-low. Add ziti and cook, stirring constantly, until edges of pasta become translucent, about 4 minutes. Off heat, stir in tomatoes and tomato sauce, scraping up any browned bits. Transfer mixture to prepared slow cooker. Cover and cook until pasta is tender, 2 to 3 hours on high.

3.Discard foil collar. Dollop ricotta over ziti and sprinkle with Mozzarella. Cover and let sit until cheese is melted, about 20 minutes. Sprinkle with basil and serve.

Mushroom Macaroni and Cheese

Prep time: 20 minutes | Cook time: 1 to 2 hours | Serves 6 to 8

1 pound (454 g) elbow macaroni or small shells
1 tablespoon extra-virgin olive oil
3 cups boiling water, plus extra as needed
2 (12-ounce / 340-g) cans evaporated milk
2 (11-ounce / 312-g) cans condensed onion soup
8 ounces (227 g) Comté cheese, shredded (2 cups)
8 ounces (227 g) Monterey Jack cheese, shredded (2 cups)
¼ cup dry white wine
¼ ounce (7 g) dried porcini mushrooms, rinsed and minced
1 teaspoon dry mustard
Salt and pepper, to taste
Vegetable oil spray

1.Line slow cooker with aluminum foil collar and lightly coat with vegetable oil spray. Microwave macaroni and oil in a bowl at 50 percent power, stirring occasionally, until macaroni begin to look toasted and blistered, 5 to 8 minutes.

2.Transfer hot macaroni to prepared slow cooker and immediately stir in 2¾ cups boiling water. Stir in evaporated milk, condensed soup, Comté, Monterey Jack, wine, mushrooms, mustard, 1 teaspoon pepper, and ½ teaspoon salt. Cover and cook until macaroni are tender, 1 to 2 hours on high.

3.Discard foil collar. Gently stir remaining ¼ cup boiling water into macaroni until combined. Season with salt and pepper to taste. Adjust consistency with extra boiling water as needed. Serve. (Macaroni can be held on warm or low setting for up to 30 minutes.)

Broccoli and Three-Cheese Lasagna

Prep time: 20 minutes | Cook time: 4 to 5 hours | Serves 6 to 8

12 ounces (340 g) broccoli florets, cut into 2-inch pieces
Salt and pepper, to taste
8 curly-edged lasagna noodles, broken in half
1 pound (454 g) whole-milk ricotta cheese
2½ ounces (71 g) Parmesan cheese, grated (1¼ cups)
¾ cup oil-packed sun-dried tomatoes, patted dry and quartered
1 large egg
1 teaspoon minced fresh oregano
1 teaspoon garlic powder
½ teaspoon red pepper flakes
3 cups jarred pasta sauce
1 pound (454 g) Mozzarella cheese, shredded (4 cups)
Vegetable oil spray

1.Line slow cooker with aluminum foil collar, then press 2 large sheets of foil into slow cooker perpendicular to one another, with extra foil hanging over edges. Lightly coat prepared slow cooker with vegetable oil spray.
2.Bring 4 quarts water to boil in a large pot. Add broccoli and 1 tablespoon salt and cook until broccoli is bright green and just tender, about 3 minutes. Transfer to a paper towel-lined plate. Let broccoli cool slightly, then chop coarsely.
3.Return water to boil, add noodles, and cook, stirring often, until al dente. Drain noodles, rinse under cold water, then spread out in a single layer over clean dish towels and let dry. (Do not use paper towels; they will stick to noodles.)
4.Combine ricotta, 1 cup Parmesan, tomatoes, egg, oregano, garlic powder, pepper flakes, ½ teaspoon salt, and ½ teaspoon pepper in bowl. Spread ½ cup pasta sauce into prepared slow cooker.
5.Arrange 4 noodle pieces in a slow cooker (they may overlap), then dollop 10 rounded tablespoons of ricotta mixture over noodles. Scatter one-third of broccoli over ricotta. Sprinkle with 1 cup Mozzarella, then spoon ½ cup sauce over top. Repeat layering of noodles, ricotta mixture, broccoli, Mozzarella, and sauce twice more.
6.For the final layer, arrange remaining 4 noodles in a slow cooker, then top with remaining 1 cup sauce and sprinkle with remaining 1 cup Mozzarella and remaining ¼ cup Parmesan. Cover and cook until lasagna is heated through, 4 to 5 hours on low.
7.Let lasagna cool for 20 minutes. (If desired, use sling to transfer lasagna to serving dish. Press edges of foil flat; discard any juices.) Serve.

Ham and Potato Casserole

Prep time: 15 minutes | Cook time: 4 to 5 hours | Serves 4

1 (10¾-ounce / 305-g) can condensed cream of mushroom soup, undiluted
½ cup 2% milk
1 tablespoon dried parsley flakes
6 medium potatoes, peeled and thinly sliced
1 small onion, chopped
1½ cups cubed fully cooked ham
6 slices process American cheese

1.In a small bowl, combine the soup, milk and parsley. In a slow cooker, layer half of the potatoes, onion, ham, cheese, and soup mixture. Repeat layers. Cover and cook on low for 4 to 5 hours or until potatoes are tender. Serve warm.

Ritzy Beef Pot Pie with Vegetables

Prep time: 30 minutes | Cook time: 7 to 8 hours | Serves 6

3 pounds (1.4 kg) boneless beef chuck-eye roast, pulled apart at seams, trimmed, and cut into 1-inch pieces
Salt and pepper, to taste
¼ cup extra-virgin olive oil, divided
12 ounces (340 g) portobello mushroom caps, gills removed, caps halved, and sliced ¼ inch thick
4 carrots, peeled, halved lengthwise, and sliced ½ inch thick
½ cup all-purpose flour
2 tablespoons tomato paste
4 garlic cloves, minced
1 tablespoon minced fresh thyme
3 cups beef broth, plus extra as needed
½ cup dry red wine
2 cups frozen pearl onions
2 tablespoons soy sauce
1 (9½ by 9-inch) sheet puff pastry, thawed
1½ cups frozen peas, thawed
¼ cup chopped fresh parsley

1.Pat beef dry with paper towels and season with salt and pepper. Heat 2 tablespoons of oil in a skillet over medium-high heat until just smoking. Brown half of beef on all sides, about 8 minutes. Transfer to slow cooker with remaining uncooked beef.

2.Heat 1 tablespoon of oil in the skillet over medium heat until shimmering. Add mushrooms, carrots, and ½ teaspoon salt, cover, and cook until vegetables are softened and mushrooms have released their liquid, about 5 minutes. Uncover and continue to cook until vegetables are dry and lightly browned, 5 to 7 minutes. Stir in flour, tomato paste, garlic, and 2 teaspoons of thyme and cook until fragrant, about 1 minute. slowly stir in 1 cup of broth and wine, scraping up any browned bits and smoothing out any lumps. Transfer to a slow cooker.

3.Stir remaining 2 cups of broth, onions, and soy sauce into a slow cooker. Cover and cook until beef is tender, 7 to 8 hours on low or 4 to 5 hours on high.

4.Preheat the oven to 400ºF (205ºC). Roll puff pastry into 12 by 9-inch rectangle on a lightly floured surface. Using a paring knife, cut pastry in half lengthwise, then into thirds widthwise to create 6 pieces. Cut four 1-inch slits in each piece and arrange upside down on parchment paper-lined baking sheet. Brush pieces with remaining 1 tablespoon of oil, sprinkle with remaining 1 teaspoon of thyme and pinch salt, and bake until puffed and lightly browned, 10 to 15 minutes, rotating sheet halfway through baking. Let pastry cool on the sheet.

5.Stir peas into filling and let sit until heated through, about 5 minutes. Adjust consistency with extra hot broth as needed. Stir in parsley and season with salt and pepper to taste. Top individual portions with pastry before serving.

Chapter 6 Soups, Stews, and Chilies

Barley Buttermilk Soup with Herbs

Prep time: 10 minutes | Cook time: 5½ to 6½ hours | Serves 4 to 6

2 tablespoons unsalted butter
2 large yellow onions, chopped
1 cup chopped celery
¾ cup pearl barley, rinsed and drained
4 cups water
2 cups buttermilk
Salt and freshly ground black pepper, to taste
¼ cup minced fresh herbs, such as cilantro, tarragon, chives, dill, thyme, or parsley, or a combination

1.Heat the butter in a large skillet over medium heat. When it is melted, add the onions and celery and cook, stirring occasionally, until the celery has softened and the onion is lightly browned, about 10 minutes. Transfer to the slow cooker. Add the barley and water; stir to combine. Cover and cook on low until the barley is very tender, 5 to 6 hours.
2.Stir in the buttermilk. Cover and cook on high until the soup is thoroughly hot, about 30 minutes longer. Season with salt and pepper. Just before serving, stir in half the herbs. Sprinkle the remaining herbs over the individual bowls as a garnish.

Lemony Red Lentil Soup

Prep time: 10 minutes | Cook time: 6 to 7 hours | Serves 6

2 tablespoons olive oil
1 medium-size yellow onion, finely chopped
2 ribs celery, chopped
2½ cups dried red lentils, picked over and rinsed (about 1 pound / 454 g)
1 teaspoon ground cumin
1 teaspoon ground turmeric
¾ teaspoon ground coriander
2 tablespoons fresh lemon juice

6 cups chicken or vegetable broth
Salt and freshly ground black pepper, to taste (optional)

1.In a large skillet, heat the olive oil over medium heat. Add the onion and celery and cook, stirring often, until just softened, about 5 minutes. Transfer to the slow cooker, along with the lentils, spices, and lemon juice. Add the broth and enough water to come about 3 inches above the vegetables. Cover and cook on high for 1 hour.
2.Turn the cooker to low and cook the soup for 5 to 6 hours. Season with salt and pepper, if desired. Add water to thin if the soup is too thick. Ladle into bowls and serve hot.

Beef Couscous Soup

Prep time: 25 minutes | Cook time: 6½ hours | Serves 8 to 12

1 pound (454 g) boneless chuck, cut into ½-inch cubes
1 to 2 tablespoons oil
1 (28-ounce / 794-g) can tomatoes
2 teaspoons garlic powder
2 carrots, sliced
2 ribs celery, sliced
4 cups water
½ cup red wine
1 small onion, coarsely chopped
4 beef bouillon cubes
1 teaspoon pepper
1 teaspoon dry oregano
½ teaspoon dry thyme
1 bay leaf
¼ to ½ cup couscous

1.Brown beef cubes in oil in the skillet.
2.Place vegetables in bottom of the slow cooker. Add beef.
3.Combine all other ingredients in a separate bowl except couscous. Pour over ingredients in a slow cooker.
4.Cover. Cook on low 6 hours. Stir in couscous. Cover and cook 30 minutes.

Green Split Pea Soup

Prep time: 10 minutes | Cook time: 12 to 15 hours | Serves 4 to 6

1 cup dried green split peas
5 cups water
⅔ cup chopped shallots
1 cup chopped carrots
1 cup chopped celery
1 bay leaf
½ teaspoon dried thyme or 1½ teaspoons chopped fresh thyme
¼ teaspoon dried sage or 1 teaspoon chopped fresh sage (optional)
Salt, to taste
Dash of cayenne pepper
Warm bread or croutons, for serving

1. Put the split peas in a colander and rinse under cold running water. Pick over, discarding any that are discolored. Put in the slow cooker along with the water, shallots, carrots, celery, bay leaf, thyme, and sage, if using. Stir to combine. Cover and cook on low until the peas are completely tender, 12 to 15 hours. Remove the bay leaf.
2. Purée the soup, using a blender, food processor, immersion blender, or the fine blade of a food mill. You may need to do this in batches. Season the soup with salt (start with about ¼ teaspoon) and a just a bit of cayenne pepper. Serve hot with warm bread or croutons.

Black Bean and Tomato Soup

Prep time: 10 minutes | Cook time: 5 to 7 hours | Serves 4 to 6

2 (15-ounce / 425-g) cans black beans, rinsed and drained
2 (4½-ounce / 128-g) cans chopped roasted green chiles
1 (14½-ounce / 411-g) can Mexican stewed tomatoes with green chiles
1 (14½-ounce / 411-g) can diced tomatoes, with their juice
1 (11-ounce / 312-g) can whole kernel corn, drained
4 green onions (white part and 2 inches of the green), sliced
2 cloves garlic, pressed
1 to 1½ tablespoons chili powder, to your taste

1 teaspoon ground cumin
For Serving:
Shredded Cheddar cheese
Sour cream

1. Put all the ingredients in the slow cooker and stir to combine. Cover and cook on low for 5 to 7 hours.
2. Add some boiling water to thin, if desired. Ladle into individual bowls and serve hot with a sprinkling of shredded Cheddar cheese and a dollop of sour cream.

Nutmeg Carrot Soup

Prep time: 15 minutes | Cook time: 6 to 8 hours | Serves 8

¼ cup olive oil
2 medium-size yellow onions, chopped
2 large russet potatoes, peeled and chopped
3 pounds (1.4 kg) carrots (about 15 medium-size), scrubbed, tops cut off, and chopped
1 or 2 small cloves garlic, pressed
½ teaspoon each dried thyme and marjoram
4 to 6 cups water or chicken broth, plus more as needed
2 heaping tablespoons honey
½ to 1 teaspoon freshly grated nutmeg, to your taste
Sea salt and freshly ground black pepper, to taste

1. Heat the oil in a large skillet over medium heat. Add the onions and cook until softened, 6 to 8 minutes, stirring often to cook evenly.
2. Put the potatoes, carrots, garlic, and herbs in the slow cooker; add the onions and oil, scraping them out of the pan. Add enough of the water to cover everything. Cover and cook on high for 1 hour.
3. Turn the cooker to low and cook until the vegetables are soft, 5 to 7 hours. Purée in batches in a food processor or right in the slow cooker with a handheld immersion blender; the soup will be nice and thick. Stir in the honey and grate the nutmeg right over the crock. Season with salt and pepper. Keep warm on low without letting it come to a boil until serving. Ladle the hot soup into bowls and enjoy.

Traditional Beef Vegetable Soup

Prep time: 25 minutes | Cook time: 6 to 9 hours | Serves 8 to 10

1 to 2 pounds (454 to 907 g) beef short ribs
2 quarts water
1 teaspoon salt
1 teaspoon celery salt
1 small onion, chopped
1 cup diced carrots
½ cup diced celery
2 cups diced potatoes
1 (1-pound / 454-g) can whole-kernel corn, undrained
1 (1-pound / 454-g) can diced tomatoes and juice

1. Combine meat, water, salt, celery salt, onion, carrots, and celery in a slow cooker.
2. Cover. Cook on low 4 to 6 hours.
3. Debone meat, cut into bite-sized pieces, and return to pot.
4. Add potatoes, corn, and tomatoes.
5. Cover and cook on high 2 to 3 hours.

Lentil and Beef Soup

Prep time: 20 minutes | Cook time: 8 hours | Serves 10

1 pound (454 g) extra-lean ground beef
1 medium onion, chopped
2 cups cubed potatoes
1 cup chopped celery
1 cup diced carrots
1 cup dry lentils, rinsed
½ cup medium-sized pearl barley
8 cups water
2 teaspoons beef bouillon granules
½ teaspoon salt
½ teaspoon lemon pepper seasoning
2 (14½-ounce / 411-g) cans low-sodium stewed tomatoes, undrained

1. Brown ground beef with onions in a skillet. Drain.
2. Combine all ingredients except tomatoes in a slow cooker.
3. Cook on low 6 hours, or until tender.
4. Add tomatoes. Cook on low 2 more hours.

Beef Alphabet Soup

Prep time: 10 minutes | Cook time: 6½ to 8½ hours | Serves 5 to 6

½ pound (227 g) beef stewing meat or round steak, cubed
1 (14½-ounce / 411-g) can stewed tomatoes
1 (8-ounce / 227-g) can tomato sauce
1 cup water
1 envelope dry onion soup mix
1 (10-ounce / 283-g) package frozen vegetables, partially thawed
½ cup alphabet noodles, uncooked

1. Combine meat, tomatoes, tomato sauce, water, and soup mix in a slow cooker.
2. Cover. Cook on low 6 to 8 hours. Turn to high.
3. Stir in vegetables and noodles. Add more water if mixture is too dry and thick.
4. Cover. Cook on high 30 minutes, or until vegetables are tender.

Garlic and Onion Soup

Prep time: 10 minutes | Cook time: 6 to 7 hours | Serves 4

4 heads garlic
1 large yellow onion, chopped
3 (14-ounce / 397-g) cans chicken broth
1 (6-ounce / 170-g) can tomato paste
3 tablespoons extra-virgin olive oil
Hot fresh crusty bread, for serving

1. Fill a small deep saucepan with water and bring to a boil. Separate the garlic heads into cloves and toss them into the boiling water; blanch for 1 minute exactly. Drain the garlic cloves in a colander and rinse under cold running water; peel with a paring knife.
2. Combine the garlic cloves, onion, broth, and tomato paste in the slow cooker and stir to blend. Cover and cook on low for 6 to 7 hours.
3. Purée the soup with a handheld immersion blender or transfer to a food processor or blender and purée in batches. Before serving, add the olive oil. Ladle into soup bowls and serve hot with fresh crusty bread. You can drizzle the top of the soup with a bit more olive oil if you like.

Black-Eyed Pea and Beef Soup

Prep time: 25 minutes | Cook time: 8 to 10 hours | Serves 6

1 (16-ounce / 454-g) package dried black-eyed peas
1 (10-ounce / 283-g) can condensed bean and bacon soup
3 to 4 cups water
4 large carrots, peeled and sliced
3 pounds (1.4 kg) beef chuck roast, cut into 2-inch cubes
½ teaspoon salt
½ teaspoon pepper

1.Rinse and drain the peas.
2.Combine all ingredients in a slow cooker.
3.Cook on low 8 to 10 hours, or until peas and beef are tender.

Hearty Italian Vegetable Soup

Prep time: 15 minutes | Cook time: 7½ to 8½ hours | Serves 6

3 tablespoons olive oil
1 medium-size yellow onion, chopped
2 small carrots, diced
2 ribs celery, chopped
2 small zucchini, ends trimmed and cubed
1 (15-ounce / 425-g) can red kidney beans, rinsed, drained, and half the beans mashed
1 teaspoon salt
1 bay leaf
Freshly ground black pepper, to taste
¼ cup packed fresh flat-leaf parsley leaves, chopped
1 (28-ounce / 794-g) can whole tomatoes, mashed, with their juice
1 (10-ounce / 283-g) package frozen baby lima beans
2½ cups chicken broth
5 leaves Swiss chard, chopped, or ½ small head Napa cabbage, cored and chopped
½ cup dry red wine
⅓ cup elbow macaroni or little shells
Freshly grated Parmesan cheese, for serving

1.In a large skillet, heat the olive oil over medium heat. Add the onion, carrots, celery, and zucchini and cook, stirring often, until just softened, about 5 minutes. Transfer to the slow cooker and add the kidney beans, salt, bay leaf, pepper, parsley, tomatoes and their juice, limas, and broth. Add water to come about 1 inch above the vegetables. Cover and cook on low for 5 hours.
2.Add the Swiss chard and wine, cover, and continue to cook on low for another 2 to 3 hours. Remove the bay leaf.
3.Stir in the pasta, cover, and cook on high until the pasta is just tender, about 30 minutes. Ladle into soup bowls and serve hot with lots of Parmesans.

Creamy Artichoke and Leek Soup

Prep time: 10 minutes | Cook time: 6 to 7 hours | Serves 6

6 tablespoons (¾ stick) unsalted butter, cut into 4 or 5 pieces
1 small white onion, chopped
3 leeks (white part and 1 inch of the green), washed well and thinly sliced
3 (10-ounce / 283-g) packages frozen artichoke hearts, thawed
6 cups chicken broth
Salt and white pepper, to taste
1 cup heavy cream
Croutons, for serving (optional)

1.Place the butter, onion, and leeks in the slow cooker. Turn to high, cover, and sweat the vegetables for 30 minutes.
2.Add the artichoke hearts and broth, cover, and cook on low for 5 to 6 hours.
3.Purée with a handheld immersion blender or transfer to a food processor or blender and purée in batches. Strain the soup by pushing it with a spatula through a large-mesh strainer to remove any fibers. Season with salt and pepper. Return the soup to the cooker, stir in the cream, cover, and cook on low until heated through, about 20 minutes; do not boil.
4.Ladle the hot soup into bowls and garnish with croutons, if desired.

Beef Barley Soup with Veggies

Prep time: 10 minutes | Cook time: 5 to 7 hours | Serves 12

1 pound (454 g) lean stewing meat, cut into bite-sized pieces
½ cup onions, chopped
½ cup cut green beans, fresh or frozen
½ cup corn, fresh or frozen
4 cups fat-free, low-sodium beef broth
2 (14½-ounce / 411-g) cans low-sodium stewed tomatoes
1 (12-ounce / 340-g) can low-sodium V8 juice
⅔ cup pearl barley, uncooked
1 cup water

1. Combine all ingredients in a slow cooker.
2. Cover. Cook on high 5 to 7 hours, until vegetables are cooked to your liking.

White Bean and Bacon Soup

Prep time: 15 minutes | Cook time: 8¼ to 9¼ hours | Serves 4 to 6

2 cups dried navy or great northern beans, picked over, soaked overnight, and drained
2 to 3 strips bacon, cooked, drained, and chopped
1 small yellow onion, finely chopped
1 rib celery, minced
1 small carrot, minced
1 bouquet garni: ½ teaspoon dried oregano, 3 sprigs fresh flat-leaf parsley, ½ fresh sage leaf, and 1 bay leaf, wrapped in cheesecloth and tied with kitchen twine
6 cups chicken broth or water
Salt, to taste
¼ teaspoon freshly ground black pepper, or more to taste
½ cup heavy cream (optional)

1. Combine the beans, bacon, onion, celery, carrot, bouquet garni, and broth in the slow cooker. Cover and cook on low for 8 to 9 hours.
2. Remove the bouquet garni and discard. Purée about one-third of the soup in a food processor or with a handheld immersion blender. Season with salt, then add the pepper and cream, if using, cover, and continue to cook on low 15 minutes longer. Ladle into soup bowls and serve hot.

Italian Beef Minestrone

Prep time: 15 minutes | Cook time: 6 hours | Serves 12

1 pound (454 g) extra-lean ground beef
1 large onion, chopped
1 clove garlic, minced
2 (15½-ounce / 439-g) cans low-sodium stewed tomatoes
1 (15-ounce / 425-g) can kidney beans, drained
1 (10-ounce / 283-g) package frozen corn
2 ribs celery, sliced
2 small zucchini, sliced
1 cup macaroni, uncooked
2½ cups hot water
2 beef bouillon cubes
½ teaspoon salt
2 teaspoons Italian seasoning

1. Brown ground beef in nonstick skillet.
2. Combine browned ground beef, onion, garlic, stewed tomatoes, kidney beans, corn, celery, zucchini, and macaroni in a slow cooker.
3. Dissolve bouillon cubes in hot water. Combine with salt and Italian seasoning. Add to a slow cooker.
4. Cover. Cook on low 6 hours.

Ground Beef Macaroni Soup

Prep time: 10 minutes | Cook time: 6¼ to 8¼ hours | Serves 6

1 pound (454 g) extra-lean ground beef
¼ teaspoon black pepper
¼ teaspoon dried oregano
¼ teaspoon seasoned salt
1 envelope dry onion soup mix
3 cups hot water
1 (8-ounce / 227-g) can tomato sauce
1 tablespoon low-sodium soy sauce
1 cup carrots, sliced
1 cup celery, sliced
1 cup macaroni, cooked
¼ cup grated Parmesan cheese

1. Combine all ingredients except macaroni and Parmesan cheese in a slow cooker.
2. Cook on low 6 to 8 hours.
3. Turn to high. Add macaroni and Parmesan cheese.
4. Cook for another 15 to 20 minutes.

Cream of Zucchini Soup

Prep time: 10 minutes | Cook time: 6 to 7 hours | Serves 4

6 tablespoons (¾ stick) unsalted butter, cut into 3 or 4 pieces
1 large yellow onion, chopped
½ teaspoon curry powder
1½ pounds (680 g) zucchini, ends trimmed, and cut into chunks
2 heaping tablespoons white basmati rice or long-grain white rice
1 tablespoon chopped fresh basil
3 cups chicken or vegetable broth
Salt and freshly ground black pepper, to taste
1 cup half-and-half
Croutons, for serving (optional)

1. Put the butter, onion, curry powder, and zucchini in the slow cooker, cover, and cook on high to sweat the vegetables for 30 minutes.
2. Add the rice, basil, and broth, cover, and cook on low for 5 to 6 hours.
3. Purée with a handheld immersion blender or transfer to a food processor or blender and purée in batches. Season with salt and pepper. Stir in the half-and-half, cover, and continue to cook on low until heated through, 20 minutes; do not boil.
4. Ladle the hot soup into bowls and garnish with croutons, if desired.

Mushroom and Bacon Soup

Prep time: 10 minutes | Cook time: 3 hours | Serves 8

8 strips bacon, cut into ½-inch dice
1 large onion, finely chopped
1 teaspoon dried sage leaves, crushed
1 pound (454 g) cremini mushrooms, sliced
1 pound (454 g) shiitake mushrooms, stems removed, and caps sliced
1 ounce (28 g) dried porcini mushrooms
¼ cup soy sauce
3 cups chicken broth
1 cup heavy cream
½ cup snipped fresh chives, for garnish

1. Sauté the bacon in a large skillet over medium heat until crisp and remove it from the pan to drain.
2. Add the onion and sage to the pan and sauté until the onion is softened. Add the cremini and shiitake mushrooms and toss until the mixture is combined.
3. Transfer the contents of the skillet to the insert of a slow cooker. Add the porcini mushrooms, soy sauce, broth, and bacon.
4. Cover and cook on high for 3 hours or on low for 5 to 6 hours. At the end of the cooking time, add the cream and stir to combine.
5. Serve the soup garnished with the chives.

Thyme Onion Soup

Prep time: 10 minutes | Cook time: 7½ to 8½ hours | Serves 8

½ cup (1 stick) unsalted butter
2 tablespoons olive oil
5 large sweet onions, such as Vidalia, thinly sliced
2 tablespoons sugar
1 tablespoons dried thyme
1 teaspoon salt
½ teaspoon freshly ground black pepper
1 bay leaf
½ cup white wine
5 cups beef stock
1½ cups finely shredded Gruyère cheese, for garnish

1. Turn a slow cooker on high, add the butter and oil to the insert, cover until the butter is melted.
2. Remove the cover and add the onions, sugar, thyme, salt, pepper, and bay leaf. Stir the onions until they are coated with the butter and seasonings.
3. Cover and cook on high for 7 to 8 hours, until they are caramelized to a deep golden brown.
4. Remove the cover and add the wine and beef stock. Cover and cook the soup on high for an additional 30 minutes or on low for an additional 1 hour.
5. Remove the bay leaf before serving and garnish each serving with a sprinkling of Gruyère cheese.

Butternut Squash Soup with Thyme

Prep time: 10 minutes | Cook time: 3 hours | Serves 8

4 tablespoons (½ stick) unsalted butter
1 cup finely chopped sweet onion
½ cup finely chopped carrot
½ cup finely chopped celery
2 teaspoons dried thyme
8 cups 1-inch pieces peeled and deseeded butternut squash
4 cups chicken or vegetable broth
Salt and freshly ground black pepper, to taste

1.Melt the butter in a large skillet over medium-high heat. Add the onion, carrot, celery, and thyme and sauté until the vegetables are softened, 3 to 4 minutes.
2.Transfer the contents of the skillet to the insert of a slow cooker. Add the squash and broth, and season with salt and pepper.
3.Cover the slow cooker and cook on high for 3 hours or on low for 6 hours. At the end of the cooking time, stir the soup and season with salt and pepper. If you would like to purée the soup, use an immersion blender, or cool the soup and purée it in a blender.
4.Serve warm from the cooker.

Spiced Beef Stew

Prep time: 25 minutes | Cook time: 8½ hours | Serves 10

6 tablespoons all-purpose flour
1½ teaspoons salt, divided
1 teaspoon pepper, divided
2 pounds (907 g) beef stew meat
¼ cup olive oil
4 medium potatoes, peeled and cubed
6 medium carrots, sliced
2 medium onions, halved and sliced
4 celery ribs, sliced
2 (14½-ounce / 411-g) cans beef broth
2 (11½-ounce / 326-g) cans V8 juice
6 garlic cloves, minced
2 teaspoons Worcestershire sauce
2 bay leaves
1 teaspoon dried thyme

½ teaspoon dried basil
½ teaspoon paprika
6 tablespoons cornstarch
½ cup cold water

1.Combine the flour, 1 teaspoon salt and ½ teaspoon pepper in a large resealable plastic bag. Add beef, a few pieces at a time, and shake to coat.
2.Brown the beef in oil in batches in a large skillet. Transfer the meat and drippings to a slow cooker. Add the potatoes, carrots, onion and celery. Combine the beef broth, juice, garlic, Worcestershire sauce, bay leaves, thyme, basil, paprika and remaining salt and pepper; pour over top.
3.Cover; cook on low for 8-10 hours or until the meat and vegetables are tender. Combine the cornstarch and cold water until smooth; stir into stew. Cover and cook 30 minutes longer or until thickened. Discard bay leaves.

Red Pear and Pumpkin Soup

Prep time: 10 minutes | Cook time: 3 hours | Serves 8

4 tablespoons (½ stick) unsalted butter
½ cup finely chopped sweet onion
½ cup finely chopped celery
½ cup finely chopped carrot
2 medium red pears, peeled, cored, and finely chopped
½ teaspoon ground ginger
2 (15-ounce / 425-g) cans pumpkin purée
3 cups chicken broth
Salt and freshly ground black pepper, to taste
1 cup heavy cream

1.Melt the butter in a medium skillet over medium-high heat. Add the onion, celery, carrot, pears, and ginger and sauté until the vegetables begin to soften, about 3 minutes. Transfer the contents of the skillet to the insert of a slow cooker.
2.Stir in the pumpkin and broth. Cover and cook on high for 3 hours or on low for 5 to 6 hours.
3.Season with salt and pepper. Stir in the cream, cover, and leave on warm for 30 minutes before serving.

Creamy Cheddar Potato Soup

Prep time: 15 minutes | Cook time: 3 hours | Serves 8 to 10

4 tablespoons (½ stick) unsalted butter
2 medium leeks, finely chopped, using the white and some of the tender green parts
4 large russet potatoes, peeled and cut into ½-inch dice
4 cups chicken broth
1 cup whole milk
2 cups finely shredded sharp Cheddar cheese
6 green onions, finely chopped, using the white and some of the tender green parts
8 strips bacon, cooked crisp, drained, and crumbled
Salt and freshly ground black pepper, to taste
1 cup sour cream, for garnish

1.Heat the butter in a large skillet over medium-high heat. Add the leeks and sauté until softened, 2 to 3 minutes. Transfer the leeks to the insert of a slow cooker and add the potatoes and broth. Cover the slow cooker and cook on high for 3 hours or on low for 5 to 6 hours, until the potatoes are tender. Using an immersion blender, purée the soup, or cool the soup and purée it in a blender.
2.Reduce the heat to low and add the milk, cheese, green onions, and bacon. Cover the slow cooker and cook for an additional 1 hour. Season with salt and pepper.
3.Serve the soup garnished with a dollop of sour cream.

Leek and Potato Soup

Prep time: 10 minutes | Cook time: 3 hours | Serves 8 to 10

4 tablespoons (½ stick) unsalted butter
4 leeks, finely chopped, using the white and a bit of the tender green parts
4 large russet potatoes, peeled and cut into 1-inch chunks
3 cups chicken broth
Salt and freshly ground black pepper, to taste
1 cup heavy cream
½ cup snipped fresh chives, for garnish

1.Turn a slow cooker on high, add the butter to the insert, and cover until the butter is melted. Add the leeks and toss with the butter. Add the potatoes and broth. Cover the slow cooker and cook the soup on high for 3 hours or on low for 5 to 6 hours, until the potatoes are tender.
2.Purée the soup with an immersion blender, or mash with a potato masher. Season with salt and pepper. Stir in the cream and turn off the slow cooker. Cool the soup, then refrigerate until chilled.
3.Serve the soup in chilled bowls and garnish with the chives.

Peppery Beef Stew

Prep time: 25 minutes | Cook time: 6 to 8 hours | Serves 8

2 pounds (907 g) boneless beef chuck roast, cut in half
2 tablespoons olive oil
2 large onions, coarsely chopped
2 large green peppers, coarsely chopped
4 jalapeño peppers, deseeded and minced
1 habanero pepper, deseeded and minced
3 (14½-ounce / 411-g) cans diced tomatoes, undrained
½ cup water
6 garlic cloves, minced
2 tablespoons minced fresh cilantro
4 teaspoons beef bouillon granules
2 teaspoons pepper
1½ teaspoons ground cumin
1 teaspoon dried oregano
½ cup pimiento-stuffed olives, coarsely chopped
Hot cooked rice (optional)

1.In a large skillet, brown beef in oil on all sides. Transfer meat to a slow cooker. Add onions and peppers. Combine tomatoes, water, garlic, cilantro, beef bouillon, pepper, cumin and oregano; pour over vegetables.
2.Cover; cook on low for 6 to 8 hours or until meat is tender. Remove beef; cool slightly. Skim fat from cooking juices; stir in olives. Shred beef with two forks and return to slow cooker; heat through. Serve with rice if desired.

Creamy Carrot and Broccoli Soup

Prep time: 15 minutes | Cook time: 2½ to 3 hours | Serves 6 to 8

2 tablespoons unsalted butter
1 medium onion, finely chopped
3 medium carrots, cut into ½-inch dice
2 bunches broccoli (about 1½ pounds / 680 g), stems trimmed and cut into florets
1 teaspoon baking soda
3 cups chicken or vegetable broth
Salt and freshly ground black pepper, to taste
1 cup heavy cream

1. Turn a slow cooker on high, add the butter to the insert, and cover until the butter is melted. Add the onion, carrots, and broccoli and toss the vegetables in the butter. Dissolve the baking soda in the broth and add to the vegetables.
2. Cook on high for 2½ to 3 hours or on low for 5 to 6 hours.
3. Season with salt and pepper and stir in the cream. Turn off the slow cooker and let the soup rest for 15 minutes to come to serving temperature.

Ginger Lentil Stew

Prep time: 20 minutes | Cook time: 6 to 8 hours | Serves 8

2 large onions, thinly sliced, divided
2 tablespoons canola oil
2 tablespoons minced fresh ginger
3 garlic cloves, minced
8 plum tomatoes, chopped
2 teaspoons ground coriander
1½ teaspoons ground cumin
¼ teaspoon cayenne pepper
3 cups vegetable broth
2 cups water
2 cups dried lentils, rinsed
1 (4-ounce / 113-g) can chopped green chilies
¾ cup heavy whipping cream
2 tablespoons butter
1 teaspoon cumin seeds
6 cups hot cooked basmati or jasmine rice
Sliced green onions or minced fresh cilantro (optional)

1. In a large skillet, sauté half of the onions in oil until tender. Add ginger and garlic; sauté for 1 minute. Add the tomatoes, coriander, cumin and cayenne; cook and stir 5 minutes longer.
2. In a slow cooker, combine the vegetable broth, water, lentils, green chilies, tomato mixture and remaining onion. Cover and cook on low for 6 to 8 hours or until lentils are tender.
3. Just before serving, stir cream into a slow cooker. In a small skillet, heat butter over medium heat. Add cumin seeds; cook and stir for 1 to 2 minutes or until golden brown. Add to lentil mixture.
4. To serve, spoon over rice. Sprinkle with green onions or cilantro if desired.

Garbanzo Bean Soup

Prep time: 15 minutes | Cook time: 6 hours | Serves 8

3 tablespoons olive oil
1 large sweet onion, such as Vidalia, finely chopped
3 stalks celery, finely chopped
2 carrots, finely chopped
3 cloves garlic, finely chopped
2 tablespoons finely chopped fresh rosemary
1 (14- to 15-ounce / 397- to 425-g) can crushed tomatoes, with their juice
4 cups vegetable broth
2 (14- to 15-ounce / 397- to 425-g) cans garbanzo beans, drained and rinsed
2 cups cooked small pasta, such as ditalini or tubetti
½ cup freshly grated Pecorino-Romano cheese, for garnish

1. Heat the oil in a skillet over medium-high heat. Add the onion, celery, carrots, garlic, and rosemary and sauté until the vegetables begin to soften and are fragrant, 3 to 4 minutes.
2. Add the tomatoes and sauté for another minute to incorporate. Transfer the contents of the skillet to the insert of a slow cooker and add the broth and garbanzo beans.
3. Cover and cook on low for 6 hours or on high for 3 hours. Remove the cover, stir in the pasta, and cook for an additional 20 minutes on low or 10 minutes on high.
4. Serve the soup garnished with the cheese.

Rosemary White Bean Soup

Prep time: 15 minutes | Cook time: 8 to 9 hours | Serves 8

3 tablespoons extra-virgin olive oil
4 ounces (113 g) spicy Italian ham or Capicola, cut into ½-inch dice
1 medium onion, finely chopped
2 cloves garlic, minced
3 stalks celery with leaves, finely chopped
3 medium carrots, finely chopped
2 teaspoons finely minced fresh rosemary
1 (14- to 15-ounce / 397- to 425-g) can plum tomatoes, crushed and drained
2 cups dried beans, picked over for stones, soaked, or 2 (14- to 15-ounce / 397- to 425-g) cans small white beans, drained and rinsed
6 cups chicken or vegetable broth
Salt and freshly ground black pepper, to taste

1.Heat the oil in a skillet over medium-high heat.
2.Add the ham and sauté until it begins to get crisp, about 3 minutes. Add the onion, garlic, celery, carrots, and rosemary and sauté until the vegetables begin to soften, about 3 minutes. Add the tomatoes and stir to combine.
3.Transfer the contents of the skillet to the insert of a slow cooker. Stir in the beans and the broth.
4.Cover the slow cooker and cook on low for 8 to 9 hours, until the beans are tender. Season with salt and pepper before serving.

Spicy Chicken and Bean Chili

Prep time: 15 minutes | Cook time: 8 to 10 hours | Serves 8

3 tablespoons olive oil
2 medium onions, finely chopped
1 medium red bell pepper, deseeded and finely chopped
1 medium green bell pepper, deseeded and finely chopped
4 chipotle chiles in adobo, finely chopped
1 teaspoon ground cumin
1 teaspoon dried oregano
8 cups chicken broth
4 (6-inch) corn tortillas, torn into small pieces
2 (14- to 15-ounce / 397- to 425-g) cans small white beans, drained and rinsed
3 cups cooked chicken or turkey
1 (16-ounce / 454-g) package frozen corn, thawed
½ cup finely chopped fresh cilantro
2 cups finely shredded mild Cheddar or Monterey Jack cheese, for garnish
2 cups sour cream, for garnish

1.Heat the oil in a large skillet over medium-high heat. Add the onions, bell peppers, chiles, cumin, and oregano and sauté until the vegetables are softened, 5 to 7 minutes.
2.Transfer the contents of the skillet to the insert of a slow cooker. Add the broth, tortillas, beans, chicken, and corn.
3.Cover the slow cooker and cook on low for 8 to 10 hours, until the chili is thick and the beans and vegetables are tender. Stir in the cilantro.
4.Serve each bowl garnished with cheese and sour cream.

Red Potato and Celery Stew

Prep time: 25 minutes | Cook time: 8½ to 9½ hours | Serves 10

3 cups cubed red potatoes (about 4 medium)
2 cups chopped celery (about 4 ribs)
2 medium leeks (white portion only), cut into ½-inch pieces
1¾ cups coarsely chopped peeled parsnips (about 2 medium)
1½ cups chopped carrots (about 3 medium)
1 (28-ounce / 794-g) can Italian crushed tomatoes
1 (14½-ounce / 411-g) can vegetable broth
2 teaspoons sugar
½ teaspoon salt
½ teaspoon dried thyme
½ teaspoon dried rosemary, crushed
3 tablespoons cornstarch
3 tablespoons cold water
10 round loaves sourdough bread (8 to 9 ounces / 227 to 255 g each)

1.In a slow cooker, combine the first 11 ingredients. Cook, covered, on low 8 to 9 hours or until vegetables are tender.
2.In a small bowl, mix the cornstarch and water until smooth. Stir into stew. Cook, covered, on high 30 minutes or until thickened.
3.Cut a thin slice off the top of each bread loaf. Hollow out the bottoms of the loaves, leaving ½-in.-thick shells (save removed bread for another use). Serve stew in bread bowls.

Turkey and Black Bean Chili

Prep time: 15 minutes | Cook time: 8 to 10 hours | Serves 8

2 tablespoons olive oil
1 medium onion, chopped
2 cloves garlic, minced
1½ teaspoons dried oregano
2 teaspoons ancho chile powder
½ teaspoon ground cumin
2 Anaheim chiles, deseeded and finely chopped
1 medium red bell pepper, deseeded and chopped
1½ teaspoons salt
2 teaspoons cornmeal
6 cups chicken or turkey broth
1 (16-ounce / 454-g) package frozen corn, thawed
2 (14- to 15-ounce / 397- to 425-g) cans black beans, rinsed and drained
3 cups shredded cooked turkey or chicken
¼ cup chopped fresh cilantro

1. Heat the oil in a large skillet over medium-high heat. Add the onion, garlic, oregano, chile powder, and cumin and sauté until the spices are fragrant. Add the chiles, bell pepper, and salt and sauté until the vegetables are softened.
2. Transfer the contents of the skillet to the insert of a slow cooker. Stir in the cornmeal, broth, corn, beans, and turkey.
3. Cover the slow cooker and cook on low for 8 to 10 hours, until the chili is thickened and the vegetables are tender.
4. Stir in the cilantro before serving.

Vegetable and Black-Eyed Pea Chili

Prep time: 20 minutes | Cook time: 6 to 8 hours | Serves 4 to 6

1 cup finely chopped onions
1 cup finely chopped carrots
1 cup finely chopped red or green pepper, or mixture of two
1 garlic clove, minced
4 teaspoons chili powder
1 teaspoon ground cumin
2 tablespoons chopped cilantro

1 (14½-ounce / 411-g) can diced tomatoes
3 cups black-eyed peas, cooked or 2 (15-ounce / 425-g) cans black-eyed peas, drained
1 (4-ounce / 113-g) can chopped green chilies
¾ cup orange juice
¾ cup water or broth
1 tablespoon cornstarch
2 tablespoons water
½ cup shredded Cheddar cheese
2 tablespoons chopped cilantro

1. Combine all ingredients except cornstarch, 2 tablespoons water, cheese, and cilantro.
2. Cover. Cook on low 6 to 8 hours, or high 4 hours.
3. Dissolve cornstarch in water. Stir into soup mixture 30 minutes before serving.
4. Garnish individual servings with cheese and cilantro.

Lamb and Carrot Stew

Prep time: 20 minutes | Cook time: 7 to 9 hours | Serves 6

½ cup all-purpose flour
½ teaspoon salt
¼ teaspoon pepper
1½ pounds (680 g) lamb stew meat, cubed
2 shallots, sliced
2 tablespoons olive oil
½ cup red wine
2 (14½-ounce / 411-g) cans beef broth
2 medium potatoes, cubed
1 large sweet potato, peeled and cubed
2 large carrots, cut into 1-inch pieces
2 medium parsnips, peeled and cubed
1 garlic clove, minced
1 tablespoon mint jelly
4 bacon strips, cooked and crumbled

1. In a large resealable plastic bag, combine the flour, salt and pepper. Add the meat, a few pieces at a time, and shake to coat. In a large skillet, brown meat and shallots in oil in batches.
2. Transfer to a slow cooker. Add wine to the skillet, stirring to loosen browned bits from pan. Bring to a boil. Reduce heat; simmer, uncovered, for 1-2 minutes. Add to a slow cooker.
3. Stir in the broth, potatoes, sweet potato, carrots, parsnips and garlic. Cover and cook on low for 7 to 9 hours or until meat is tender. Stir in jelly; sprinkle with bacon.

Chicken Sausage and Lentil Stew

Prep time: 15 minutes | Cook time: 8 to 10 hours | Serves 6

1 (32-ounce / 907-g) carton reduced-sodium chicken broth
1 (28-ounce / 794-g) can diced tomatoes, undrained
3 fully cooked spicy chicken sausage links (3 ounces / 85 g each), cut into ½-inch slices
1 cup dried lentils, rinsed
1 medium onion, chopped
1 medium carrot, chopped
1 celery rib, chopped
2 garlic cloves, minced
½ teaspoon dried thyme

1. In a slow cooker, combine all ingredients. Cover; cook on low for 8 to 10 hours or until lentils are tender.

Mushroom and Beef Stew

Prep time: 25 minutes | Cook time: 4 to 5 hours | Serves 8

¼ cup all-purpose flour
2 pounds (907 g) boneless beef chuck roast, trimmed and cut into 1-inch cubes
2 tablespoons canola oil
1 (10¾-ounce / 305-g) can condensed tomato soup, undiluted
1 cup water or red wine
2 reduced-sodium beef bouillon cubes
3 teaspoons Italian seasoning
1 bay leaf
½ teaspoon coarsely ground pepper
6 white onions or yellow onions, quartered
4 medium potatoes, cut into 1½-inch slices
3 medium carrots, cut into 1-inch slices
12 large fresh mushrooms
½ cup sliced celery

1. Place flour in a large resealable plastic bag. Add beef, a few pieces at a time, and shake to coat.
2. In a large skillet, brown meat in oil in batches; drain. Transfer to a slow cooker. Combine the tomato soup, water or wine, bouillon and seasonings; pour over beef. Add the onions, potatoes, carrots, mushrooms and celery.
3. Cover and cook on low for 4 to 5 hours or until meat is tender. Discard bay leaf. Serve with noodles or French bread.

Sour and Sweet Beef Stew

Prep time: 25 minutes | Cook time: 8 to 10 hours | Serves 8

2 pounds (907 g) beef top round steak, cut into 1-inch cubes
2 tablespoons olive oil
1 (15-ounce / 425-g) can tomato sauce
2 large onions, chopped
4 medium carrots, thinly sliced
1 large green pepper, cut into 1-inch pieces
1 cup canned pineapple chunks, drained
½ cup cider vinegar
¼ cup packed brown sugar
¼ cup light corn syrup
2 teaspoons chili powder
2 teaspoons paprika
½ teaspoon salt
Hot cooked rice (optional)

1. In a large skillet, brown beef in oil in batches; drain. Transfer to a slow cooker.
2. In a large bowl, combine the tomato sauce, onions, carrots, green pepper, pineapple, vinegar, brown sugar, corn syrup, chili powder, paprika and salt; pour over beef.
3. Cover and cook on low for 8 to 10 hours or until beef is tender. Serve with rice if desired.

Macaroni Bean Stew

Prep time: 10 minutes | Cook time: 5 to 6 hours | Serves 6

1 cup chopped tomatoes
¾ cup macaroni shells, uncooked
¼ cup chopped onions
¼ cup chopped green bell peppers
1 teaspoon dried basil leaves
1 teaspoon Worcestershire sauce
1 clove garlic, chopped
1 (15-ounce / 425-g) can kidney beans, drained
1 (8-ounce / 227-g) can garbanzo beans, drained
1 (14½-ounce / 411-g) can fat-free chicken broth

1. Combine all ingredients in a slow cooker.
2. Cook on low 5 to 6 hours.

Pork and Butternut Squash Stew

Prep time: 20 minutes | Cook time: 8½ to 10½ hours | Serves 6

⅓ cup plus 1 tablespoon all-purpose flour, divided
1 tablespoon paprika
1 teaspoon salt
1 teaspoon ground coriander
1½ pounds (680 g) boneless pork shoulder butt roast, cut into 1-inch cubes
1 tablespoon canola oil
2¾ cups cubed peeled butternut squash
1 (14½-ounce / 411-g) can diced tomatoes, undrained
1 cup frozen corn, thawed
1 medium onion, chopped
2 tablespoons cider vinegar
1 bay leaf
2½ cups reduced-sodium chicken broth
1⅔ cups frozen shelled edamame, thawed

1. In a large resealable plastic bag, combine ⅓ cup flour, paprika, salt and coriander. Add pork, a few pieces at a time, and shake to coat.
2. In a large skillet, brown pork in oil in batches; drain. Transfer to a slow cooker. Add squash, tomatoes, corn, onion, vinegar and bay leaf. In a small bowl, combine broth and the remaining flour until smooth; stir into slow cooker.
3. Cover and cook on low for 8 t0 10 hours or until pork and vegetables are tender. Stir in edamame; cover and cook 30 minutes longer. Discard the bay leaf.

Beef and Pumpkin Stew

Prep time: 25 minutes | Cook time: 6½ to 8½ hours | Serves 6

1 tablespoon canola oil
1 beef top round steak (1½ pounds / 680 g), cut into 1-inch cubes
1½ cups cubed peeled pie pumpkin or sweet potatoes
3 small red potatoes, peeled and cubed
1 cup cubed acorn squash
1 medium onion, chopped
2 (14½-ounce / 411-g) cans reduced-sodium beef broth
1 (14½-ounce / 411-g) can diced tomatoes, undrained

2 bay leaves
2 garlic cloves, minced
2 teaspoons reduced-sodium beef bouillon granules
½ teaspoon chili powder
½ teaspoon pepper
¼ teaspoon ground allspice
¼ teaspoon ground cloves
¼ cup water
3 tablespoons all-purpose flour

1. In a large skillet, heat oil over medium-high heat. Brown beef in batches; remove with a slotted spoon to a slow cooker. Add the pumpkin, potatoes, squash and onion. Stir in the broth, tomatoes and seasonings. Cover and cook on low for 6 to 8 hours or until meat is tender.
2. Remove bay leaves. In a small bowl, mix water and flour until smooth; gradually stir into stew. Cover and cook on high for 30 minutes or until liquid is thickened.

Black Bean and Turkey Sausage Stew

Prep time: 20 minutes | Cook time: 5½ to 7½ hours | Serves 6

3 (15-ounce / 425-g) cans black beans, drained and rinsed
1 (14½-ounce / 411-g) can fat-free, reduced-sodium chicken broth
1 cup celery, sliced
2 (4-ounce / 113-g) cans green chilies, chopped
3 cloves garlic, minced
1½ teaspoons dried oregano
¾ teaspoon ground coriander
½ teaspoon ground cumin
¼ teaspoon ground red pepper (not cayenne)
1 pound (454 g) link turkey sausage, thinly sliced and cooked

1. Combine all ingredients in a slow cooker except sausage.
2. Cover. Cook on low 5 to 7 hours.
3. Remove 1½ cups of the bean mixture and purée in blender. Return to slow cooker.
4. Add sliced sausage.
5. Cover. Cook on low 30 minutes.

Turkey Sausage and Navy Bean Stew

Prep time: 20 minutes | Cook time: 8 to 9 hours | Serves 6

½ pound (227 g) turkey sausage, removed from casing
1 large onion, chopped
2 garlic cloves, minced
¾ cup chopped carrots
1 fennel bulb, chopped
½ cup chopped celery
1 (10¾-ounce / 305-g) can fat-free, reduced-sodium chicken broth
3 medium tomatoes, peeled, deseeded, and chopped
1 teaspoon dried basil
1 teaspoon dried oregano
¼ teaspoon salt
1 cup shell pasta, uncooked
1 (15-ounce / 425-g) can navy beans, drained and rinsed
½ cup low-fat Parmesan cheese

1. In the nonstick skillet, brown turkey sausage, onion, and garlic. Drain well.
2. Combine all ingredients except cheese in a slow cooker.
3. Cook on low 8 to 9 hours.
4. Sprinkle with cheese to serve.

Vegetable and Rice Stew

Prep time: 20 minutes | Cook time: 8 to 9 hours | Serves 12

1 pound (454 g) dry beans, assorted
2 cups fat-free vegetable broth
½ cup white wine
⅓ cup soy sauce
⅓ cup unsweetened apple or pineapple juice
Vegetable stock or water
½ cup diced celery
½ cup diced parsnips
½ cup diced carrots
½ cup sliced mushrooms
1 onion, sliced
1 teaspoon dried basil
1 teaspoon parsley flakes
1 bay leaf
3 cloves garlic, minced
1 teaspoon black pepper
1 cup rice or pasta, cooked

1. Sort and rinse beans and soak overnight in water. Drain. Place in a slow cooker.
2. Add vegetable juice, wine, soy sauce, and apple or pineapple juice.
3. Cover with vegetable stock or water.
4. Cover. Cook on high 2 hours.
5. Add vegetables, herbs, and spices.
6. Cover cooker. Cook on low 5 to 6 hours, or until carrots and parsnips are tender.
7. Add cooked rice or pasta.
8. Cover. Cook 1 hour more.

Veggie and Brown Rice Stew

Prep time: 15 minutes | Cook time: 9 to 11 hours | Serves 10

5 to 6 potatoes, cubed
3 carrots, cubed
1 onion, chopped
½ cup chopped celery
2 cups canned diced or stewed tomatoes
3 chicken bouillon cubes, dissolved in 3 cups water
1½ teaspoons dried thyme
½ teaspoon dried parsley
½ cup brown rice, uncooked
1 pound (454 g) frozen green beans
1 pound (454 g) frozen corn
1 (15-ounce / 425-g) can butter beans
1 (46-ounce / 1.3-kg) can V8 juice

1. Combine potatoes, carrots, onion, celery, tomatoes, chicken stock, thyme, parsley, and rice in a slow cooker.
2. Cover. Cook on high 2 hours. purée one cup of mixture and add back to the slow cooker to thicken the soup.
3. Stir in beans, corn, butter beans, and juice.
4. Cover. Cook on high 1 more hour, then reduce to low and cook 6 to 8 more hours.

Beef and Kidney Bean Stew

Prep time: 15 minutes | Cook time: 6 hours | Serves 4 to 6

¾ cup sliced onion
1 pound (454 g) ground beef
¼ cup long-grain rice, uncooked
3 cups diced raw potatoes
1 cup diced celery
2 cups canned kidney beans, drained
1 teaspoon salt
⅛ teaspoon pepper
¼ teaspoon chili powder
¼ teaspoon Worcestershire sauce
1 cup tomato sauce
½ cup water

1. Brown onions and ground beef in a skillet. Drain.
2. Layer ingredients in a slow cooker in order given.
3. Cover. Cook on low 6 hours, or until potatoes and rice are cooked.

Pinto Bean and Beef Chili

Prep time: 15 minutes | Cook time: 8 to 10 hours | Serves 8 to 10

3 tablespoons vegetable oil
2 medium onions, finely chopped
1 jalapeño pepper, deseeded and finely chopped
1 teaspoon ancho chile powder
½ teaspoon dried oregano
2 pounds (907 g) boneless beef short ribs or chuck, cut into ½-inch pieces
3 cups beef broth
1 (28- to 32-ounce / 794- to 907-g) can crushed tomatoes, with their juice
2 (14- to 15-ounce / 397- to 425-g) cans pinto beans, drained and rinsed

1. Heat 2 tablespoons of the oil in a large skillet over medium-high heat. Add the onions, jalapeño, chile powder, and oregano and sauté until the onions become soft, about 3 minutes.
2. Transfer the contents of the skillet to the insert of a slow cooker. Heat the remaining 1 tablespoon of oil in the same skillet over high heat.
3. Add the meat, a few pieces at a time, and brown on all sides. Transfer the browned meat to the slow-cooker insert. Add the broth, tomatoes, and beans to the slow-cooker insert.
4. Cover and cook on low for 8 to 10 hours or on high for 4 to 5 hours, until the beef is tender and the sauce is thickened.
5. Serve the chili from the cooker set on warm.

Oregano Ground Beef Chili

Prep time: 10 minutes | Cook time: 6 to 7 hours | Serves 8

2 tablespoons vegetable oil
2 pounds (907 g) 15% lean ground beef
2 teaspoons ancho chile powder
1 teaspoon dried oregano
½ teaspoon ground cumin
Salt, to taste
Pinch of cayenne pepper
2 teaspoons cornmeal
2 cups beef broth
4 cups tomato sauce
Freshly ground black pepper, to taste
Tortilla chips, for garnish
Shredded Cheddar cheese, for garnish
Chopped red onion, for garnish

1. Heat the oil in a large skillet over high heat. Add the beef and brown, breaking up any large pieces.
2. Transfer the meat to the insert of a slow cooker. Add the chile powder, oregano, cumin, 2 teaspoons salt, and the cayenne to the same skillet and cook until the spices are fragrant, 30 to 45 seconds.
3. Add the cornmeal to the pan and stir until the mixture thickens. Add the broth and whisk until smooth. Transfer the contents of the skillet to the slow-cooker insert and stir in the tomato sauce.
4. Cover and cook on low for 6 to 7 hours, until the chili is thickened. Season with salt and pepper.
5. Serve the chili in bowls and garnish with tortilla chips, shredded Cheddar cheese, and chopped red onion.

Lone Star Beef Sirloin Chili

Prep time: 15 minutes | Cook time: 4 to 5 hours | Serves 8 to 10

2½ pounds (1.1 kg) beef sirloin, cut into ½-inch pieces
2 teaspoons salt
Pinch of cayenne pepper (optional)
4 tablespoons olive oil
2 large sweet onions, such as Vidalia, coarsely chopped
2 cloves garlic, minced
2 tablespoons finely chopped jalapeño
2 teaspoons ancho chile powder
½ teaspoon ground cumin
½ teaspoon dried oregano
¼ cup cornmeal
2 cups beef broth
1 (12-ounce / 340-g) bottle Lone Star or other beer
1 (14- to 15-ounce / 397- to 425-g) can tomato purée
2 (14- to 15-ounce / 397- to 425-g) cans black beans, drained and rinsed
½ cup chopped fresh cilantro

1. Sprinkle the beef evenly with the salt and cayenne (if using). Heat 2 tablespoons of the oil in a large skillet over medium-high heat. Add the beef in batches and brown on all sides.
2. Transfer the meat to the insert of a slow cooker.
3. Lower the heat to medium-low and heat the remaining 2 tablespoons oil. Add the onions, garlic, jalapeño, chile powder, cumin, and oregano and sauté until the onions are softened, about 5 minutes, being careful to stir the mixture so the chile powder doesn't burn. Add the cornmeal and stir until blended with the other ingredients, and cook for 1 minute. Stir in the broth, whisking, and bring to a boil.
4. Transfer the contents of the skillet to the slow-cooker insert. Add the beer, tomato purée, and beans. Cover and cook on high for 4 to 5 hours or on low for 8 to 10 hours, until the meat is tender and the sauce is thickened.
5. Skim off any fat from the top of the chili and stir in the cilantro before serving.

Pork and Black Bean Chili

Prep time: 10 minutes | Cook time: 6 to 8 hours | Serves 8

1 pound (454 g) pork tenderloin, cut into 1-inch chunks
1 (16-ounce / 454-g) jar thick chunky salsa
3 (15-ounce / 425-g) cans black beans, rinsed and drained
½ cup chicken broth
1 medium red bell pepper, chopped
1 medium onion, chopped
1 teaspoon ground cumin
2 to 3 teaspoons chili powder
1 to 1½ teaspoons dried oregano
¼ cup sour cream

1. Combine all ingredients except sour cream in a slow cooker.
2. Cover. Cook on low 6 to 8 hours, or until pork is tender.
3. Garnish individual servings with sour cream.

Vegetable Chili

Prep time: 20 minutes | Cook time: 6 to 8 hours | Serves 6

1 medium butternut squash, peeled and cubed
2 medium carrots, peeled and diced
1 medium onion, diced
3 teaspoons chili powder, or more to taste
2 (14-ounce / 397-g) cans diced tomatoes
1 (4-ounce / 113-g) can chopped mild green chilies
1 teaspoon salt (optional)
1 cup vegetable broth
2 (16-ounce / 454-g) cans black beans, drained and rinsed
Sour cream (optional)

1. In a slow cooker, layer ingredients in order given—except sour cream.
2. Cover. Cook on low 6 to 8 hours, or until vegetables are tender.
3. Stir before serving.
4. Top individual servings with dollops of sour cream.
5. Serve with crusty French bread.

Veggie and Cashew Chili

Prep time: 20 minutes | Cook time: 8½ hours | Serves 8 to 10

2 tablespoons oil
2 cups minced celery
1½ cups chopped green pepper
1 cup minced onions
4 garlic cloves, minced
5½ cups stewed tomatoes
2 (1-pound / 454-g) cans kidney beans, undrained
1½ to 2 cups raisins
¼ cup wine vinegar
1 tablespoon chopped parsley
2 teaspoons salt
1½ teaspoons dried oregano
1½ teaspoons cumin
¼ teaspoon pepper
¼ teaspoon Tabasco sauce
1 bay leaf
¾ cup cashews
1 cup shredded cheese (optional)

1. Combine all ingredients except cashews and cheese in a slow cooker.
2. Cover. Simmer on low for 8 hours. Add cashews and simmer 30 minutes.
3. Garnish individual servings with shredded cheese.

Hearty Garden Chili

Prep time: 15 minutes | Cook time: 6 to 8 hours | Serves 10

¾ pound (340 g) onions, chopped
1 teaspoon garlic, minced
1 tablespoon olive oil
¾ cup chopped celery
1 large carrot, peeled and thinly sliced
1 large green bell pepper, chopped
1 small zucchini, sliced
¼ pound (113 g) fresh mushrooms, sliced
1¼ cups water
1 (14-ounce / 397-g) can kidney beans, drained
1 (14-ounce / 397-g) can low-sodium diced tomatoes, with their juice
1 teaspoon lemon juice
⅛ teaspoon dried oregano

1 teaspoon ground cumin
1 teaspoon chili powder
1 teaspoon salt
1 teaspoon black pepper

1. Sauté onions and garlic in olive oil in a large skillet over medium heat until tender.
2. Add remaining fresh veggies. Sauté 2 to 3 minutes. Transfer to a slow cooker.
3. Add remaining ingredients.
4. Cover. Cook on low 6 to 8 hours.

Pinto Bean Chili with Mushrooms

Prep time: 20 minutes | Cook time: 6 to 8 hours | Serves 8

1 cup dried pinto or kidney beans
3 cups water
1 tablespoon vegetable oil
2 cups chopped onions
1 green bell pepper, deseeded and chopped
2 heaping cups sliced fresh mushrooms (about 10 ounces / 283 g)
1 cup thinly sliced carrots
2 cups fresh or canned unsalted tomatoes, chopped
1 (6-ounce / 170-g) can unsalted tomato paste
¾ cup water
2 tablespoons chili powder
1 large dried bay leaf
1 tablespoon vinegar
1 to 2 teaspoons finely minced garlic

1. Place beans and 3 cups water in a saucepan. Bring to a boil and cook 2 minutes. Do not drain. Let sit 1 hour.
2. Pour beans into a slow cooker. If water does not cover beans, add additional water to cover them.
3. Cover cooker. Cook on high 2 hours.
4. Heat oil in the skillet. Add onion and green pepper. Cook until onions are transparent. Drain. Add to a slow cooker.
5. Add remaining ingredients.
6. Cover. Cook on low 4 to 6 hours.
7. Remove bay leaf before serving.
8. Serve over brown rice or potatoes.

Brown Sugar Beef Chili

Prep time: 15 minutes | Cook time: 2 hours | Serves 8

1 pound (454 g) extra-lean ground beef
½ cup brown sugar
2 tablespoons prepared mustard
1 medium onion, chopped
2 (14-ounce / 397-g) cans kidney beans, drained
1 pint low-sodium tomato juice
½ teaspoon salt
¼ teaspoon black pepper
1 teaspoon chili powder

1. Brown lean ground beef and onion in a nonstick skillet over medium heat. Stir brown sugar and mustard into meat.
2. Combine all ingredients in a slow cooker.
3. Cover. Cook on high 2 hours. If it's convenient, stir several times during cooking.

Hamburger Chili with Beans

Prep time: 15 minutes | Cook time: 8 to 10 hours | Serves 12

½ pound (227 g) lean hamburger or ground turkey
½ pound (227 g) sausage
1 onion, chopped
1 (15-ounce / 425-g) can kidney beans or chili beans, undrained
1 (15-ounce / 425-g) can ranch-style beans, undrained
1 (15-ounce / 425-g) can pinto beans, undrained
1 (14½-ounce / 411-g) can stewed tomatoes, undrained
1 (15-ounce / 425-g) can tomato sauce
1 envelope dry chili seasoning mix
3 tablespoons brown sugar
3 tablespoons chili powder

1. Brown hamburger, sausage, and onion together in a nonstick skillet.
2. Combine all ingredients in a large slow cooker. Mix well.
3. Cook on low 8 to 10 hours.

Corn and Beef Chili

Prep time: 15 minutes | Cook time: 5 to 6 hours | Serves 4 to 6

1 pound (454 g) ground beef
½ cup chopped onions
½ cup chopped green peppers
½ teaspoon salt
⅛ teaspoon pepper
¼ teaspoon dried thyme
1 (14½-ounce / 411-g) can diced tomatoes with Italian herbs
1 (6-ounce / 170-g) can tomato paste, diluted with 1 can water
2 cups frozen whole-kernel corn
1 (16-ounce / 454-g) can kidney beans
1 tablespoon chili powder
Sour cream, for serving
Shredded cheese, for serving

1. Sauté ground beef, onions, and green peppers in a deep saucepan. Drain and season with salt, pepper, and thyme.
2. Stir in tomatoes, tomato paste, and corn.
3. Heat until corn is thawed. Add kidney beans and chili powder. Pour into a slow cooker. Cover. Cook on low 5 to 6 hours.
4. Top individual servings with dollops of sour cream, or sprinkle with shredded cheese.

Slow Cooker Beef Chili

Prep time: 15 minutes | Cook time: 4 to 6 hours | Serves 4

1 pound (454 g) ground beef
1 onion, chopped
1 (15-ounce / 425-g) can chili, with or without beans
1 (14½-ounce / 411-g) can diced tomatoes with green chilies, or with basil, garlic, and oregano
1 cup tomato juice
Chopped onion, for serving
Shredded Cheddar cheese, for serving

1. Brown ground beef and onion in the skillet. Drain and put in a slow cooker.
2. Add chili, diced tomatoes, and tomato juice.
3. Cover. Cook on low 4 to 6 hours.
4. Serve with onion and cheese on top of each individual serving.

Potato and Beef Chili

Prep time: 20 minutes | Cook time: 4 hours | Serves 8

1 pound (454 g) ground beef
½ cup chopped onions, or 2 tablespoons dried minced onions
½ cup chopped green peppers
1 tablespoon poppy seeds (optional)
1 teaspoon salt
½ teaspoon chili powder
1 package au gratin or scalloped potato mix
1 cup hot water
1 (15-ounce / 425-g) can kidney beans, undrained
1 (16-ounce / 454-g) can stewed tomatoes
1 (4-ounce / 113-g) can mushroom pieces, undrained

1.Brown ground beef in skillet. Remove meat and place in a slow cooker. Sauté onions and green peppers in drippings until softened.
2.Combine all ingredients in a slow cooker.
3.Cover. Cook on high 4 hours, or until liquid is absorbed and potatoes are tender.

Bacon and Beef Chili

Prep time: 20 minutes | Cook time: 9 to 10 hours | Serves 15

8 bacon strips, diced
2½ pounds (1.1 kg) beef stewing meat, cubed
1 (28-ounce / 794-g) can stewed tomatoes
1 (14½-ounce / 411-g) can stewed tomatoes
2 (8-ounce / 227-g) cans tomato sauce
1 (16-ounce / 454-g) can kidney beans, rinsed and drained
2 cups sliced carrots
1 medium onion, chopped
1 cup chopped celery
½ cup chopped green pepper
¼ cup minced fresh parsley
1 tablespoon chili powder
1 teaspoon salt
½ teaspoon ground cumin
¼ teaspoon pepper

1.Cook bacon in the skillet until crisp. Drain on paper towel.
2.Brown beef in bacon drippings in the skillet.
3.Combine all ingredients in a slow cooker.
4.Cover. Cook on low 9 to 10 hours, or until meat is tender. Stir occasionally.

Indian-Style Chili

Prep time: 10 minutes | Cook time: 5½ to 6½ hours | Serves 4 to 6

2 tablespoons olive oil
2 medium-size red onions, chopped
3 cloves garlic, minced
2 tablespoons grated fresh ginger
1 to 2 canned jalapeños en escabeche, to your taste, chopped
2 teaspoons ground coriander
1¼ teaspoons ground cumin
½ teaspoon cayenne pepper
¼ teaspoon ground turmeric
1 (14½-ounce / 411-g) can diced tomatoes, with their juice
3 tablespoons tomato paste
1 cup water
3 (15-ounce / 425-g) cans red kidney beans, rinsed and drained
½ teaspoon salt, or more to taste
½ cup evaporated milk or heavy cream
For Serving:
Chopped red onion
Chopped fresh cilantro
Plain yogurt
Warm chapatis

1.Heat the olive oil in a large skillet over medium-high heat, then cook the onions, stirring, until softened, about 5 minutes. Add the garlic, ginger, jalapeños, and spices, and cook, stirring, until the onions are browned. Transfer to the slow cooker, add the tomatoes with their juice, tomato paste, water, and kidney beans, and stir to combine. Cover and cook on low for 5 to 6 hours.
2.Stir in the salt and evaporated milk, cover, and continue to cook on low for another 30 minutes.
3.Serve the chili in bowls with the toppings and warm chapatis, if you can find them.

Chapter 7 Side Dishes

Lemon Braised Artichokes

Prep time: 10 minutes | Cook time: 8 to 9 hours | Serves 4

4 artichokes
¼ cup lemon juice (2 lemons)
1 tablespoon extra-virgin olive oil
6 tablespoons unsalted butter
3 garlic cloves, minced
¼ teaspoon salt

3. Using chef's knife, cut off stems so artichokes sit upright, then trim off the top quarter of each artichoke. Using kitchen shears, trim off the top portion of outer leaves. Toss artichokes with 2 tablespoons lemon juice and oil in a bowl, then place right side up in a slow cooker. Add ½ cup water, cover, and cook until outer leaves of artichokes pull away easily and tip of paring knife inserted into stem end meets no resistance, 8 to 9 hours on low or 5 to 6 hours on high.
4. Microwave remaining 2 tablespoons lemon juice, butter, garlic, and salt in the bowl until butter is melted, about 30 seconds. Whisk butter mixture to combine, then divide evenly among 4 serving bowls. Remove artichokes from the slow cooker, letting any excess cooking liquid drain back into insert, and place artichokes in bowls with butter. Serve.

Braised Green Beans with Capers

Prep time: 15 minutes | Cook time: 7 to 8 hours | Serves 4 to 6

1 onion, halved and thinly sliced
2 tablespoons extra-virgin olive oil
3 garlic cloves, thinly sliced
2 teaspoons minced fresh oregano or ½ teaspoon dried
Salt and pepper, to taste
⅛ teaspoon red pepper flakes
½ cup water
⅓ cup tomato paste
2 pounds (907 g) green beans, trimmed

2 tablespoons capers, rinsed and minced
1 tablespoon chopped fresh parsley

1. Microwave onion, 1 tablespoon oil, garlic, oregano, ¾ teaspoon salt, and pepper flakes in bowl, stirring occasionally, until onion is softened, about 5 minutes; transfer to a slow cooker. Stir in water and tomato paste, then stir in green beans. Cover and cook until green beans are tender, 7 to 8 hours on low or 4 to 5 hours on high.
2. Stir in remaining 1 tablespoon oil, capers, and parsley. Season with salt and pepper to taste. Serve. (Green beans can be held on warm or low setting for up to 2 hours.)

Coconut Curried Butternut Squash

Prep time: 20 minutes | Cook time: 4 to 5 hours | Serves 9

1 cup chopped carrots
1 small onion, chopped
1 tablespoon olive oil
1½ teaspoons brown sugar
1½ teaspoons curry powder
1 garlic clove, minced
½ teaspoon ground cinnamon
¼ teaspoon ground ginger
⅛ teaspoon salt
1 medium butternut squash (about 2½ pounds / 1.1 kg), cut into 1-inch cubes
2½ cups vegetable broth
¾ cup coconut milk
½ cup uncooked basmati or jasmine rice

1. In a large skillet, sauté carrots and onion in oil until onion is tender. Add the brown sugar, curry, garlic, cinnamon, ginger and salt. Cook and stir 2 minutes longer.
2. In a slow cooker, combine the butternut squash, broth, coconut milk, rice and carrot mixture. Cover and cook on low for 4 to 5 hours or until rice is tender.

Creamy Mashed Cauliflower

Prep time: 10 minutes | Cook time: 7 to 8 hours | Serves 8 to 10

2 heads cauliflower (4 pounds / 1.8 kg), cored and cut into 2-inch florets
½ cup boiling water, plus extra as needed
Salt and pepper, to taste
¼ cup heavy cream
3 tablespoons minced fresh chives

1. Combine cauliflower, boiling water, and 1½ teaspoons salt in a slow cooker. Press 16 by 12-inch sheet of parchment paper firmly onto cauliflower, folding down edges as needed. Cover and cook until cauliflower is very tender, 7 to 8 hours on low or 4 to 5 hours on high.
2. Discard parchment. Mash cauliflower with potato masher until almost completely broken down. Stir in cream and chives and season with salt and pepper to taste. Serve. (Cauliflower can be held on warm or low setting for up to 2 hours; adjust consistency with extra hot water as needed before serving.)

Braised Sweet and Sour Red Cabbage

Prep time: 15 minutes | Cook time: 5 to 6 hours | Serves 4 to 6

1 head red cabbage (2 pounds / 907 g), cored and thinly sliced
1 tablespoon vegetable oil
Salt and pepper, to taste
4 slices bacon, finely chopped
1 onion, finely chopped
1 teaspoon minced fresh thyme or ¼ teaspoon dried
½ teaspoon toasted caraway seeds
¼ teaspoon ground cinnamon
¼ teaspoon ground allspice
1½ cups apple cider
2 tablespoons packed brown sugar, plus extra for seasoning
3 bay leaves
2 tablespoons cider vinegar, plus extra for seasoning

1. Microwave cabbage, oil, and ½ teaspoon salt in

covered bowl, stirring occasionally, until cabbage is softened, 15 to 20 minutes. Drain cabbage and transfer to a slow cooker.
2. Cook bacon in 12-inch skillet over medium-high heat until crisp, about 5 minutes. Add onion and cook until softened and lightly browned, 5 to 7 minutes. Stir in thyme, caraway seeds, cinnamon, and allspice and cook until fragrant, about 30 seconds. Stir in ½ cup cider, scraping up any browned bits; transfer to a slow cooker.
3. Stir remaining 1 cup cider, sugar, and bay leaves into a slow cooker. Cover and cook until cabbage is tender, 5 to 6 hours on low or 3 to 4 hours on high.
4. Discard bay leaves. Stir in vinegar and season with salt, pepper, extra sugar, and extra vinegar to taste. Serve. (Cabbage can be held on warm or low setting for up to 2 hours.)

Cabbage Poriyal

Prep time: 10 minutes | Cook time: 3 hours | Serves 6

3 tablespoons coconut oil
2 teaspoons black mustard seeds
2 tablespoons chopped fresh curry leaves
1 teaspoon cumin seeds
2 dried Kashmiri chiles, broken into small pieces
2-inch piece fresh ginger, finely grated
½ teaspoon turmeric
1 teaspoon salt
½ teaspoon freshly ground black pepper
4 cups shredded savoy cabbage
2 fresh green chiles, sliced
½ cup freshly grated coconut
¼ cup water
Juice of 1 lemon

1. Heat the oil in a frying pan (or in the slow cooker if you have a sear setting). Add the mustard seeds, followed by the curry leaves, cumin seeds, and dried chiles. Sauté until the spices sizzle and become aromatic, about 30 seconds.
2. Pour into the slow cooker. Add the ginger, turmeric, salt, and black pepper. Stir in the cabbage, green chiles, fresh coconut, and water.
3. Cover and cook on low for 3 hours, or on high for 1 hour.
4. When the dish is cooked, squeeze in the lemon juice. Mix and serve with fresh boiled rice.

Marmalade Glazed Carrots

Prep time: 10 minutes | Cook time: 5 to 6 hours | Serves 6 to 8

3 pounds (1.4 kg) carrots, peeled and sliced ¼ inch thick on bias
1 tablespoon sugar
Salt and pepper, to taste
½ cup orange marmalade
2 tablespoons unsalted butter, softened

1.Combine carrots, ¾ cup water, sugar, and ¼ teaspoon salt in a slow cooker. Cover and cook until carrots are tender, 5 to 6 hours on low or 3 to 4 hours on high.
2.Drain carrots and return to now-empty slow cooker. Stir in marmalade and butter. Season with salt and pepper to taste. Serve. (Carrots can be held on warm or low setting for up to 2 hours.)

Parmesan Ratatouille

Prep time: 20 minutes | Cook time: 3 to 4 hours | Serves 8 to 10

2 pounds (907 g) eggplant, cut into ½-inch pieces
1½ pounds (680 g) zucchini, cut into 1-inch pieces
2 red bell peppers, stemmed, deseeded, and cut into ½-inch pieces
2 onions, chopped
½ cup extra-virgin olive oil
1 tablespoon sugar
2 garlic cloves, minced
2 teaspoons herbes de Provence
1 (28-ounce / 794-g) can diced tomatoes, drained
1 teaspoon instant tapioca
Salt and pepper, to taste
¼ cup grated Parmesan cheese
¼ cup chopped fresh basil

1.Adjust oven rack 4 inches from broiler element and heat broiler. Line 2 rimmed baking sheets with aluminum foil and spray with vegetable oil spray. Toss eggplant, zucchini, bell peppers, and onions with 6 tablespoons oil, sugar, garlic, and herbes de Provence in a large bowl. Divide vegetables evenly between prepared sheets and spread in a single layer. Broil, 1 sheet at a time, until vegetables begin to brown, 10 to 12 minutes, rotating sheet halfway through broiling. Transfer vegetables and tomatoes to a slow cooker.
2.Stir tapioca, 2½ teaspoons salt, and 1 teaspoon pepper into vegetables. Cover and cook until vegetables are tender, 3 to 4 hours on low or 2 to 3 hours on high. Stir in Parmesan, basil, and remaining 2 tablespoons oil. Season with salt and pepper to taste. Serve. (Ratatouille can be held on warm or low setting for up to 2 hours; adjust consistency with hot water as needed before serving.)

Braised Cauliflower with Lemon-Caper Dressing

Prep time: 10 minutes | Cook time: 2 to 3 hours | Serves 4 to 6

4 garlic cloves, peeled and smashed
2 sprigs fresh thyme
Salt and pepper, to taste
⅛ teaspoon red pepper flakes
1 head cauliflower (2 pounds / 907 g)
2 tablespoons extra-virgin olive oil
2 teaspoons grated lemon zest plus 1 tablespoon juice
2 teaspoons capers, rinsed and minced
1 tablespoon minced fresh parsley

1.Combine 1 cup water, garlic, thyme sprigs, ½ teaspoon salt, and pepper flakes in a slow cooker. Trim outer leaves of cauliflower and cut stem flush with bottom of head. Cut head into 8 equal wedges, keeping core and florets intact. Place wedges cut side down in slow cooker (wedges may overlap). Cover and cook until cauliflower is tender, 2 to 3 hours on high.
2.Whisk oil, lemon zest and juice, capers, and parsley together in a bowl. Season with salt and pepper to taste. Using a slotted spoon, transfer cauliflower to the serving dish, brushing away any garlic cloves or thyme sprigs that stick to cauliflower. Drizzle cauliflower with dressing. Serve.

Thyme-Braised Fennel with Orange

Prep time: 10 minutes | Cook time: 8 to 9 hours | Serves 4 to 6

2 garlic cloves, peeled and smashed
2 sprigs fresh thyme
1 teaspoon juniper berries
Salt and pepper, to taste
2 fennel bulbs, stalks discarded, bulbs halved, and each half cut into 4 wedges
2 tablespoons extra-virgin olive oil
2 teaspoons grated orange zest plus 1 tablespoon juice
1 teaspoon minced fresh tarragon

1.Combine 1 cup water, garlic, thyme sprigs, juniper berries, and ½ teaspoon salt in a slow cooker. Place fennel wedges cut side down in slow cooker (wedges may overlap). Cover and cook until fennel is tender, 8 to 9 hours on low or 5 to 6 hours on high.
2.Whisk oil, orange zest and juice, and tarragon together in the bowl. Season with salt and pepper to taste. Using a slotted spoon, transfer fennel to the serving dish, brushing away any garlic cloves, thyme sprigs, or juniper berries that stick to fennel. Drizzle fennel with dressing. Serve.

Garlicky Collard Greens

Prep time: 10 minutes | Cook time: 9 to 10 hours | Serves 4 to 6

1 onion, finely chopped
6 garlic cloves, minced
1 tablespoon vegetable oil
Salt and pepper, to taste
½ teaspoon red pepper flakes
2 pounds (907 g) collard greens, stemmed and cut into 1-inch pieces
4 cups chicken broth
1 (12-ounce / 340-g) smoked ham hock, rinsed
2 tablespoons cider vinegar, plus extra for seasoning
Hot sauce, for serving

1.Lightly coat slow cooker with vegetable oil spray. Microwave onion, garlic, oil, 1 teaspoon salt, and pepper flakes in bowl, stirring occasionally, until onion is softened, about 5 minutes; transfer to prepared slow cooker. Stir in collard greens and broth. Nestle ham hock into a slow cooker. Cover and cook until collard greens are tender, 9 to 10 hours on low or 6 to 7 hours on high.
2.Transfer ham hock to cutting board, let cool slightly, then shred into bite-size pieces using 2 forks; discard fat, skin, and bones. Stir ham and vinegar into collard greens. Season with salt, pepper, and extra vinegar to taste. Serve with hot sauce. (Collard greens can be held on warm or low setting for up to 2 hours.)

Braised Swiss Chard with Mushrooms

Prep time: 20 minutes | Cook time: 1 to 2 hours | Serves 4 to 6

2 pounds (907 g) Swiss chard, stems finely chopped, leaves cut into 1-inch pieces
4 ounces (113 g) shiitake mushrooms, stemmed and sliced ¼ inch thick
3 garlic cloves, minced
2 teaspoons grated fresh ginger
2 teaspoons toasted sesame oil
Salt and pepper, to taste
⅛ teaspoon red pepper flakes
1 tablespoon rice vinegar
1 tablespoon unsalted butter
1 teaspoon sugar
2 tablespoons chopped dry-roasted peanuts
2 scallions, thinly sliced

1.Lightly coat slow cooker with vegetable oil spray. Microwave chard stems, mushrooms, garlic, 1 teaspoon ginger, 1 teaspoon oil, ¼ teaspoon salt, and pepper flakes in bowl, stirring occasionally, until vegetables are softened, about 5 minutes; transfer to prepared slow cooker. Stir in chard leaves, cover, and cook until chard is tender, 1 to 2 hours on high.
2.Stir in vinegar, butter, sugar, remaining 1 teaspoon ginger, and remaining 1 teaspoon oil. Season with salt and pepper to taste. (Swiss chard can be held on warm or low setting for up to 2 hours.) Sprinkle with peanuts and scallions before serving.

Garlic Hash Browns

Prep time: 20 minutes | Cook time: 3 to 4 hours | Serves 12

1 large red onion, chopped
1 small sweet red pepper, chopped
1 small green pepper, chopped
¼ cup butter, cubed
1 tablespoon olive oil
4 garlic cloves, minced
1 (30-ounce / 850-g) package frozen shredded hash brown potatoes
½ teaspoon salt
½ teaspoon pepper
3 drops hot pepper sauce (optional)
2 teaspoons minced fresh parsley

1. In a large skillet, sauté onion and peppers in butter and oil until crisp-tender. Add garlic; cook 1 minute longer. Stir in the hash browns, salt, pepper and pepper sauce if desired.
2. Transfer to a slow cooker coated with cooking spray. Cover and cook on low for 3 to 4 hours or until heated through. Sprinkle with parsley before serving.

Coconut-Pecan Sweet Potatoes

Prep time: 10 minutes | Cook time: 5 to 6 hours | Serves 6

¼ cup packed brown sugar
2 tablespoons flaked coconut
2 tablespoons chopped pecans, toasted
1 teaspoon vanilla extract
½ teaspoon salt
¼ teaspoon ground cinnamon
2 pounds (907 g) sweet potatoes, peeled and cut into ¾-inch cubes
1 tablespoon butter, melted
½ cup miniature marshmallows

1. In a small bowl, mix the first six ingredients. Place sweet potatoes in a slow cooker coated with cooking spray; sprinkle with brown sugar mixture. Drizzle with butter.
2. Cook, covered, on low 5 to 6 hours or until the sweet potatoes are tender. Turn off the slow cooker. Sprinkle the marshmallows over potatoes; let stand, covered, 5 minutes before serving.

Honey Glazed Peas and Carrots

Prep time: 15 minutes | Cook time: 5¼ hours | Serves 12

1 pound (454 g) carrots, sliced
1 large onion, chopped
¼ cup water
¼ cup butter, cubed
¼ cup honey
4 garlic cloves, minced
1 teaspoon salt
1 teaspoon dried marjoram
⅛ teaspoon white pepper
1 (16-ounce / 454-g) package frozen peas

1. In a slow cooker, combine the first nine ingredients. Cook, covered, on low 5 hours. Stir in the peas. Cook, covered, on high 15 to 25 minutes or until the vegetables are tender.

Roasted Beets with Oranges and Walnuts

Prep time: 10 minutes | Cook time: 6 to 7 hours | Serves 4 to 6

1½ pounds (680 g) beets, trimmed
2 oranges
¼ cup white wine vinegar
2 tablespoons extra-virgin olive oil
1 tablespoon honey
Salt and pepper, to taste
¼ cup toasted and chopped walnuts
2 tablespoons minced fresh chives

1. Wrap beets individually in aluminum foil and place in a slow cooker. Add ½ cup water, cover, and cook until beets are tender, 6 to 7 hours on low or 4 to 5 hours on high.
2. Transfer beets to cutting board and carefully remove foil (watch for steam). When beets are cool enough to handle, rub off skins with paper towels and cut into ½-inch-thick wedges.
3. Cut away peel and pith from oranges. Quarter oranges, then slice crosswise into ½-inch-thick pieces. Whisk vinegar, oil, and honey together in large bowl. Add beets and orange pieces, along with any accumulated juices, and toss to coat. Season with salt and pepper to taste. Sprinkle with walnuts and chives. Serve.

Cinnamon Brown Sugar Carrots

Prep time: 10 minutes | Cook time: 6 to 8 hours | Serves 6

2 pounds (907 g) fresh baby carrots
½ cup peach preserves
¼ cup packed brown sugar
½ cup butter, melted
1 teaspoon vanilla extract
½ teaspoon ground cinnamon
¼ teaspoon salt
⅛ teaspoon ground nutmeg
2 tablespoons cornstarch
2 tablespoons water
Toasted chopped pecans (optional)

1.Place carrots in a slow cooker. Combine the preserves, brown sugar, butter, vanilla, cinnamon, salt and nutmeg. Combine cornstarch and water until smooth; stir into preserve mixture. Pour over carrots.
2.Cover and cook on low for 6 to 8 hours or until tender. Stir carrots; sprinkle with pecans if desired.

Simple Harvard Beets

Prep time: 10 minutes | Cook time: 7 to 8 hours | Serves 6

2 pounds (907 g) small fresh beets, peeled and halved
½ cup sugar
¼ cup packed brown sugar
2 tablespoons cornstarch
½ teaspoon salt
¼ cup orange juice
¼ cup cider vinegar
2 tablespoons butter
1½ teaspoons whole cloves

1.Place beets in a slow cooker. In a small bowl, combine the sugar, brown sugar, cornstarch and salt. Stir in orange juice and vinegar. Pour over beets; dot with butter. Place cloves on a double thickness of cheesecloth; bring up corners of cloth and tie with string to form a bag. Place bag in a slow cooker.
2.Cover and cook on low for 7 to 8 hours or until tender. Discard spice bag.

Buttery Leeks with Thyme

Prep time: 10 minutes | Cook time: 1 to 1½ hours | Serves 6 to 8

4 leeks, split lengthwise and rinsed well
Coarse salt and freshly ground pepper, to taste
4 to 6 thyme sprigs
2 dried bay leaves
6 tablespoons unsalted butter, cut into small pieces
2½ cups low-sodium chicken broth
¼ cup extra-virgin olive oil
Juice of 1 lemon

1.Preheat a slow cooker.
2.Arrange leeks in the slow cooker. Season generously with salt and pepper, scatter with thyme and bay leaves, and dot with butter. Pour in broth. Cover and cook on high until leeks are tender and easily pierced with the tip of a knife, 1 to 1½ hours (or on low for 2½ hours). Discard bay leaves. Drizzle leeks with oil and lemon juice before serving.

Creamy Mashed Potatoes

Prep time: 10 minutes | Cook time: 2 to 3 hours | Serves 10

3¾ cups boiling water
1½ cups 2% milk
1 (8-ounce / 227-g) package cream cheese, softened
½ cup butter, cubed
½ cup sour cream
4 cups mashed potato flakes
1 teaspoon garlic salt
¼ teaspoon pepper
Minced fresh parsley (optional)

1.In a greased slow cooker, whisk the boiling water, milk, cream cheese, butter and sour cream until smooth. Stir in the potato flakes, garlic salt and pepper. Cover and cook on low for 2 to 3 hours or until heated through. Sprinkle with parsley if desired.

Sweet Potato Roast with Crème Fraîche

Prep time: 10 minutes | Cook time: 3 to 3½ hours | Serves 6 to 8

3 tablespoons unsalted butter, room temperature
1 teaspoon onion powder
1 teaspoon garlic powder
1½ teaspoons dried sage
Coarse salt and freshly ground pepper, to taste
6 sweet potatoes, scrubbed and pierced with a fork
½ cup crème fraîche
1 tablespoon mixed fresh herbs, such as flat-leaf parsley, tarragon, and chives, plus more for garnish
Finely grated zest of 1 lemon

1.Preheat a slow cooker.
2.In a bowl, combine butter, onion powder, garlic powder, sage, 2 teaspoons salt, and ½ teaspoon pepper. Rub sweet potatoes with butter mixture, dividing evenly. Tightly wrap each sweet potato in parchment paper, then aluminum foil; transfer to the slow cooker. Cover and cook on high until tender when pierced with a knife, 3 to 3½ hours (or on low for 6 to 7); larger potatoes will take longer to cook.
3.Combine crème fraîche, mixed herbs, and lemon zest in a small bowl. Season with salt and pepper. Spread herbed crème fraîche on a serving platter, and top with sliced potatoes and more herbs.

Butter Mushrooms

Prep time: 10 minutes | Cook time: 4 to 5 hours | Serves 6

1 pound (454 g) medium fresh mushrooms
1 large onion, sliced
½ cup butter, melted
1 envelope Italian salad dressing mix

1.In a slow cooker, layer mushrooms and onion. Combine butter and salad dressing mix; pour over vegetables. Cover and cook on low for 4 to 5 hours or until vegetables are tender. Serve with a slotted spoon.

Garlic and Thyme Braised Baby Artichokes

Prep time: 20 minutes | Cook time: 1½ hours | Serves 6

3 lemons, 2 halved and 1 thinly sliced
12 baby artichokes, trimmed
3 cups low-sodium chicken broth
1 cup dry white wine
1 head garlic, peeled and cut in half crosswise
¼ cup extra-virgin olive oil
6 thyme sprigs
1 tablespoon coarse salt
1 tablespoon black peppercorns

1.Preheat a slow cooker.
2.Fill a large bowl halfway with cold water. Squeeze lemon halves into water, then add lemons to bowl. Remove tough outer leaves from artichokes, halve artichokes, and remove any prickly chokes. Transfer halved artichokes to lemon water.
3.In a small saucepan, bring broth and wine to a boil over high. Place artichokes and garlic in the slow cooker. slowly pour broth mixture over artichokes, then top with oil. Add thyme, salt, peppercorns, and lemon slices. Cover and cook on high until artichokes are tender when pierced with a knife, about 1½ hours (or on low for 3 hours). Transfer artichokes, garlic, braising liquid, and aromatics to a platter, and serve.

Thyme Garlic Tomatoes

Prep time: 15 minutes | Cook time: 5 to 6 hours | Serves 4 to 6

6 ripe tomatoes, cored and halved crosswise
½ cup extra-virgin olive oil
6 garlic cloves, peeled and smashed
2 teaspoons minced fresh thyme or ¾ teaspoon dried
Salt and pepper, to taste

1.Combine tomatoes, oil, garlic, thyme, ¾ teaspoon salt, and ¼ teaspoon pepper in a slow cooker. Cover and cook until tomatoes are tender and slightly shriveled around edges, 5 to 6 hours on low or 3 to 4 hours on high.
2.Let tomatoes cool in oil for at least 15 minutes or up to 4 hours. Season with salt and pepper to taste. Serve.

Buttered Parsley Red Potatoes

Prep time: 10 minutes | Cook time: 2½ to 3 hours | Serves 6

1½ pounds (680 g) medium red potatoes
¼ cup water
¼ cup butter, melted
3 tablespoons minced fresh parsley
1 tablespoon lemon juice
1 tablespoon minced chives
Salt and pepper, to taste

1.Cut a strip of peel from around the middle of each potato. Place potatoes and water in a slow cooker. Cover and cook on high for 2½ to 3 hours or until tender (do not overcook); drain.
2.In a small bowl, combine the butter, parsley, lemon juice and chives. Pour over the potatoes and toss to coat. Season with salt and pepper.

Greek Green Beans with Tomatoes

Prep time: 20 minutes | Cook time: 3 hours | Serves 6 to 8

Coarse salt and freshly ground black pepper, to taste
3 tablespoons extra-virgin olive oil
1 large onion, finely chopped
3 garlic cloves, thinly sliced
⅛ teaspoon red-pepper flakes
1½ teaspoons dried oregano
3 plum tomatoes, peeled and coarsely chopped
1½ pounds (680 g) fresh mature green beans, trimmed and halved if large
1 cup low-sodium chicken broth
1 lemon, cut into wedges, for serving

1.Preheat a slow cooker.
2.Heat oil in a large skillet over medium. Add onion and garlic, and sauté until onion is soft, about 10 minutes. Add red-pepper flakes, oregano, 1 teaspoon salt, ¼ teaspoon black pepper, and tomatoes, and sauté until tomatoes begin to break down, about 5 minutes.
3.Place beans and a pinch of salt in the slow cooker. Spoon tomato mixture over beans in a slow cooker. Pour in broth. Cover and cook on low until beans are tender, about 3 hours. Season with salt and black pepper. Serve with lemon wedges on the side.

Cheesy Scalloped Potatoes

Prep time: 15 minutes | Cook time: 6 to 7 hours | Serves 6 to 8

3 tablespoons unsalted butter, plus more for slow cooker
1 sweet onion, finely chopped
Coarse salt and freshly ground black pepper, to taste
1 tablespoon minced garlic
¼ cup all-purpose flour
1½ cups half-and-half
1 teaspoon dry mustard
Pinch cayenne pepper
1 teaspoon fresh thyme leaves, plus 2 sprigs
2 cups coarsely grated Gruyère cheese (8 ounces / 227 g)
8 Yukon Gold potatoes (about 2½ pounds / 1.1 kg), peeled and sliced paper-thin

1.Butter the insert of a slow cooker.
2.In a large saucepan, melt butter over medium heat. Add onion and sauté until translucent, about 8 minutes. Season with salt. Add garlic and cook 1 minute more. Add flour and cook, stirring constantly, about 2 minutes. Gradually whisk in half-and-half; cook, stirring, until sauce thickens and comes to a boil. Add mustard, ½ teaspoon salt, ¼ teaspoon black pepper, cayenne, 1 teaspoon thyme, and 1 cup cheese. Reduce heat and continue whisking 2 to 3 minutes more. Remove from heat.
3.Season potatoes with salt and black pepper. Layer half the potatoes evenly on the bottom of the slow cooker, overlapping slightly. Pour half the cheese sauce over layer, spreading to cover evenly. Repeat layering potatoes and cheese sauce. Sprinkle with remaining 1 cup cheese and the thyme sprigs. Cover and cook on low until potatoes are tender when pierced with a knife, 6 to 7 hours (or on high for 3 to 3½ hours). Remove lid and allow potatoes to rest for 15 minutes before serving.

India-Spiced Chickpeas and Potatoes

Prep time: 20 minutes | Cook time: 10 hours | Serves 6

1 tablespoon rapeseed oil
2 teaspoons cumin seeds
2 bay leaves
2¾-inch piece cassia bark
2 medium onions, thinly sliced
1 teaspoon salt
1 tablespoon freshly grated ginger
6 garlic cloves, finely chopped
2 fresh green chiles, chopped
2 cups dried chickpeas, washed
2 red potatoes, peeled and diced
2 medium tomatoes, finely chopped
1 teaspoon Kashmiri chili powder
2 teaspoons ground coriander seeds
½ teaspoon turmeric
4 cups hot water
1 tablespoon fresh lemon juice
Roughly chopped fresh coriander leaves, for garnish
1 teaspoon chaat masala
2 fresh green chiles, sliced lengthwise

1. Heat the oil in a frying pan (or in the slow cooker if you have a sear setting). Add the cumin seeds, bay leaves, and cassia bark, and cook until fragrant, about 1 minute.
2. Stir in the sliced onions and salt, and cook for 5 to 6 minutes. Add the ginger, garlic, and chopped chiles, and stir for 1 to 2 minutes.
3. Pour the mixture into the slow cooker with the chickpeas, potatoes, tomatoes, chili powder, coriander seeds, turmeric, and hot water.
4. Cover and cook for 10 hours on low, or for 8 hours on high. Leave on warm until ready to serve.
5. Just before serving, sprinkle with the lemon juice, chopped coriander leaves, chaat masala, and sliced green chilies.

Lemon and Parsley Fingerling Potatoes

Prep time: 10 minutes | Cook time: 5 to 6 hours | Serves 6

2 pounds (907 g) fingerling potatoes, unpeeled
2 tablespoons extra-virgin olive oil
2 scallions, white parts minced, green parts thinly sliced
3 garlic cloves, minced
Salt and pepper, to taste
1 tablespoon chopped fresh parsley
1 teaspoon grated lemon zest plus 1 tablespoon juice

1. Combine potatoes, 1 tablespoon oil, scallion whites, garlic, 1 teaspoon salt, and ¼ teaspoon pepper in a slow cooker. Cover and cook until potatoes are tender, 5 to 6 hours on low or 3 to 4 hours on high.
2. Stir in parsley, lemon zest and juice, scallion greens, and remaining 1 tablespoon oil. Season with salt and pepper to taste. Serve. (Potatoes can be held on warm or low setting for up to 2 hours.)

Balsamic Fresh Shell Beans with Herbs

Prep time: 10 minutes | Cook time: 1½ to 4 hours | Serves 6

3 tablespoons olive oil
2 shallots, minced
3 pounds (1.4 kg) fresh shell beans, shelled
1 cup water, vegetable broth, or chicken broth
Salt and freshly ground black pepper, to taste
2 to 3 teaspoons fresh chopped herbs, such as thyme, parsley, marjoram, or basil
2 to 3 teaspoons dark or white balsamic vinegar

1. In a small skillet over medium heat, warm the olive oil and cook the shallots, stirring, until softened. Put in the slow cooker along with the beans and water. Cover and cook on high for 1½ to 4 hours, depending on the size of the bean.
2. Season with salt and pepper and stir in the herbs and vinegar. Serve immediately, or refrigerate and eat cold.

Cider Butternut Squash Purée

Prep time: 15 minutes | Cook time: 5 to 6 hours | Serves 6 to 8

3 pounds (1.4 kg) butternut squash, peeled, deseeded, and cut into 1-inch pieces (8 cups)
½ cup apple cider, plus extra as needed
Salt and pepper, to taste
4 tablespoons unsalted butter, melted
2 tablespoons heavy cream, warmed
2 tablespoons packed brown sugar, plus extra for seasoning

1. Combine squash, cider, and ½ teaspoon salt in a slow cooker. Press 16 by 12-inch sheet of parchment paper firmly onto squash, folding down edges as needed. Cover and cook until squash is tender, 5 to 6 hours on low or 3 to 4 hours on high.
2. Discard parchment. Mash squash with potato masher until smooth. Stir in melted butter, cream, and sugar. Season with salt, pepper, and extra sugar to taste. Serve. (Squash can be held on warm or low setting for up to 2 hours; adjust consistency with extra hot cider as needed before serving.)

Braised Butternut Squash with Pecans

Prep time: 15 minutes | Cook time: 4 to 5 hours | Serves 4 to 6

1 cup vegetable or chicken broth
2 garlic cloves, peeled and smashed
2 sprigs fresh thyme
Salt and pepper, to taste
2 pounds (907 g) butternut squash, peeled, halved lengthwise, deseeded, and sliced 1 inch thick
2 tablespoons extra-virgin olive oil
1 teaspoon grated lemon zest plus 2 teaspoons juice
¼ cup toasted and chopped pecans
¼ cup dried cranberries
1 tablespoon minced fresh parsley

1. Combine broth, garlic, thyme sprigs, and ¼ teaspoon salt in a slow cooker. Nestle squash into a slow cooker. Cover and cook until squash is tender, 4 to 5 hours on low or 3 to 4 hours on high.
2. Using a slotted spoon, transfer squash to a serving dish, brushing away any garlic cloves or thyme sprigs that stick to squash. Whisk oil and lemon zest and juice together in the bowl. Season with salt and pepper to taste. Drizzle squash with dressing and sprinkle with pecans, cranberries, and parsley. Serve.

Braised Peas with Lettuce and Onions

Prep time: 20 minutes | Cook time: 2½ to 3½ hours | Serves 8

1 medium-size head Boston lettuce
1 sprig fresh thyme, savory, or mint
8 white boiling onions (16 if they are really tiny), peeled
½ cup (1 stick) unsalted butter, softened
½ teaspoon sugar
½ teaspoon salt
½ teaspoon ground white pepper
3½ to 4 pounds (1.6 to 1.8 kg) fresh peas in the pod (5 to 6 cups shelled peas of a uniform size), or 2 (12-ounce / 340-g) bags frozen garden peas (not petites), thawed
¼ cup water

1. Coat the slow cooker with nonstick cooking spray or butter; line the bottom and sides with the outer lettuce leaves. Reserve some leaves for the top. Open the lettuce heart, place the single herb sprig inside, and tie with kitchen twine. Put it in the cooker and add the onions.
2. In a small bowl, mash together the butter, sugar, salt, and pepper. Add to the bowl of shelled peas and, with your hands, gently squeeze the butter into the mass of peas to coat them; it is okay if some peas are bruised, but try not to crush any. Pack the peas around the heart of lettuce in the cooker and top with more lettuce leaves. Add the water. Cover and cook on high for 30 minutes to get the pot heated up.
3. Reduce the heat setting to low and cook until the peas are tender, 2 to 3 hours. At 2 hours, lift the cover to check their progress. Remove the lettuce leaves and the lettuce heart, and serve the hot peas from the crock.

Acorn Squash with Maple Orange Glaze

Prep time: 15 minutes | Cook time: 3 to 4 hours | Serves 4 to 6

2 teaspoons grated orange zest plus ½ cup juice
5 whole cloves
1 cinnamon stick
2 small acorn squashes (1 pound / 454 g each), quartered pole to pole and seeded
Salt and pepper, to taste
¼ cup maple syrup
⅛ teaspoon ground coriander
Pinch cayenne pepper
¼ cup hazelnuts, toasted, skinned, and chopped
1 tablespoon chopped fresh parsley

1. Combine 1 cup water, orange juice, cloves, and cinnamon stick in a slow cooker. Season squashes with salt and pepper and shingle cut side down in a slow cooker. Cover and cook until squashes are tender, 3 to 4 hours on low or 2 to 3 hours on high.
2. Using tongs, transfer squashes to the serving dish, brushing away any cloves that stick to squashes. Microwave maple syrup, coriander, cayenne, and orange zest in bowl until heated through, about 1 minute. Season with salt and pepper to taste. Drizzle glaze over squashes and sprinkle with hazelnuts and parsley. Serve.

Sake-Cooked Asparagus

Prep time: 10 minutes | Cook time: 1¼ to 1½ hours | Serves 4 to 5

1¼ to 1½ pounds (567 to 680 g) asparagus
1 tablespoon olive oil
1 tablespoon sake
1 teaspoon soy sauce
Pinch of brown sugar
Pinch of salt
1 to 2 teaspoons toasted sesame seeds, for garnish (optional)

1. Wash and drain the asparagus. One by one, hold each spear in both of your hands. Bend the spear at the stem end until the end snaps off. Discard the stem end. Put the asparagus in the slow cooker. Drizzle in the olive oil, sake, and soy sauce. Sprinkle with the brown sugar and salt. With your hands, gently toss the asparagus to coat them lightly with the seasonings. Cover and cook on high until tender when pierced with a sharp knife, 1¼ to 1½ hours.
2. Use a pair of tongs to place the asparagus on a serving platter. Pour the liquid from the crock over the asparagus. Sprinkle with the toasted sesame seeds just before serving.

Garlic Collard Greens and Kale

Prep time: 15 minutes | Cook time: 4 to 5 hours | Serves 4 to 6

1 bunch collards (1½ pounds / 680 g)
1 bunch kale (1½ pounds / 680 g)
3 tablespoons olive oil
4 cloves garlic or 2 small shallots, chopped
1 cup chicken, beef, or vegetable broth
1 canned chipotle pepper in adobo sauce or small dried hot pepper (optional)
Salt and freshly ground black pepper, to taste
Juice of 1 lemon
1 tablespoon cider vinegar
For Serving:
Unsalted butter
Cornbread

1. Rinse the greens well in the sink. Drain and trim off the tough stems. Cut the leaves crosswise into ½-inch-wide strips; you will have about 12 to 14 cups.
2. In a deep saucepan, heat the olive oil over medium heat. Add the garlic and cook, stirring, just 30 seconds to 1 minute. Add the greens in handfuls and toss to coat with the oil. With each addition, cover for a minute until wilted, then add some more. Transfer to the slow cooker once they've all been wilted and add the broth. If using the chipotle pepper, nestle it down in the center of the greens. Cover and cook on low until tender, 4 to 5 hours.
3. Season with salt and pepper and stir in the lemon juice and vinegar. Serve nice and hot with a pat of butter and some cornbread.

Garlic Mushrooms with Crème Fraîche

Prep time: 15 minutes | Cook time: 2 to 3 hours | Serves 6 to 10

1½ pounds (680 g) cremini or white mushrooms, stems trimmed
1 cup vegetable broth
2 tablespoons dry white or red wine
3 cloves garlic, chopped
⅓ bunch green onions (white and a few inches of green parts), chopped
1¼ teaspoons dried Italian herbs or herbes de Provence
⅓ cup crème fraîche (optional)
2 tablespoons unsalted butter
Sea salt and freshly ground black pepper, to taste

1. Combine the mushrooms, broth, wine, garlic, green onions, and herbs in the cooker; stir to mix well.
2. Cover and cook on high for 2 to 3 hours, or on low for 4 to 6 hours, until the mushrooms are tender. Check at the halfway point. Stir in the crème fraîche (if using) and butter. Season to taste and serve hot, or set aside to cool and then refrigerate, covered, in the poaching liquid. The mushrooms will keep in the refrigerator for up to 4 days.

Shoepeg Corn Casserole

Prep time: 20 minutes | Cook time: 3 to 4 hours | Serves 8

1 (14½-ounce / 411-g) can French-style green beans, drained
2 (7-ounce / 198-g) cans white or shoepeg corn
1 (10¾-ounce / 305-g) can condensed cream of mushroom soup, undiluted
1 (4½-ounce / 128-g) jar sliced mushrooms, drained
½ cup slivered almonds
½ cup shredded Cheddar cheese
½ cup sour cream
¾ cup French-fried onions

1. In a slow cooker, combine the first seven ingredients. Cover and cook on low for 3 to 4 hours or until vegetables are tender, stirring occasionally. Sprinkle with onions during the last 15 minutes of cooking.

Black-Eyed Peas with Ham

Prep time: 20 minutes | Cook time: 6 to 8 hours | Serves 12

1 (16-ounce / 454-g) package dried black-eyed peas, rinsed and sorted
½ pound (227 g) fully cooked boneless ham, finely chopped
1 medium onion, finely chopped
1 medium sweet red pepper, finely chopped
5 bacon strips, cooked and crumbled
1 large jalapeño pepper, deseeded and finely chopped
2 garlic cloves, minced
1½ teaspoons ground cumin
1 teaspoon reduced-sodium chicken bouillon granules
½ teaspoon salt
½ teaspoon cayenne pepper
¼ teaspoon pepper
6 cups water
Minced fresh cilantro (optional)
Hot cooked rice, for serving

1. In a slow cooker, combine the first 13 ingredients. Cover and cook on low for 6 to 8 hours or until peas are tender. Sprinkle with cilantro if desired. Serve with rice.

Cheesy Red Potatoes

Prep time: 15 minutes | Cook time: 5 to 6 hours | Serves 8

7 cups cubed uncooked red potatoes
1 cup (8 ounces / 227 g) 4% cottage cheese
½ cup sour cream
½ cup cubed process cheese (Velveeta)
1 tablespoon dried minced onion
2 garlic cloves, minced
½ teaspoon salt
Paprika and minced chives (optional)

1. Place the potatoes in a slow cooker. In a blender, purée cottage cheese and sour cream until smooth. Transfer to a large bowl; stir in the process cheese, onion, garlic and salt. Pour over potatoes and mix well.
2. Cover and cook on low for 5 to 6 hours or until potatoes are tender. Stir well before serving. Garnish with paprika and chives if desired.

Creamy Jalapeño Corn

Prep time: 15 minutes | Cook time: 4 to 5 hours | Serves 8

2 (16-ounce / 454-g) packages frozen corn
1 (8-ounce / 227-g) package cream cheese, softened and cubed
4 jalapeño peppers, deseeded and finely chopped
¼ cup butter, cubed
2 tablespoons water
½ teaspoon salt
¼ teaspoon pepper

1.In a slow cooker, combine all ingredients. Cover and cook on low for 4 to 5 hours or until corn is tender, stirring occasionally.

Zucchini Stuffed Sweet Onions

Prep time: 20 minutes | Cook time: 4 to 5 hours | Serves 4

4 medium sweet onions
2 small zucchini, shredded
1 large garlic clove, minced
1 tablespoon olive oil
1 teaspoon dried basil
1 teaspoon dried thyme
¼ teaspoon salt
¼ teaspoon pepper
½ cup dry bread crumbs
4 thick-sliced bacon strips, cooked and crumbled
¼ cup grated Parmesan cheese
¼ cup reduced-sodium chicken broth

1.Peel onions and cut a ¼-inch slice from the top and bottom. Carefully cut and remove the center of each onion, leaving a ½-in. shell; chop removed onion.
2.In a large skillet, sauté the zucchini, garlic and chopped onions in oil until tender and juices are reduced. Stir in the basil, thyme, salt and pepper. Remove from the heat. Stir in the bread crumbs, bacon and Parmesan cheese. Fill onion shells with the zucchini mixture.
3.Place in a greased slow cooker. Add broth to the slow cooker. Cover and cook on low for 4 to 5 hours or until onions are tender.

Cowboy Calico Beans with Ground Beef

Prep time: 30 minutes | Cook time: 4 to 5 hours | Serves 8

1 pound (454 g) 90% lean ground beef
1 large sweet onion, chopped
½ cup packed brown sugar
¼ cup ketchup
3 tablespoons cider vinegar
2 tablespoons yellow mustard
1 (16-ounce / 454-g) can butter beans, drained
1 (16-ounce / 454-g) can kidney beans, rinsed and drained
1 (15-ounce / 425-g) can pork and beans
1 (15¼-ounce / 432-g) can lima beans, rinsed and drained

1.In a large skillet, cook beef and onion over medium heat until meat is no longer pink; drain.
2.Transfer to a slow cooker. Combine the brown sugar, ketchup, vinegar and mustard; add to meat mixture. Stir in the beans. Cover and cook on low for 4 to 5 hours or until heated through.

Spanish Hominy

Prep time: 20 minutes | Cook time: 6 to 8 hours | Serves 12

4 (15½-ounce / 439-g) cans hominy, rinsed and drained
1 (14½-ounce / 411-g) can diced tomatoes, undrained
1 (10-ounce / 283-g) can diced tomatoes and green chilies, undrained
1 (8-ounce / 227-g) can tomato sauce
¾ pound (340 g) sliced bacon, diced
1 large onion, chopped
1 medium green pepper, chopped

1.In a slow cooker, combine the hominy, tomatoes and tomato sauce.
2.In a large skillet, cook bacon until crisp; remove with a slotted spoon to paper towels. Drain, reserving 1 tablespoon drippings.
3.In the same skillet, sauté onion and green pepper in drippings until tender. Stir onion mixture and bacon into hominy mixture. Cover and cook on low for 6 to 8 hours or until heated through.

Green Beans and Potatoes with Bacon

Prep time: 20 minutes | Cook time: 6 to 8 hours | Serves 10

8 bacon strips, chopped
1½ pounds (680 g) fresh green beans, trimmed and cut into 2-inch pieces (about 4 cups)
4 medium potatoes, peeled and cubed (½-inch)
1 small onion, halved and sliced
¼ cup reduced-sodium chicken broth
½ teaspoon salt
¼ teaspoon pepper

1.In a large skillet, cook bacon over medium heat until crisp, stirring occasionally. Remove to paper towels with a slotted spoon; drain, reserving 1 tablespoon drippings. Cover and refrigerate bacon until serving.
2.In a slow cooker, combine the remaining ingredients; stir in reserved drippings. Cover and cook on low for 6 to 8 hours or until potatoes are tender. Stir in bacon; heat through.

Root Vegetable Medley

Prep time: 20 minutes | Cook time: 5 to 6 hours | Serves 8

4 large carrots, cut into 1½-inch pieces
3 fresh beets, peeled and cut into 1½-inch pieces
2 medium sweet potatoes, peeled and cut into 1½-inch pieces
2 medium onions, peeled and quartered
½ cup water
2 teaspoons salt
½ teaspoon pepper
¼ teaspoon dried thyme
1 tablespoon olive oil
Fresh parsley or dried parsley flakes (optional)

1.Place the carrots, beets, sweet potatoes, onions and water in a greased slow cooker. Sprinkle with salt, pepper and thyme. Drizzle with olive oil. Cover and cook on low for 5 to 6 hours or until tender.
2.Stir vegetables and sprinkle with parsley if desired.

Creamed Broccoli

Prep time: 10 minutes | Cook time: 2½ to 3 hours | Serves 8 to 10

6 cups frozen chopped broccoli, partially thawed
1 (10¾-ounce / 305-g) can condensed cream of celery soup, undiluted
1½ cups (6 ounces / 170 g) shredded sharp Cheddar cheese, divided
¼ cup chopped onion
½ teaspoon Worcestershire sauce
¼ teaspoon pepper
1 cup crushed butter-flavored crackers
2 tablespoons butter

1.In a large bowl, combine the broccoli, cream of celery soup, 1 cup cheese, onion, Worcestershire sauce and pepper. Pour into a greased slow cooker. Sprinkle the crushed butter-flavored crackers on top; dot with butter.
2.Cover and cook on high for 2½ to 3 hours. Sprinkle with the remaining cheese. Cook 10 minutes longer or until the cheese is melted.

Bacon Hash Brown Casserole

Prep time: 15 minutes | Cook time: 4 to 5 hours | Serves 14

1 (2-pound / 907-g) package frozen cubed hash brown potatoes
2 cups cubed process cheese (Velveeta)
2 cups sour cream
1 (10¾-ounce / 305-g) can condensed cream of celery soup, undiluted
1 (10¾-ounce / 305-g) can condensed cream of chicken soup, undiluted
1 pound (454 g) sliced bacon, cooked and crumbled
1 large onion, chopped
¼ cup butter, melted
¼ teaspoon pepper

1.Place the cubed hash brown potatoes in a slow cooker. In a large bowl, combine the remaining ingredients. Pour over potatoes and mix well. Cover and cook on low for 4 to 5 hours or until potatoes are tender and heated through.

Maple Baked Beans with Bacon

Prep time: 15 minutes | Cook time: 6 to 8 hours | Serves 8

3 (15-ounce / 425-g) cans pork and beans
½ cup finely chopped onion
½ cup chopped green pepper
½ cup ketchup
½ cup maple syrup
2 tablespoons finely chopped, deseeded jalapeño pepper
½ cup crumbled cooked bacon

1.In a slow cooker, combine the first six ingredients. Cover and cook on low for 6 to 8 hours or until vegetables are tender. Just before serving, stir in bacon.

Zucchini Tomato Casserole

Prep time: 20 minutes | Cook time: 3½ to 4½ hours | Serves 6

3 medium zucchini, cut into ¼-inch slices
1 teaspoon salt, divided
½ teaspoon pepper, divided
1 medium onion, thinly sliced
1 medium green pepper, thinly sliced
3 medium tomatoes, sliced
⅔ cup condensed tomato soup, undiluted
1 teaspoon dried basil
1 cup shredded Cheddar cheese

1.Place zucchini in greased slow cooker. Sprinkle with ½ teaspoon salt and ¼ teaspoon pepper. Layer with onion, green pepper and tomatoes. In a small bowl, combine the soup, basil and remaining salt and pepper; spread over tomatoes.
2.Cover and cook on low for 3 to 4 hours or until vegetables are tender. Sprinkle with cheese. Cover and cook 30 minutes longer or until cheese is melted.

Warm Fruit Salad

Prep time: 15 minutes | Cook time: 2 hours | Serves 14 to 18

2 (29-ounce / 822-g) cans sliced peaches, drained
2 (29-ounce / 822-g) cans pear halves, drained and sliced
1 (20-ounce / 567-g) can pineapple chunks, drained
1 (15¼-ounce / 432-g) can apricot halves, drained and sliced
1 (21-ounce / 595-g) can cherry pie filling

1.In a slow cooker, combine the peaches, pears, pineapple and apricots. Top with pie filling. Cover and cook on high for 2 hours or until heated through. Serve with a slotted spoon.

Cinnamon Glazed Acorn Squash

Prep time: 15 minutes | Cook time: 3½ to 4 hours | Serves 4

¾ cup packed brown sugar
1 teaspoon ground cinnamon
1 teaspoon ground nutmeg
2 small acorn squash, halved and seeded
¾ cup raisins
4 tablespoons butter
½ cup water

1.In a small bowl, mix brown sugar, cinnamon and nutmeg; spoon into squash halves. Sprinkle with raisins. Top each with 1 tablespoon butter. Wrap each half individually in heavy-duty foil, sealing tightly.
2.Pour water into a slow cooker. Place squash in a slow cooker, cut side up (packets may be stacked). Cook, covered, on high 3½ to 4 hours or until squash is tender. Open foil carefully to allow steam to escape.

Spinach and Cheese Casserole

Prep time: 10 minutes | Cook time: 2½ hours | Serves 8

2 (10-ounce / 283-g) packages frozen chopped spinach, thawed and well drained
2 cups 4% cottage cheese
1 cup cubed process cheese (Velveeta)
¾ cup egg substitute
2 tablespoons butter, cubed
¼ cup all-purpose flour
½ teaspoon salt

1.In a slow cooker, combine all ingredients. Cover and cook on low for 2½ hours or until cheese is melted.

Chapter 8 Vegetarian Mains

Thai Butternut Squash and Tofu Curry

Prep time: 20 minutes | Cook time: 3 to 4 hours | Serves 4 to 6

1 onion, finely chopped
3 tablespoons Thai red curry paste
2 tablespoons grated fresh ginger
4 garlic cloves, minced
4 teaspoons vegetable oil
2 pounds (907 g) butternut squash, peeled, deseeded, and cut into 1-inch pieces (6 cups)
14 ounces (397 g) extra-firm tofu, cut into ¾-inch pieces
1 cup vegetable broth, plus extra as needed
2 teaspoons instant tapioca
1 red bell pepper, stemmed, deseeded, and cut into ¼-inch-wide strips
1 cup canned coconut milk
1 tablespoon lime juice, plus extra for seasoning
Salt and pepper, to taste
⅓ cup fresh cilantro leaves
¼ cup chopped dry-roasted peanuts

1.Microwave onion, curry paste, 1 tablespoon ginger, garlic, and 1 tablespoon oil in bowl, stirring occasionally, until onion is softened, about 5 minutes; transfer to a slow cooker. Stir in squash, tofu, broth, and tapioca. Cover and cook until squash is tender, 3 to 4 hours on low or 2 to 3 hours on high.
2.Microwave bell pepper with remaining 1 teaspoon oil in the bowl, stirring occasionally, until tender, about 5 minutes. Stir bell pepper, coconut milk, lime juice, and remaining 1 tablespoon ginger into a slow cooker. Cover and cook on high until heated through, about 10 minutes.
3.Adjust sauce consistency with extra hot broth as needed. Season with salt, pepper, and extra lime juice to taste. Sprinkle individual portions with cilantro and peanuts before serving.

Barley Salad with Summer Squash

Prep time: 15 minutes | Cook time: 3 to 4 hours | Serves 4 to 6

1 cup pearl barley, rinsed
3 tablespoons extra-virgin olive oil
1 teaspoon ground coriander
1 tablespoon grated lemon zest plus 1 tablespoon juice
Salt and pepper, to taste
1 pound (454 g) yellow summer squash or zucchini
10 ounces (283 g) cherry tomatoes, halved
½ cup fresh parsley leaves
⅓ cup plain yogurt
2 tablespoons minced fresh chives
1 garlic clove, minced

1.Lightly coat slow cooker with vegetable oil spray. Microwave barley, 1 tablespoon oil, and coriander in bowl, stirring occasionally, until barley is lightly toasted and fragrant, about 3 minutes; transfer to prepared slow cooker. Stir in 2¼ cups water, 2 teaspoons lemon zest, and ½ teaspoon salt. Cover and cook until barley is tender, 3 to 4 hours on low or 2 to 3 hours on high.
2.Drain barley, if needed, and transfer to large serving bowl; let cool slightly. Using vegetable peeler or mandoline, shave squash lengthwise into very thin ribbons. Add squash ribbons, tomatoes, and parsley to bowl with barley and gently toss to combine.
3.Whisk yogurt, chives, garlic, lemon juice, ¼ teaspoon salt, ¼ teaspoon pepper, remaining 2 tablespoons oil, and remaining 1 teaspoon lemon zest together in separate bowl. Add dressing to salad and toss to coat. Season with salt and pepper to taste. Serve.

Indian Coconut Vegetable Curry

Prep time: 20 minutes | Cook time: 4 to 5 hours | Serves 4 to 6

1 onion, finely chopped
3 garlic cloves, minced
1 tablespoon vegetable oil
1 tablespoon grated fresh ginger
1 tablespoon tomato paste
1 tablespoon curry powder
½ teaspoon garam masala
Salt and pepper, to taste
4 cups vegetable broth, plus extra as needed
1 pound (454 g) red potatoes, unpeeled, cut into ½-inch pieces
14 ounces (397 g) extra-firm tofu, cut into ½-inch pieces
1 tablespoon instant tapioca
1 (13½-ounce / 383-g) can coconut milk
2 cups frozen cut green beans, thawed
¼ cup minced fresh cilantro

1.Microwave onion, garlic, oil, ginger, tomato paste, curry powder, garam masala, and ½ teaspoon salt in a bowl, stirring occasionally, until onion is softened, about 5 minutes; transfer to a slow cooker. Stir in broth, potatoes, tofu, and tapioca. Cover and cook until potatoes are tender, 4 to 5 hours on low or 3 to 4 hours on high.
2.Microwave coconut milk in a bowl, whisking occasionally, until hot, about 3 minutes. Stir coconut milk and green beans into curry and let sit until heated through, about 5 minutes. Adjust consistency with extra hot broth as needed. Stir in cilantro and season with salt and pepper to taste. Serve.

Beet and Wheat Berry Salad

Prep time: 10 minutes | Cook time: 6 to 8 hours | Serves 4 to 6

1 cup wheat berries
2 garlic cloves, minced
2 teaspoons minced fresh thyme or ½ teaspoon dried
Salt and pepper, to taste
1 pound (454 g) beets, trimmed
1 Granny Smith apple, peeled, cored, halved, and sliced ¼ inch thick
4 ounces (113 g) baby arugula
3 tablespoons extra-virgin olive oil
3 tablespoons red wine vinegar
Pinch sugar
4 ounces (113 g) goat cheese, crumbled (1 cup)

1.Combine 5 cups water, wheat berries, garlic, thyme, and ½ teaspoon salt in a slow cooker. Wrap beets individually in aluminum foil and place in a slow cooker. Cover and cook until wheat berries and beets are tender, 6 to 8 hours on low or 4 to 5 hours on high.
2.Transfer beets to cutting board, open foil, and let sit until cool enough to handle. Rub off beet skins with paper towels and cut beets into ½-inch-thick wedges.
3.Drain wheat berries, transfer to a large serving bowl, and let cool slightly. Add beets, apple, arugula, oil, vinegar, ½ teaspoon salt, pinch pepper, and sugar and toss to combine. Season with salt and pepper to taste. Sprinkle with goat cheese and serve.

Red Beans and Rice with Okra

Prep time: 15 minutes | Cook time: 8 to 9 hours | Serves 4 to 6

2 tablespoons Cajun seasoning
2 tablespoons extra-virgin olive oil
3 garlic cloves, minced
4 cups vegetable broth
8 ounces (227 g) dried small red beans, picked over and rinsed
1 green bell pepper, stemmed, deseeded, and cut into ½-inch pieces
1½ cups instant white rice
2 cups frozen cut okra, thawed
2 tomatoes, cored and cut into ½-inch pieces
4 scallions, thinly sliced
Salt and pepper, to taste

1.Microwave Cajun seasoning, oil, and garlic in bowl until fragrant, about 1 minute; transfer to a slow cooker. Stir in broth, beans, and bell pepper. Cover and cook until beans are tender, 8 to 9 hours on high.
2.Stir in rice, cover, and cook on high until rice is tender, 20 to 30 minutes. Stir in okra and let sit until heated through, about 5 minutes. Stir in tomatoes and scallions, and season with salt and pepper to taste. Serve.

Mushroom and Spinach Biryani

Prep time: 20 minutes | Cook time: 2 to 3 hours | Serves 4 to 6

Sauce:
¾ cup plain yogurt
2 tablespoons chopped fresh cilantro
2 tablespoons chopped fresh mint
1 garlic clove, minced
Salt and pepper, to taste

Biryani:
1 onion, finely chopped
3 tablespoons extra-virgin olive oil
4 garlic cloves, minced
2 teaspoons garam masala
Salt and pepper, to taste
½ teaspoon turmeric
⅛ teaspoon cayenne pepper
1½ cups vegetable broth
1½ cups basmati rice, rinsed
1 pound (454 g) cremini mushrooms, trimmed and thinly sliced
6 ounces (170 g) baby spinach, coarsely chopped
¼ cup raisins
2 tablespoons chopped fresh cilantro
2 tablespoons chopped fresh mint
⅓ cup sliced almonds, toasted

1. For the sauce: Combine all ingredients in bowl and season with salt and pepper to taste. Refrigerate until ready to serve.
2. For the **Biryani:** Lightly coat slow cooker with vegetable oil spray. Microwave onion, oil, garlic, garam masala, 1 teaspoon salt, turmeric, and cayenne in bowl, stirring occasionally, until onion is softened, about 5 minutes; transfer to prepared slow cooker.
3. Microwave broth in the bowl until steaming, about 5 minutes. Stir broth and rice into a slow cooker. Spread mushrooms evenly on top of rice mixture. Gently press 16 by 12-inch sheet of parchment paper onto surface of mushrooms, folding down edges as needed. Cover and cook until rice is tender and all broth is absorbed, 2 to 3 hours on high.
4. Discard parchment. Sprinkle spinach and raisins on top of rice, cover, and let sit until spinach is wilted, about 5 minutes. Add cilantro and mint, and fluff rice with fork until combined. Season with salt and pepper to taste. Sprinkle with almonds and serve, passing sauce separately.

Spicy Potato Stuffed Peppers

Prep time: 15 minutes | Cook time: 4 hours | Serves 4

4 medium Yukon Gold potatoes
2 red bell peppers
2 green bell peppers
1 teaspoon rapeseed oil
1 teaspoon cumin seeds
1 cup frozen peas
1 teaspoon salt
1 fresh green chile, finely chopped
1 teaspoon garam masala
1 tablespoon fenugreek leaves
1-inch piece fresh ginger, grated
1 tablespoon finely chopped fresh coriander leaves

1. Boil the potatoes with the skin on until they're soft (about 15 minutes), then leave to cool. (I always boil potatoes with the skin on, as it stops them taking on too much water and becoming mushy.) Peel off their skins and dice the potatoes.
2. Preheat the slow cooker on high and make sure the 4 peppers will fit into the cooker side by side.
3. Heat the oil in a small frying pan, and then toast the cumin seeds until fragrant, about 1 minute. Add the peas to soften.
4. Put the toasted cumin and peas in a large bowl. Then add the cooked potatoes with the salt, chile, garam masala, fenugreek leaves, ginger, and fresh coriander leaves, and mix together. Taste the filling and adjust the seasoning.
5. Slice the tops off the peppers, keeping the stalks intact. Remove the seeds and discard. Divide the potato mixture into 4 portions and stuff each of the peppers.
6. If you have a tray for the inside of your slow cooker, place this inside. If not, crumple up some foil to make a little tray for the peppers to sit on.
7. Place the stuffed peppers on the tray inside the cooker. Replace the top of each of the peppers. Pour about ¼ to ⅓ cup of water into the cooker outside of the tray (so the peppers are not sitting in the water).
8. Cook on low for 4 hours, or for 2 hours on high.

Rosemary Cauliflower and Lentils

Prep time: 10 minutes | Cook time: 8 hours | Serves 2

1 cup cauliflower florets
1 cup lentils
1 tablespoon fresh rosemary
1 tablespoon roasted garlic
Zest of 1 lemon
1 tablespoon extra-virgin olive oil
⅛ teaspoon sea salt
Freshly ground black pepper, to taste
3 cups low-sodium vegetable broth
Juice of 1 lemon
¼ cup roughly chopped fresh parsley

1. Put the cauliflower, lentils, rosemary, garlic, lemon zest, and olive oil in the slow cooker. Season with the salt and black pepper.
2. Pour the vegetable broth over the cauliflower and lentils. Cover and cook on low for 8 hours.
3. Just before serving, drizzle the cauliflower and lentils with the lemon juice and sprinkle the parsley over the top.

Tomato and Pine Nut Stuffed Spiced Eggplants

Prep time: 15 minutes | Cook time: 5 to 6 hours | Serves 4

1 onion, finely chopped
2 tablespoons extra-virgin olive oil
3 garlic cloves, minced
2 teaspoons minced fresh oregano or ½ teaspoon dried
¼ teaspoon ground cinnamon
Salt and pepper, to taste
⅛ teaspoon cayenne pepper
1 (14½-ounce / 411-g) can diced tomatoes, drained
2 ounces (57 g) Pecorino Romano cheese, grated (1 cup)
¼ cup pine nuts, toasted
1 tablespoon red wine vinegar
2 (10-ounce / 283-g) Italian eggplants, halved lengthwise
2 tablespoons minced fresh parsley

1. Microwave onion, 1 tablespoon oil, garlic, oregano, cinnamon, ¼ teaspoon salt, and cayenne in bowl, stirring occasionally, until onion

is softened, about 5 minutes; transfer to a slow cooker. Stir in tomatoes, ¾ cup Pecorino, pine nuts, and vinegar. Season eggplant halves with salt and pepper and nestle cut side down into slow cooker (eggplants may overlap slightly). Cover and cook until eggplants are tender, 5 to 6 hours on low or 3 to 4 hours on high.
2. Transfer eggplant halves cut side up to serving dish. Using 2 forks, gently push eggplant flesh to sides of each half to make room for filling. Stir remaining 1 tablespoon oil into tomato mixture and season with salt and pepper to taste. Mound tomato mixture evenly into eggplants and sprinkle with parsley and remaining ¼ cup Pecorino. Serve.

Carrot Farro Risotto with Goat Cheese

Prep time: 15 minutes | Cook time: 3 to 4 hours | Serves 4

1 onion, finely chopped
1 tablespoon unsalted butter
2 garlic cloves, minced
Salt and pepper, to taste
2½ cups vegetable broth, plus extra as needed
¼ cup dry white wine
1 cup whole farro
3 carrots, peeled and finely grated
4 ounces (113 g) goat cheese, crumbled (1 cup)
4 ounces (113 g) baby spinach

1. Lightly coat slow cooker with vegetable oil spray. Microwave onion, butter, garlic, and ¼ teaspoon salt in bowl, stirring occasionally, until onion is softened, about 5 minutes; transfer to prepared slow cooker.
2. Microwave 2 cups broth and wine in the bowl until steaming, about 5 minutes. Stir broth mixture, farro, and carrots into a slow cooker. Cover and cook until farro is tender, 3 to 4 hours on low or 2 to 3 hours on high.
3. Microwave remaining ½ cup broth in bowl until steaming, about 5 minutes. Stir broth and goat cheese into farro until mixture is creamy but still somewhat thin. Stir in spinach, 1 handful at a time, until slightly wilted. Cover and cook on high until spinach is completely wilted, about 15 minutes. Adjust risotto consistency with extra hot broth as needed. Season with salt and pepper to taste. Serve.

Barbecued Kabocha Squash

Prep time: 15 minutes | Cook time: 6 to 8 hours | Serves 2

1 teaspoon extra-virgin olive oil
½ kabocha squash, deseeded, peeled, and cut into 2-by-1-inch pieces
1 red onion, halved and thinly sliced
1 small sweet potato, cut into 1-inch pieces
1 cup tomato sauce
½ cup low-sodium vegetable broth
1 teaspoon Dijon mustard
1 teaspoon smoked paprika
1 teaspoon garlic powder
1 teaspoon onion powder
1 teaspoon maple syrup or honey
⅛ teaspoon sea salt

1.Grease the inside of the slow cooker with the olive oil.
2.Put the squash, red onion, and sweet potato into the slow cooker.
3.In a small bowl, whisk together the tomato sauce, vegetable broth, mustard, paprika, garlic powder, onion powder, maple syrup, and salt. Pour this mixture over the vegetables.
4.Cover and cook on low for 6 to 8 hours, or until the squash is very tender. Serve.

Summer Squash, Kale, and Quinoa Stew

Prep time: 10 minutes | Cook time: 4 hours | Serves 2

½ cup quinoa
½ cup canned chickpeas, drained and rinsed
1 cup diced summer squash
4 cups fresh kale
1 cup canned plum tomatoes, roughly chopped
2 cups low-sodium vegetable broth
1 tablespoon Italian herb blend
⅛ teaspoon sea salt

1.Put all the ingredients into the slow cooker, stirring to mix them together thoroughly.
2.Cover and cook on low for 4 hours.

Curried Sweet Potatoes and Broccoli

Prep time: 10 minutes | Cook time: 6 to 8 hours | Serves 2

2 medium sweet potatoes, cut into 1-inch pieces
1 cup broccoli florets
½ cup diced onions
1 cup light coconut milk
1 teaspoon minced fresh ginger
1 teaspoon minced garlic
Pinch red pepper flakes
1 tablespoon curry powder
1 teaspoon garam masala
¼ cup toasted cashews

1.Put the sweet potatoes, broccoli, and onions into the slow cooker.
2.In a small bowl, whisk together the coconut milk, ginger, garlic, red pepper flakes, curry powder, and garam masala. Pour this mixture over the vegetables.
3.Cover and cook on low for 6 to 8 hours until the vegetables are very tender but not falling apart.
4.Just before serving, add the cashews and stir thoroughly.

Smoky Mixed Bean Chili

Prep time: 10 minutes | Cook time: 6 to 8 hours | Serves 2

1 (16-ounce / 454-g) can mixed beans, drained and rinsed
1 cup frozen roasted corn kernels, thawed
1 cup canned fire-roasted diced tomatoes, undrained
½ cup diced onion
2 garlic cloves, minced
1 teaspoon ground cumin
1 teaspoon smoked paprika
1 teaspoon dried oregano
⅛ teaspoon sea salt

1.Put all the ingredients in the slow cooker. Give them a quick stir to combine.
2.Cover and cook on low for 6 to 8 hours.

Moroccan Chickpea and Chard Stew

Prep time: 15 minutes | Cook time: 8 hours | Serves 2

½ bunch Swiss chard, stems diced and leaves roughly chopped
1 (16-ounce / 454-g) can chickpeas, drained and rinsed
½ cup diced onion
½ cup diced carrots
¼ cup diced dried apricots
2 tablespoons roughly chopped preserved lemons (optional)
1 tablespoon tomato paste
1 teaspoon minced fresh ginger
¼ teaspoon red pepper flakes
½ teaspoon smoked paprika
½ teaspoon ground cinnamon
¼ teaspoon ground cumin
⅛ teaspoon sea salt

1. Put all the ingredients into the slow cooker. Stir everything together thoroughly.
2. Cover and cook on low for 8 hours.

Chickpea Tagine with Vegetables

Prep time: 20 minutes | Cook time: 8 to 9 hours | Serves 4 to 6

2 onions, finely chopped
3 tablespoons extra-virgin olive oil, plus extra for drizzling
8 garlic cloves, minced
4 teaspoons paprika
2 teaspoons garam masala
4 cups vegetable broth, plus extra as needed
2 cups water
1 pound (454 g) dried chickpeas, picked over and rinsed
2 (2-inch) strips orange zest
2 red bell peppers, stemmed, deseeded, and cut into ¼-inch-wide strips
2 cups jarred whole baby artichokes packed in water, halved, rinsed, and patted dry
½ cup pitted kalamata olives, coarsely chopped
½ cup golden raisins
½ cup plain Greek yogurt
½ cup minced fresh cilantro
2 tablespoons honey
Salt and pepper, to taste

1. Microwave onions, 2 tablespoons oil, garlic, paprika, and garam masala in bowl, stirring occasionally, until onions are softened, about 5 minutes; transfer to a slow cooker. Stir in broth, water, chickpeas, and orange zest. Cover and cook until chickpeas are tender, 8 to 9 hours on high.
2. Microwave bell peppers with remaining 1 tablespoon oil in the bowl, stirring occasionally, until tender, about 5 minutes. Discard orange zest. Stir bell peppers, artichokes, olives, and raisins into tagine. Cover and cook on high until heated through, about 10 minutes.
3. Whisk ½ cup hot cooking liquid and yogurt together in bowl (to temper), then stir mixture back into slow cooker. Stir in cilantro and honey. Adjust consistency with extra hot broth as needed. Season with salt and pepper to taste. Serve, drizzling individual portions with extra oil.

Chickpea and Seitan Curry

Prep time: 10 minutes | Cook time: 6 to 8 hours | Serves 2

1 teaspoon extra-virgin olive oil
8 ounces (227 g) seitan, cut into bite-size pieces
1 (15-ounce / 425-g) can chickpeas, drained and rinsed
½ cup minced onion
1 teaspoon minced garlic
2 tablespoons tomato paste
1 teaspoon minced fresh ginger
½ teaspoon garam masala
1 teaspoon curry powder
Pinch red pepper flakes
½ teaspoon sea salt
1 cup light coconut milk

1. Grease the inside of the slow cooker with the olive oil.
2. Put all the ingredients into the slow cooker and stir to mix thoroughly.
3. Cover and cook on low for 6 to 8 hours.

Black Bean Spinach Enchiladas

Prep time: 10 minutes | Cook time: 6 to 8 hours | Serves 2

1 (15-ounce / 425-g) can black beans, drained and rinsed
¼ cup low-fat cream cheese
¼ cup low-fat Cheddar cheese
½ cup minced onion
1 teaspoon minced garlic
1 teaspoon ground cumin
1 teaspoon smoked paprika
2 cups shredded fresh spinach
1 teaspoon extra-virgin olive oil
1 cup enchilada sauce, divided
4 corn tortillas
¼ cup fresh cilantro, for garnish

1.In a large bowl, mix together the beans, cream cheese, Cheddar cheese, onion, garlic, cumin, paprika, and spinach.
2.Grease the inside of the slow cooker with the olive oil.
3.Pour ¼ cup of enchilada sauce into the crock, spreading it across the bottom. Place one corn tortilla on top of the sauce. Top the tortilla with one-third of the black bean and spinach mixture. Top this with a second corn tortilla and then slather it with ¼ cup of enchilada sauce. Repeat this layering, finishing with a corn tortilla and the last ¼ cup of enchilada sauce.
4.Cover and cook on low for 6 to 8 hours. Garnish with the cilantro just before serving.

Veggie Tofu Stir-Fry

Prep time: 15 minutes | Cook time: 4 to 6 hours | Serves 2

1 teaspoon extra-virgin olive oil
½ cup brown rice
1 cup water
Pinch sea salt
1 (16-ounce / 454-g) block tofu, drained and cut into 1-inch pieces
1 green bell pepper, cored and cut into long strips
½ onion, halved and thinly sliced
1 cup chopped green beans, cut into 1-inch pieces
2 carrots, cut into ½-inch dice

2 tablespoons low-sodium soy sauce
1 tablespoon hoisin sauce
1 tablespoon freshly squeezed lime juice
1 teaspoon minced garlic
Pinch red pepper flakes

1.Grease the inside of the slow cooker with the olive oil.
2.Put the brown rice, water, and salt in the slow cooker and gently stir so all the rice grains are submerged.
3.Put the tofu, bell pepper, onion, green beans, and carrots over the rice.
4.In a measuring cup or glass jar, whisk together the soy sauce, hoisin sauce, lime juice, garlic, and red pepper flakes. Pour this mixture over the tofu and vegetables.
5.Cover and cook on low for 4 to 6 hours, until the rice has soaked up all the liquid and the vegetables are tender.

Spinach Mushroom Cheese Quiche

Prep time: 10 minutes | Cook time: 8 hours | Serves 2

1 teaspoon butter, at room temperature, or extra-virgin olive oil
4 eggs
1 teaspoon fresh thyme
⅛ teaspoon sea salt
Freshly ground black pepper, to taste
2 slices whole-grain bread, crusts removed and cut into 1-inch cubes
½ cup diced button mushrooms
2 tablespoons minced onion
1 cup shredded spinach
½ cup shredded Swiss cheese

1.Grease the inside of the slow cooker with the butter.
2.In a small bowl, whisk together the eggs, thyme, salt, and a few grinds of the black pepper.
3.Put the bread, mushrooms, onions, spinach, and cheese in the slow cooker. Pour the egg mixture over the top and stir gently to combine.
4.Cover and cook on low for 8 hours or overnight.

Seitan Tikka Masala with Green Beans

Prep time: 10 minutes | Cook time: 6 hours | Serves 2

8 ounces (227 g) seitan, cut into bite-size pieces
1 cup chopped green beans
1 cup diced onion
1 cup fire-roasted tomatoes, drained
1 teaspoon ground coriander
1 teaspoon ground cumin
1 teaspoon smoked paprika
⅛ teaspoon red pepper flakes
1 teaspoon minced fresh ginger
1 cup low-sodium vegetable broth
2 tablespoons coconut cream
¼ cup minced fresh cilantro, for garnish

1.Put the seitan, green beans, onion, tomatoes, coriander, cumin, paprika, red pepper flakes, ginger, and vegetable broth in the slow cooker. Gently stir the ingredients together to combine.
2.Cover and cook on low for 6 hours.
3.Allow to the dish to rest, uncovered, for 10 minutes, then stir in the coconut cream and garnish the dish with the cilantro.

Tempeh and Vegetable Shepherd's Pie

Prep time: 10 minutes | Cook time: 8 hours | Serves 2

1 cup frozen peas, thawed
1 cup diced carrots
½ cup minced onions
8 ounces (227 g) tempeh
⅛ teaspoon sea salt
Freshly ground black pepper, to taste
1½ cups prepared mashed potatoes
2 tablespoons shredded sharp Cheddar cheese

1.Put the peas, carrots, onions, and tempeh in the slow cooker and gently stir to combine. Season the mixture with the salt and black pepper.
2.Spread the prepared mashed potatoes over the tempeh and vegetable mixture.
3.Cover and cook on low for 8 hours.
4.Sprinkle with the cheese just before serving.

Tempeh and Corn Stuffed Bell Peppers

Prep time: 10 minutes | Cook time: 6 to 8 hours | Serves 2

1 teaspoon extra-virgin olive oil
8 ounces (227 g) tempeh, crumbled
1 cup frozen corn kernels, thawed
¼ cup minced onions
1 teaspoon minced garlic
1 teaspoon ground cumin
1 teaspoon smoked paprika
2 tablespoons Pepper Jack cheese
⅛ teaspoon sea salt
4 narrow red bell peppers

1.Grease the inside of the slow cooker with the olive oil.
2.In a medium bowl, combine the tempeh, corn, onions, garlic, cumin, paprika, cheese, and salt.
3.Cut the tops off each of the peppers and set the tops aside. Scoop out and discard the seeds and membranes from inside each pepper. Divide the tempeh filling among the peppers. Return the tops to each of the peppers.
4.Nestle the peppers into the slow cooker.
5.Cover and cook on low for 6 to 8 hours, until the peppers are very tender.

Red Tofu Curry and Green Beans

Prep time: 15 minutes | Cook time: 6 hours | Serves 2

1 teaspoon extra-virgin olive oil
16 ounces (454 g) firm tofu, drained and cut into 1-inch pieces
2 cups chopped green beans
½ red onion, halved and thinly sliced
1 plum tomato, diced
1 teaspoon minced fresh ginger
1 teaspoon minced garlic
2 teaspoons Thai red curry paste
1 cup coconut milk
1 cup low-sodium vegetable broth

1.Grease the inside of the slow cooker with the olive oil.
2.Put all the ingredients into the slow cooker and stir gently.
3.Cover and cook on low for 6 hours.

Vegetarian Bean Cassoulet

Prep time: 10 minutes | Cook time: 6 to 8 hours | Serves 2

1 teaspoon extra-virgin olive oil
2 (15-ounce / 425-g) cans navy beans, drained and rinsed
16 ounces (454 g) vegan sausage, cut into 1-inch pieces
1 cup minced onion
¼ cup minced celery
1 tablespoon minced garlic
1 teaspoon minced fresh sage
1 cup low-sodium vegetable broth

1.Grease the inside of the slow cooker with the olive oil.
2.Put the beans, sausage, onion, celery, garlic, and sage in the slow cooker. Stir to mix thoroughly. Pour in the vegetable broth.
3.Cover and cook on low for 6 to 8 hours, until the beans are very tender but not falling apart.

Curried Coconut Quinoa

Prep time: 15 minutes | Cook time: 3 to 4 hours | Serves 6

2 cups coconut milk
1 cup uncooked quinoa
⅓ cup hot water
1 (14-ounce / 397-g) can chickpeas, drained and rinsed
1 tablespoon tomato purée
1 tablespoon freshly grated ginger
1 teaspoon turmeric
1 teaspoon chili powder
1 teaspoon sea salt
2 garlic cloves, minced
1 sweet potato, peeled and chopped
1 large broccoli crown, cut into florets
1 tomato, diced
1 fresh green chile, chopped
½ white onion, finely diced (about 1 cup)
Shredded fresh coconut, for garnish
Handful fresh coriander leaves, chopped

1.Wash the quinoa in a few changes of water to rid it of its external coating, which can be bitter.

2.Add all ingredients except the shredded coconut, and the coriander leaves to the slow cooker, and stir until everything is mixed.
3.Cover and cook on high for 3 to 4 hours, or for 6 hours on low, until the sweet potato is cooked through. Stir halfway through cooking, if you can.
4.Top with coconut shreds and coriander leaves, and serve hot.

Indian Spiced Potatoes and Cauliflower

Prep time: 15 minutes | Cook time: 3 hours | Serves 6

1 large cauliflower, cored and cut into florets
2 tablespoons mustard oil
2 teaspoons mustard seeds
2 teaspoons cumin seeds
1 onion, finely chopped
3 garlic cloves, finely chopped
2 red potatoes, peeled and cut into 1½-inch cubes
7 to 8 ounces (198 to 227 g) canned tomatoes
1 tablespoon freshly grated ginger
1 teaspoon salt
1 teaspoon turmeric
1 teaspoon chili powder
1 or 2 fresh green chiles, finely chopped
1 teaspoon dried fenugreek leaves
1 teaspoon garam masala
Handful fresh coriander leaves, chopped

1.Prepare your cauliflower and make sure it's thoroughly dry before cooking.
2.Heat the oil in a frying pan (or in the slow cooker if you have a sear setting). Add the mustard seeds, and as they sizzle, add the cumin seeds.
3.Add the onions and garlic, and cook for 1 minute before adding the potatoes and cauliflower to the slow cooker along with the tomatoes, ginger, salt, turmeric, chili powder, chopped chiles, and dried fenugreek leaves.
4.Turn the cooker to low and cook for 3 hours, or for 2 hours on high. Give the dish a stir in the first hour, and it will release enough liquid to cook.
5.Before serving, sprinkle with garam masala and fresh coriander leaves.

Spice Stuffed Baby Eggplants

Prep time: 15 minutes | Cook time: 4 hours | Serves 6

12 baby eggplants
4 dried red chiles
2 tablespoons coriander seeds
1 teaspoon mustard seeds
1 teaspoon cumin seeds
½ teaspoon fenugreek seeds
1 teaspoon fennel seeds
1 tablespoon nigella seeds
¼ teaspoon carom seeds
½ teaspoon turmeric
1 teaspoon mango powder
Sea salt, to taste
3 tablespoons mustard oil
2 onions, sliced
Handful fresh coriander leaves, chopped

1.Preheat the slow cooker on high.
2.Wash the eggplants and cut lengthwise, but leave the top intact.
3.Heat a dry frying pan on medium-high and add the red chiles, coriander seeds, mustard seeds, cumin seeds, fenugreek seeds, fennel seeds, nigella seeds, and carom seeds to the pan. Toast until fragrant, about 1 minute. Remove and put into a coffee grinder and blend to a fine powder.
4.Empty into a medium bowl and mix in the turmeric, mango powder, and salt. Add some water to make a thick paste.
5.Rub about 1 teaspoon of the paste into each of the eggplants with your fingers so the flesh is covered inside and out.
6.Heat the mustard oil in the same frying pan (or in the slow cooker if you have a sear setting). Add the sliced onions and cook for 5 minutes. Add any remaining spice paste. Mix for a minute or two and add a splash of water if needed. Then pour the onion mixture into the slow cooker.
7.Place the stuffed eggplants into the cooker and cover. Cook on low for 4 hours, or on high for 2 to 3 hours.
8.Turn the eggplants a few times during cooking, if possible.
9.Check the seasoning and sprinkle in the coriander leaves.

Roasted Cauliflower with Tomato Cashew Sauce

Prep time: 15 minutes | Cook time: 4 to 5 hours | Serves 6

1 red onion, sliced
1-inch piece fresh ginger, cut into strips
4 garlic cloves, sliced
2 tomatoes, roughly chopped
1 fresh green chile, chopped
5 tablespoons raw cashews, soaked in water for 2 hours and drained
1 large head cauliflower, outer leaves trimmed
2 tablespoons ghee or rapeseed oil
1 teaspoon cumin seeds
1 teaspoon coriander seeds
1 teaspoon salt
1 teaspoon Kashmiri chili powder
1 teaspoon turmeric
1 teaspoon garam masala
⅔ cup hot water
1 tablespoon dried fenugreek leaves
Handful fresh coriander leaves, chopped

1.Preheat the slow cooker on high for 15 minutes, or use the sauté setting if you have one. Add the onions, ginger, garlic, tomatoes, and green chile. Stir and cook for 10 minutes.
2.Add the drained cashews and place the head of cauliflower on top of everything.
3.Heat the ghee or rapeseed oil, if using, in a frying pan and toast the cumin and coriander seeds until they are fragrant. Pour them over the cauliflower head and sprinkle in the salt, chili powder, turmeric, and garam masala.
4.Add the water. Cover and cook on low for 4 to 5 hours, or on high for 2 to 3 hours.
5.When it's cooked (you can check by sticking a sharp knife through the middle), transfer the cauliflower head to a shallow oven-proof dish. Using an immersion or regular blender, blend the cooking liquid that's left in the slow cooker to make a smooth sauce. It should be like a thick batter; if it's too thick, you can add a little hot water.
6.Check and adjust the salt, if required. Add the dried fenugreek leaves and then pour the sauce over the cauliflower head. Place in the oven at 400ºF (205ºC) for 5 to 10 minutes to crisp up.
7.Sprinkle on some fresh coriander leaves and serve in chunky wedges.

Almond Vegetable Korma

Prep time: 20 minutes | Cook time: 2 to 3 hours | Serves 6

1 tablespoon vegetable oil
3 cloves
3 green cardamom pods
1-inch piece cassia bark
1 to 3 dried red chiles
2 onions, minced
2 garlic cloves, minced
1 tablespoon freshly grated ginger
1 teaspoon turmeric
1 tablespoon ground coriander seeds
Sea salt, to taste
⅓ cup hot water
⅓ cup creamed coconut
2 heaped tablespoons ground almonds
1 teaspoon ground white poppy seeds
1 cup cauliflower florets
1 carrot, peeled and chopped
1 red bell pepper, deseeded and diced
1 cup peeled, deseeded, and chopped winter squash (such as butternut or pumpkin)
½ cup frozen peas, thawed
½ cup green beans
1 teaspoon garam masala
Handful fresh coriander leaves, finely chopped
3 tablespoons slivered almonds
1 lemon, quartered

1. Heat the oil in a frying pan (or in the slow cooker if you have a sear setting). Add the cloves, cardamom pods, cassia bark, and dried red chiles. Cook for a few minutes until fragrant. Add the minced onions and sauté gently over medium heat for about 5 to 10 minutes.
2. Set the slow cooker on high and pour the mixture inside. Add the garlic and ginger and cook for a few minutes. Then stir in the turmeric, ground coriander seeds, and salt. Pour in the hot water, creamed coconut, ground almonds, and poppy seeds, and then stir.
3. Add the cauliflower, carrot, pepper, and squash. Cover and cook on high for 2 to 3 hours, or on low for 4 to 5 hours.
4. Add the peas and green beans and cook on high for another hour.
5. When the dish is cooked, add the garam masala and stir through. Top with fresh coriander leaves, slivered almonds, and a squeeze of lemon juice for added freshness.

Eggplant and Potato Curry

Prep time: 10 minutes | Cook time: 2 hours | Serves 6

2 tablespoons mustard oil

2 teaspoons mustard seeds

2 teaspoons cumin seeds

1 onion, finely sliced

7 to 8 ounces (198 to 227 g) canned tomatoes

1 teaspoon turmeric

1 fresh green chile, finely chopped

1 tablespoon freshly grated ginger

2 eggplants, about 1 pound (454 g) total, cut into

1-inch lengths

2 red potatoes, peeled and cut into 1-inch lengths

1 teaspoon sea salt

1 teaspoon garam masala

Handful fresh coriander leaves, chopped

1. Heat the oil in a frying pan (or in the slow cooker if you have a sear setting). Add the mustard seeds, and as they are sizzling add the cumin seeds until they become fragrant.
2. Turn the slow cooker to high and add the spices with the sliced onion, tomatoes, turmeric, chopped chile, and grated ginger.
3. Stir in the eggplant and potatoes. Cover and cook on high for 2 hours, or for 3 to 4 hours on low.
4. When you are ready to serve, add the salt, garam masala, and fresh coriander leaves.

Chapter 9 Poultry

Chicken and Mushroom Stew

Prep time: 15 minutes | Cook time: 6 to 8 hours | Serves 4

1 (10¾-ounce / 305-g) can 98% fat-free cream of mushroom soup
1½ cups water
4 boneless, skinless chicken breast halves
½ teaspoon salt
¼ teaspoon black pepper
½ pound (227 g) fresh medium-sized white mushrooms, or a variety of mushrooms, including portabella, cut-up
1 cup baby carrots
2 ribs celery, cut into small pieces
½ teaspoon garlic powder

1. Combine soup and water in a slow cooker.
2. Cut chicken into 2-inch chunks. Sprinkle with salt and pepper. Place in a slow cooker.
3. Add mushrooms, carrots, celery, and garlic powder. Stir gently to mix.
4. Cover. Cook on low 6 to 8 hours or until chicken is done and internal temperature reaches 170°F (77°C).
5. Serve with rice.

Savory Rubbed Roast Chicken

Prep time: 10 minutes | Cook time: 6 hours | Serves 4 to 5

Seasoning Mix:
1 tablespoon salt
2 teaspoons paprika
1½ teaspoons onion powder
1½ teaspoons garlic powder
1½ teaspoons dried basil
1 teaspoon dry mustard
1 teaspoon cumin
2 teaspoons pepper
½ teaspoon dried thyme
½ teaspoon savory
2 tablespoons butter
2 cups chopped onions
1 cup chopped green pepper

1 roasting chicken
¼ cup flour
1 to 2 cups chicken stock

1. Combine seasoning mix ingredients in a small bowl.
2. Melt butter over high heat in the skillet. When butter starts to sizzle, add chopped onions and peppers, and 3 tablespoons seasoning mix. Cook until onions are golden brown. Cool.
3. Stuff cavity of chicken with cooled vegetables.
4. Sprinkle outside of chicken with 1 tablespoon seasoning mix. Rub in well.
5. Place chicken in a large slow cooker.
6. Cover. Cook on low 6 hours.
7. Empty vegetable stuffing and juices into a saucepan. Whisk in flour and 1 cup stock. Cook over high heat until thickened. Add more stock if you prefer a thinner gravy.

Creamed Nutmeg Chicken

Prep time: 15 minutes | Cook time: 3 hours | Serves 6

6 boneless chicken breast halves
Oil
¼ cup chopped onions
¼ cup minced parsley
2 (10¾-ounce / 305-g) cans cream of mushroom soup
½ cup sour cream
½ cup milk
1 tablespoon ground nutmeg
¼ teaspoon sage
¼ teaspoon dried thyme
¼ teaspoon crushed rosemary

1. Brown chicken in skillet in oil. Reserve drippings and place chicken in a slow cooker.
2. Sauté onions and parsley in drippings until onions are tender.
3. Stir in remaining ingredients. Mix well. Pour over chicken.
4. Cover. Cook on low 3 hours, or until juices run clear.
5. Serve over mashed or fried potatoes, or rice.

Salsa Curry Chicken

Prep time: 15 minutes | Cook time: 3 to 4½ hours | Serves 10

10 skinless, bone-in chicken breast halves, divided
1 (16-ounce / 454-g) jar salsa, your choice of heat
1 medium onion, chopped
2 tablespoons curry powder
1 cup sour cream

1. Place half the chicken in the slow cooker.
2. Combine salsa, onion, and curry powder in a medium-sized bowl. Pour half the sauce over the meat in the cooker.
3. Repeat Steps 1 and 2.
4. Cover and cook on high for 3 hours. Or cook on high for 1½ hours and then turn cooker to low and cook 3 more hours.
5. Remove chicken to serving platter and cover to keep warm.
6. Add sour cream to slow cooker and stir into salsa until well blended. Serve over the chicken.

Chicken and Potato Bake

Prep time: 15 minutes | Cook time: 4½ to 5½ hours | Serves 6 to 8

¼ cup chopped green peppers
½ cup chopped onions
1½ cups diced Velveeta cheese
7 to 8 medium potatoes, sliced
Salt, to taste
1 (10¾-ounce / 305-g) can cream of celery soup
1 cup milk
3 to 4 whole boneless, skinless chicken breasts

1. Place layers of green peppers, onions, cheese, and potatoes and a sprinkling of salt in a slow cooker.
2. Sprinkle salt over chicken breasts and lay on top of potatoes.
3. Combine soup and milk and pour into a slow cooker, pushing meat down into liquid.
4. Cover. Cook on high 1½ hours. Reduce temperature to low and cook 3 to 4 hours. Test that potatoes are soft. If not, continue cooking on low another hour and test again, continuing to cook until potatoes are finished.

Soy Braised Chicken

Prep time: 10 minutes | Cook time: 2¼ to 2¾ hours | Serves 8

4 whole chicken breasts, halved
1 (10¾-ounce / 305-g) can cream of mushroom or chicken soup
¼ cup soy sauce
¼ cup oil
¼ cup wine vinegar
¾ cup water
½ teaspoon minced garlic
1 teaspoon ground ginger
½ teaspoon dried oregano
1 tablespoon brown sugar

1. Place chicken in a slow cooker.
2. Combine remaining ingredients. Pour over chicken.
3. Cover. Cook on low 2 to 2½ hours. Uncover and cook 15 minutes more. Serve with rice.

Creamy Lemon Garlic Chicken

Prep time: 15 minutes | Cook time: 3 to 4 hours | Serves 6

1 cup vegetable broth
1½ teaspoons grated lemon peel
3 tablespoons lemon juice
2 tablespoons capers, drained
3 garlic cloves, minced
½ teaspoon pepper
6 boneless skinless chicken breast halves (6 ounces / 170 g each)
2 tablespoons butter
2 tablespoons all-purpose flour
½ cup heavy whipping cream
Hot cooked rice

1. In a small bowl, combine the first six ingredients. Place chicken in a slow cooker; pour broth mixture over chicken. Cook, covered, on low 3 to 4 hours or until chicken is tender.
2. Remove chicken from slow cooker; keep warm. In a large saucepan, melt butter over medium heat. Stir in flour until smooth; gradually whisk in cooking juices. Bring to a boil, stirring constantly; cook and stir 1-2 minutes or until thickened. Remove from heat and stir in cream. Serve chicken and rice with sauce.

Roasted Chicken and Vegetables

Prep time: 15 minutes | Cook time: 8 to 10 hours | Serves 6

2 carrots, sliced
2 onions, sliced
2 celery ribs, cut into 1-inch pieces
3 pounds (1.4 kg) chicken, whole or cut up
2 teaspoons salt
½ teaspoon dried coarse black pepper
1 teaspoon dried basil
½ cup water, chicken broth, or white cooking wine

1. Place vegetables in bottom of the slow cooker. Place chicken on top of vegetables. Add seasonings and water.
2. Cover. Cook on low 8 to 10 hours, or on high 3½ to 5 hours (use 1 cup liquid if cooking on high). Serve.

Fruity Chicken Curry

Prep time: 20 minutes | Cook time: 4¼ to 6¼ hours | Serves 5

1 (2½- to 3½-pound / 1.1- to 1.6-kg) fryer chicken, cut up
Salt and pepper, to taste
1 tablespoon curry powder
1 garlic clove, crushed or minced
1 tablespoon butter, melted
½ cup chicken broth
2 tablespoons finely chopped onion
1 (29-ounce / 822-g) can cling peaches
½ cup pitted prunes
3 tablespoons cornstarch
3 tablespoons cold water
Peanuts
Shredded coconut
Fresh pineapple chunks

1. Sprinkle chicken with salt and pepper. Place in a slow cooker.
2. Combine curry, garlic, butter, broth, and onions in a bowl.
3. Drain peaches, reserving syrup. Add ½ cup syrup to curry mixture. Pour over chicken.
4. Cover. Cook on low 4 to 6 hours. Remove chicken from pot. Turn on high.

5. Stir in prunes.
6. Dissolve cornstarch in cold water. Stir into the pot.
7. Cover. Cook on high 10 minutes, or until thickened. Add peaches. Add cooked chicken.
8. Serve over rice. Offer remaining ingredients as condiments.

Hawaiian Huli Huli Chicken

Prep time: 5 minutes | Cook time: 4 to 5 hours | Serves 4

⅔ cup pineapple juice
½ cup packed brown sugar
½ cup ketchup
¼ cup lime juice (2 limes)
¼ cup soy sauce
6 garlic cloves, minced
2 tablespoons grated fresh ginger
4 (10-ounce / 283-g) chicken leg quarters, trimmed
Salt and pepper, to taste

1. Bring pineapple juice, sugar, ketchup, lime juice, soy sauce, garlic, and ginger to simmer in a medium saucepan over medium heat and cook until thickened and measures 1 cup, 15 to 20 minutes.
2. Lightly coat slow cooker with vegetable oil spray. Transfer ½ cup sauce to prepared slow cooker; reserve remaining sauce separately. Season chicken with salt and pepper, add to the slow cooker, and turn to coat evenly with sauce. Cover and cook until chicken is tender, 4 to 5 hours on low.
3. Adjust oven rack 6 inches from broiler element and heat broiler. Set wire rack in aluminum foil-lined rimmed baking sheet and coat with vegetable oil spray. Transfer chicken to prepared rack; discard cooking liquid. Broil chicken until browned, about 10 minutes, flipping chicken halfway through broiling.
4. Brush chicken with ¼ cup reserved sauce and continue to broil until chicken is lightly charred, about 5 minutes, flipping and brushing chicken with remaining ¼ cup sauce halfway through broiling. Serve.

Creamy Chicken in White Wine

Prep time: 5 minutes | Cook time: 6 to 8 hours | Serves 4 to 6

2 to 3 pounds (907 g to 1.4 kg) chicken breasts or pieces
1 (10¾-ounce / 305-g) can cream of mushroom soup
1 (10¾-ounce / 305-g) can French onion soup
1 cup dry white wine or chicken broth

1. Put chicken in a slow cooker.
2. Combine soups and wine. Pour over chicken.
3. Cover. Cook on low 6 to 8 hours.
4. Serve over rice, pasta, or potatoes.

Mushroom Chicken Alfredo

Prep time: 20 minutes | Cook time: 4 to 5 hours | Serves 4

4 bone-in chicken breast halves (12 to 14 ounces / 340 to 397 g each), skin removed
2 tablespoons canola oil
1 (10¾-ounce / 305-g) can condensed cream of chicken soup, undiluted
1 (10¾-ounce / 305-g) can condensed cream of mushroom soup, undiluted
1 cup chicken broth
1 small onion, chopped
1 (6-ounce / 170-g) jar sliced mushrooms, drained
¼ teaspoon garlic salt
¼ teaspoon pepper
8 ounces (227 g) fettuccine
1 (8-ounce / 227-g) package cream cheese, softened and cubed
Shredded Parmesan cheese (optional)

1. In a large skillet, brown chicken in oil in batches. Transfer to a slow cooker. In a large bowl, combine the soups, broth, onion, mushrooms, garlic salt and pepper; pour over meat. Cover and cook on low for 4 to 5 hours or until chicken is tender.
2. Cook fettuccine according to package directions; drain. Remove chicken from slow cooker and keep warm. Turn slow cooker off and stir in cream cheese until melted. Serve with fettucine. Top with Parmesan cheese if desired.

Basil Chicken

Prep time: 5 minutes | Cook time: 5 to 6 hours | Serves 6

6 boneless, skinless chicken breast halves
2 (10¾-ounce / 305-g) cans broccoli cheese soup
2 cups milk
1 small onion, chopped
½ to 1 teaspoon salt
½ to 1 teaspoon dried basil
⅛ teaspoon pepper

1. Place chicken pieces in a slow cooker.
2. Combine remaining ingredients. Pour over chicken.
3. Cover. Cook on high 1 hour. Reduce heat to low. Cook 5 to 6 hours.
4. Serve over noodles.

Lemon-Dill Chicken

Prep time: 20 minutes | Cook time: 4 to 5 hours | Serves 6

2 medium onions, coarsely chopped
2 tablespoons butter, softened
¼ teaspoon grated lemon peel
1 broiler/fryer chicken (4 to 5 pounds / 1.8 to 2.3 kg)
¼ cup chicken stock
4 sprigs fresh parsley
4 fresh dill sprigs
3 tablespoons lemon juice
1 teaspoon salt
1 teaspoon paprika
½ teaspoon dried thyme
¼ teaspoon pepper

1. Place onions on the bottom of a slow cooker. In a small bowl, mix butter and lemon peel.
2. Tuck wings under chicken; tie drumsticks together. With fingers, carefully loosen skin from chicken breast; rub butter mixture under the skin. Secure skin to underside of breast with toothpicks. Place chicken over onions, breast side up. Add stock, parsley and dill.
3. Drizzle lemon juice over the chicken; sprinkle with seasonings. Cook, covered, on low 4 to 5 hours (a thermometer inserted in thigh should read at least 175ºF (79ºC)).
4. Remove chicken from slow cooker; tent with foil. Let stand 15 minutes before carving.

Honey Butter Baked Chicken

Prep time: 15 minutes | Cook time: 3 hours | Serves 4

4 skinless, bone-in chicken breast halves
2 tablespoons butter, melted
2 tablespoons honey
2 teaspoons prepared mustard
2 teaspoons curry powder
Salt and pepper, to taste (optional)

1. Spray slow cooker with nonstick cooking spray and add chicken
2. Mix butter, honey, mustard, and curry powder together in a small bowl. Pour sauce over chicken.
3. Cover and cook on high 3 hours, or on low 5 to 6 hours.

Picnic Chicken

Prep time: 5 minutes | Cook time: 6 to 7 hours | Serves 4

2 pounds (907 g) or 4 large chicken thighs
¼ cup dill pickle relish
¼ cup Dijon mustard
¼ cup mayonnaise
½ cup chicken broth

1. Rinse chicken well. Pat dry. Place in a slow cooker with the skin side up.
2. In a mixing bowl, stir together the relish, mustard, and mayonnaise. When well blended, stir in chicken broth. Mix well.
3. Pour sauce over chicken.
4. Cover cooker and cook on low 6 to 7 hours, or until chicken is tender but not dry or mushy.

Garlic and Citrus Chicken

Prep time: 15 minutes | Cook time: 5 to 6 hours | Serves 6

6 skinless, bone-in chicken breast halves
1½ teaspoons dry thyme
6 cloves garlic, minced
1 cup orange juice concentrate
2 tablespoons balsamic vinegar

1. Rub thyme and garlic over chicken. (Reserve any leftover thyme and garlic.) Place chicken in a slow cooker.
2. Mix orange juice concentrate and vinegar together in a small bowl. Stir in reserved thyme and garlic. Spoon over chicken.
3. Cover and cook on low 5 to 6 hours, or on high 2½ to 3 hours, or until chicken is tender but not dry.

Oregano-Lemon Chicken

Prep time: 5 minutes | Cook time: 4 to 6 hours | Serves 6

3½ to 4 pounds (1.6 to 1.8 kg) chicken, cut up
Half a stick (¼ cup) butter, melted
1 envelope dry Italian salad dressing mix
2 tablespoons lemon juice
1 to 2 tablespoons dried oregano

1. Place chicken in bottom of the slow cooker. Mix butter, dressing mix, and lemon juice together and pour over top.
2. Cover and cook on high for 4 to 6 hours, or until chicken is tender but not dry.
3. Baste occasionally with sauce mixture and sprinkle with oregano 1 hour, or just before, serving.

Asian Ginger Chicken

Prep time: 15 minutes | Cook time: 3 to 5 hours | Serves 6

6 chicken breast halves, uncooked, cut up
1 cup diced carrots
½ cup minced onion
½ cup low-sodium soy sauce
¼ cup rice vinegar
¼ cup sesame seeds
1 tablespoon ground ginger, or ¼ cup grated ginger
¾ teaspoon salt
1 teaspoon sesame oil
2 cups broccoli florets
1 cup cauliflower florets

1. Combine all ingredients except broccoli and cauliflower in a slow cooker.
2. Cover. Cook on low 3 to 5 hours. Stir in broccoli and cauliflower and cook an additional hour.
3. Serve over brown rice.

Lemon Pepper Chicken

Prep time: 5 minutes | Cook time: 6 to 8 hours | Serves 4

1 onion, chopped
1 pound (454 g) boneless, skinless chicken thighs
1 teaspoon lemon pepper
½ teaspoon dried oregano
½ cup plain yogurt

1.Combine first 3 ingredients in a slow cooker. Cover and cook on low 6 to 8 hours, or until chicken is tender.
2.Just before serving, remove chicken and shred with two forks.
3.Add shredded chicken back into a slow cooker and stir in oregano and yogurt.
4.Serve as a filling for pita bread.

Mango Pineapple Chicken Tacos

Prep time: 25 minutes | Cook time: 5 to 6 hours | Serves 16

2 medium mangoes, peeled and chopped
1½ cups cubed fresh pineapple or canned pineapple chunks, drained
2 medium tomatoes, chopped
1 medium red onion, finely chopped
2 small Anaheim peppers, deseeded and chopped
2 green onions, finely chopped
1 tablespoon lime juice
1 teaspoon sugar
4 pounds (1.8 kg) bone-in chicken breast halves, skin removed
3 teaspoons salt
¼ cup packed brown sugar
32 taco shells, warmed
¼ cup minced fresh cilantro

1.In a large bowl, combine the first eight ingredients. Place chicken in a slow cooker; sprinkle with salt and brown sugar. Top with mango mixture. Cover and cook on low for 5 to 6 hours or until chicken is tender.
2.Remove chicken; cool slightly. Strain cooking juices, reserving mango mixture and ½ cup

juices. Discard remaining juices. When cool enough to handle, remove chicken from bones; discard bones.
3.Shred chicken with two forks. Return chicken and reserved mango mixture and cooking juices to slow cooker; heat through. Serve in taco shells; sprinkle with cilantro.

Chicken Cordon Bleu

Prep time: 10 minutes | Cook time: 6 to 8 hours | Serves 4

4 boneless, skinless chicken breast halves
½ pound (227 g) deli-sliced cooked ham
½ pound (227 g) baby Swiss cheese, sliced
1 (10¾-ounce / 305-g) can cream of chicken soup
1 box dry stuffing mix, prepared according to box directions

1.Layer all ingredients in the order they are listed into your slow cooker.
2.Cover and cook on low 6 to 8 hours, or until chicken is tender but not dry.

Apricot-Dijon-Glazed Chicken

Prep time: 10 minutes | Cook time: 5 to 6 hours | Serves 6

1 (11½-ounce / 326-g) can apricot nectar
2 tablespoons Dijon mustard
1 clove garlic, minced
¼ teaspoon fresh grated ginger
¼ teaspoon cayenne pepper
¼ teaspoon ground allspice
¼ teaspoon turmeric
¼ teaspoon ground cardamom
6 boneless, skinless chicken breast halves
4 cups prepared couscous or wild rice (blended is good, too)

1.Combine all ingredients except chicken and couscous in a slow cooker.
2.Add chicken, turning it to make sure all sides are covered in sauce.
3.Cover. Cook on low 5 to 6 hours, or on high 2½ to 3 hours.
4.Remove chicken and arrange over warm couscous or rice. Pour the sauce over the chicken and serve.

Jamaican-Inspired Brown Chicken Stew

Prep time: 25 minutes | Cook time: 6 to 8 hours | Serves 8

¼ cup ketchup
3 garlic cloves, minced
1 tablespoon sugar
1 tablespoon hot pepper sauce
1 teaspoon browning sauce (optional)
1 teaspoon dried basil
1 teaspoon dried thyme
1 teaspoon paprika
½ teaspoon salt
½ teaspoon dried oregano
½ teaspoon ground allspice
½ teaspoon pepper
8 bone-in chicken thighs (about 3 pounds / 1.4 kg), skin removed
1 pound (454 g) fully cooked andouille chicken sausage links, sliced
1 medium onion, finely chopped
2 medium carrots, finely chopped
2 celery ribs, finely chopped

1.In a large resealable plastic bag, combine ketchup, garlic, sugar, pepper sauce and, if desired, browning sauce; stir in seasonings. Add chicken thighs, sausage and vegetables. Seal bag and turn to coat. Refrigerate 8 hours or overnight.
2.Transfer contents of bag to a slow cooker. Cook, covered, on low 6 to 8 hours or until chicken is tender.

Pineapple Teriyaki Chicken

Prep time: 5 minutes | Cook time: 6 to 8 hours | Serves 5 to 6

2 to 3 pounds (907 g to 1.4 kg) skinless chicken pieces
1 (20-ounce / 567-g) can pineapple chunks
Dash of ground ginger
1 cup teriyaki sauce

1.Place chicken in a slow cooker. Pour remaining ingredients over chicken.
2.Cover. Cook on low 6 to 8 hours, or on high 4 to 6 hours.

Stuffed Chicken with Bacon and Feta

Prep time: 10 minutes | Cook time: 1½ to 3 hours | Serves 4

¼ cup crumbled cooked bacon
¼ cup crumbled feta cheese
4 boneless, skinless chicken breast halves
2 (14½-ounce / 411-g) cans diced tomatoes
1 tablespoon dried basil

1.In a small bowl, mix bacon and cheese together lightly.
2.Cut a pocket in the thicker side of each chicken breast. Fill each with ¼ of the bacon and cheese. Pinch shut and secure with toothpicks.
3.Place chicken in a slow cooker. Top with tomatoes and sprinkle with basil.
4.Cover and cook on high 1½ to 3 hours, or until chicken is tender, but not dry or mushy.

Raspberry Chicken Drumsticks

Prep time: 5 minutes | Cook time: 5¼ to 6¼ hours | Serves 3

3 tablespoons soy sauce
⅓ cup red raspberry fruit spread or jam
5 chicken drumsticks or chicken thighs
2 tablespoons cornstarch
2 tablespoons cold water

1.Mix soy sauce and raspberry spread or jam together in a small bowl until well blended.
2.Brush chicken with the sauce and place in a slow cooker. Spoon remainder of the sauce over top.
3.Cook on low 5 to 6 hours, or until chicken is tender but not dry.
4.Mix together cornstarch and cold water in a small bowl until smooth. Then remove chicken to a serving platter and keep warm. Turn the slow cooker to high and stir in cornstarch and water to thicken. When thickened and bubbly, after about 10 to 15 minutes, spoon sauce over chicken before serving.

Chicken Parmesan

Prep time: 10 minutes | Cook time: 4 to 4½ hours | Serves 8

8 boneless, skinless chicken breast halves (about 2 pounds / 907 g)
½ cup water
1 cup fat-free mayonnaise
½ cup grated fat-free Parmesan cheese
2 teaspoons dried oregano
¼ teaspoon black pepper
¼ teaspoon paprika

1.Place chicken and water in a slow cooker.
2.Cover. Cook on high 2 hours.
3.Mix remaining ingredients. Spread over chicken.
4.Cover. Cook on high 2 to 2½ hours.

Cornbread Chicken Bake

Prep time: 20 minutes | Cook time: 3 to 4 hours | Serves 6

5 cups cubed cornbread
¼ cup butter, cubed
1 large onion, chopped (about 2 cups)
4 celery ribs, chopped (about 2 cups)
3 cups shredded cooked chicken
1 (10¾-ounce / 305-g) can condensed cream of chicken soup, undiluted
1 (10¾-ounce / 305-g) can condensed cream of mushroom soup, undiluted
½ cup reduced-sodium chicken broth
1 teaspoon poultry seasoning
½ teaspoon salt
½ teaspoon rubbed sage
¼ teaspoon pepper

1.Preheat oven to 350°F (180°C). Place bread cubes on an ungreased 15x10-in. baking pan. Bake 20 to 25 minutes or until toasted. Cool on baking pan.
2.In a large skillet, heat butter over medium-high heat. Add onion and celery; cook and stir 6 to 8 minutes or until tender. Transfer to a greased slow cooker. Stir in corn bread, chicken, soups, broth and seasonings.
3.Cook, covered, on low 3 to 4 hours or until heated through.

Sticky Sesame Chicken

Prep time: 5 minutes | Cook time: 4 to 8 hours | Serves 4

1 tablespoon hot chili sesame oil
4 large chicken thighs
3 cloves garlic, sliced
½ cup brown sugar
3 tablespoons soy sauce

1.Spread oil around the bottom of your slow cooker.
2.Rinse chicken well and remove excess fat. Pat dry. Place in your slow cooker.
3.Sprinkle garlic slices over top of the chicken. Crumble brown sugar over top. Drizzle with soy sauce.
4.Cover and cook on low 4 to 8 hours, or until thighs are tender, but not dry.
5.Serve over rice, prepared with the juice from the cooked chicken instead of water.

Thai Sesame Chicken Thighs

Prep time: 20 minutes | Cook time: 5 to 6 hours | Serves 8

8 bone-in chicken thighs (about 3 pounds / 1.4 kg), skin removed
½ cup salsa
¼ cup creamy peanut butter
2 tablespoons lemon juice
2 tablespoons reduced-sodium soy sauce
1 tablespoon chopped deseeded jalapeño pepper
2 teaspoons Thai chili sauce
1 garlic clove, minced
1 teaspoon minced fresh ginger
2 green onions, sliced
2 tablespoons sesame seeds, toasted
Hot cooked basmati rice (optional)

1.Place chicken in a slow cooker. In a small bowl, combine the salsa, peanut butter, lemon juice, soy sauce, jalapeño, Thai chili sauce, garlic and ginger; pour over chicken.
2.Cover and cook on low for 5 to 6 hours or until chicken is tender. Sprinkle with green onions and sesame seeds. Serve with rice if desired.

Chicken with Apple and Chardonnay Gravy

Prep time: 20 minutes | Cook time: 6 to 8 hours | Serves 6

6 chicken leg quarters
½ teaspoon salt
¼ teaspoon pepper
2 large sweet apples, peeled and cut into wedges
1 large sweet onion, chopped
2 celery ribs, chopped
½ cup chardonnay
1 envelope brown gravy mix
2 large garlic cloves, minced
1 teaspoon each minced fresh oregano, rosemary and thyme
Hot mashed potatoes

1. Sprinkle chicken with salt and pepper. Place half of the chicken in a slow cooker. In a bowl, combine the apples, onion and celery; spoon half of the mixture over chicken. Repeat layers.
2. In the same bowl, whisk wine, gravy mix, garlic and herbs until blended; pour over top. Cover and cook on low for 6 to 8 hours or until chicken is tender.
3. Remove chicken to a serving platter; keep warm. Cool the apple mixture slightly; skim fat. In a blender, cover and process apple mixture in batches until smooth. Transfer to a saucepan and heat through over medium heat, stirring occasionally. Serve with chicken and mashed potatoes.

Braised Apple Balsamic Chicken

Prep time: 15 minutes | Cook time: 4 to 5 hours | Serves 4

4 bone-in chicken thighs (about 1½ pounds / 680 g), skin removed
½ cup chicken broth
¼ cup apple cider or juice
¼ cup balsamic vinegar
2 tablespoons lemon juice
½ teaspoon salt
½ teaspoon garlic powder
½ teaspoon dried thyme
½ teaspoon paprika
½ teaspoon pepper
2 tablespoons butter
2 tablespoons all-purpose flour

1. Place chicken in a slow cooker. In a small bowl, combine the broth, cider, vinegar, lemon juice and seasonings; pour over meat. Cover and cook on low for 4 to 5 hours or until chicken is tender.
2. Remove chicken; keep warm. Skim fat from cooking liquid. In a small saucepan, melt butter; stir in flour until smooth. Gradually add cooking liquid. Bring to a boil; cook and stir for 2 to 3 minutes or until thickened. Serve with chicken.

Rotisserie-Style Chicken with Carrots

Prep time: 25 minutes | Cook time: 6 to 7 hours | Serves 6

4 teaspoons seasoned salt
4 teaspoons poultry seasoning
1 tablespoon paprika
1½ teaspoons onion powder
1½ teaspoons brown sugar
1½ teaspoons salt-free lemon-pepper seasoning
¾ teaspoon garlic powder
1 broiler/fryer chicken (4 pounds / 1.8 kg)
1 pound (454 g) carrots, halved lengthwise and cut into 1½-inch lengths
2 large onions, chopped
2 tablespoons cornstarch

1. In a small bowl, combine the first seven ingredients. Carefully loosen skin from chicken breast; rub 1 tablespoon spice mixture under the skin. Rub remaining spice mixture over chicken. In another bowl, toss carrots and onions with cornstarch; transfer to a slow cooker. Place chicken on vegetables.
2. Cover and cook on low for 6 to 7 hours or until a thermometer inserted in thigh reads 180ºF (82ºC). Remove chicken and vegetables to a serving platter; cover and let stand for 15 minutes before carving. Skim fat from cooking juices. Serve with chicken and vegetables.

Ginger Peach Glazed Chicken Thighs

Prep time: 15 minutes | Cook time: 4 to 5 hours | Serves 10

10 boneless skinless chicken thighs (about 2½ pounds / 1.1 kg)
1 cup sliced peeled fresh or frozen peaches
1 cup golden raisins
1 cup peach preserves
⅓ cup chili sauce
2 tablespoons minced crystallized ginger
1 tablespoon reduced-sodium soy sauce
1 tablespoon minced garlic
Hot cooked rice (optional)

1. Place chicken in a slow cooker coated with cooking spray. Top with peaches and raisins. In a small bowl, combine the preserves, chili sauce, ginger, soy sauce and garlic. Spoon over the top.
2. Cover and cook on low for 4 to 5 hours or until chicken is tender. Serve with rice if desired.

Mushroom Chicken Cacciatore

Prep time: 10 minutes | Cook time: 4½ to 5½ hours | Serves 6 to 8

4 tablespoons extra-virgin olive oil
1 pound (454 g) cremini mushrooms, quartered
2 teaspoons salt
Pinch red pepper flakes
1 teaspoon dried oregano
3 cloves garlic, minced
¼ cup dried porcini mushrooms, crumbled
¼ cup red wine
1 (28- to 32-ounce / 794- to 907-g) can crushed tomatoes, with their juice
10 chicken thighs, skin and bones removed

1. Heat 2 tablespoons of the oil in a large skillet over high heat. Add the mushrooms, 1 teaspoon of the salt, red pepper flakes, oregano, and garlic and sauté until the liquid in the pan has evaporated, about 7 to 10 minutes.
2. Add the porcini and the wine to a small bowl and allow the porcini to soften. Add the wine mixture and the tomatoes to the skillet.
3. Transfer the contents of the pan to the insert of a slow cooker.

4. Sprinkle the chicken evenly with the remaining 1 teaspoon salt. Heat the remaining 2 tablespoons oil in the same skillet over high heat. Add the chicken to the skillet and brown on all sides, 15 to 20 minutes.
5. Transfer the browned meat to the slow-cooker insert, submerging it in the sauce. Cover and cook on low for 4 to 5 hours, until the chicken is tender and cooked through. Skim off any fat from the top of the sauce.
6. Serve from the cooker set on warm.

Sour Cream Chicken Enchiladas

Prep time: 10 minutes | Cook time: 2 hours | Serves 8

1 tablespoon vegetable oil
1 large yellow onion, chopped
1 (24- to 32-ounce / 680- to 907-g) can green chile enchilada sauce
1 dozen soft corn tortillas, each one cut into 4 strips
2½ to 3 cups cooked boneless, skinless chicken, cut into ¾-inch pieces
4 cups finely shredded Monterey Jack cheese
2 cups sour cream (reduced fat is okay)

1. In a large skillet, heat the oil over medium-high heat, then add the onion and cook, stirring, until softened, about 5 minutes. Set aside.
2. Pour about ½ cup of the enchilada sauce into the slow cooker; tilt to spread it around. In layers, add one-quarter of the tortilla strips, one-quarter of the remaining sauce, one-third of the sautéed onion, one-third of the chicken, and one-quarter of the cheese. Repeat the layers two more times, ending with the cheese. Finish the casserole with the remaining tortilla strips, sauce, and cheese.
3. Spoon the sour cream over the surface of the casserole in big dollops. Use a spatula or the back of a large spoon to gently spread it all around without disturbing the layers. Cover and cook on high for 2 hours, or on low for 4 to 5 hours.
4. To serve, use a long-handled spoon to reach down through all the layers for each serving. Make sure each diner gets some of the sour cream.

Easy Tandoori Chicken

Prep time: 5 minutes | Cook time: 4 hours | Serves 6

1½ cups plain yogurt
2 teaspoons fresh lemon juice
1 teaspoon ground coriander
½ teaspoon ground cumin
½ teaspoon ground cardamom
½ teaspoon turmeric
1 teaspoon sweet paprika
2 cloves garlic, minced
1 teaspoon freshly grated ginger
1 (3- to 4-pound / 1.4- to 1.8-kg) chicken, cut into 8 pieces and skin removed

1. Combine the yogurt, lemon juice, coriander, cumin, cardamom, turmeric, paprika, garlic, and ginger in a 1-gallon zipper-top plastic bag.
2. Add the chicken in the bag and marinate for at least 8 hours and up to 24 hours. Put the chicken and the marinade in the insert of a slow cooker.
3. Cover and cook on high for 4 hours, until the chicken is cooked through. Remove the chicken from the pot and serve warm or at room temperature.

Jerk Chicken

Prep time: 5 minutes | Cook time: 2½ to 3 hours | Serves 8

2 teaspoons jerk seasoning
1½ cups mango nectar
½ cup firmly packed light brown sugar
2 tablespoons dark corn syrup
2 tablespoons rice vinegar
8 chicken breast halves, skin and bones removed

1. Add the jerk seasoning, nectar, sugar, corn syrup, and rice vinegar to the insert of a slow cooker and stir to combine.
2. Add the chicken breasts and turn to coat in the sauce. Cover and cook on high for 2½ to 3 hours, until the chicken is cooked through.
3. Serve the chicken hot, warm, or at room temperature.

Tarragon Chicken Marsala

Prep time: 15 minutes | Cook time: 3 to 4 hours | Serves 6

¾ cup all-purpose flour or rice flour, for dredging
6 boneless, skin-on chicken breast halves (about 2 pounds / 907 g)
3 tablespoons unsalted butter or ghee
2 medium-size shallots, minced
8 ounces (227 g) sliced white or cremini mushrooms
1 (14½-ounce / 411-g) can low-sodium chicken broth
Sea salt and freshly ground black pepper, to taste
Marsala Gravy:
2 (1.2-ounce / 34-g) packages chicken gravy mix, such as Knorr
⅓ cup dry Marsala wine
2 teaspoons finely chopped fresh tarragon

1. Put the flour in a shallow dish or pie plate. One piece at a time, dredge the chicken in the flour, coating both sides and shaking off any excess flour.
2. Heat the butter in a large skillet over medium-high heat. When the butter is foaming, add the chicken, skin side down. Cook the chicken until it is a deep golden brown on both sides, about 5 minutes per side.
3. Transfer the chicken pieces to the slow cooker. Add the shallots and mushrooms to the skillet and cook over high heat, stirring, until they are slightly brown. Transfer to the crock. Add the broth to the skillet and bring to a boil, stirring, to dissolve any brown particles that are stuck to the pan. Pour the broth over the chicken in the crock. Season with salt and pepper. Cover and cook on high for 3 to 4 hours, until the chicken pulls apart easily.
4. Ladle 2 cups of the liquid out of the crockpot and into a saucepan. Discard any remaining liquid. Add the two gravy packets, Marsala, and tarragon to the saucepan and whisk well. Cook over medium-high heat, whisking constantly, and bring to a boil. Reduce the heat to a simmer and cook for 2 minutes, until thickened and smooth. While the gravy simmers, remove the chicken breasts and mushrooms from the crock, discard the skin, and shred or chop the meat into large pieces. Serve the gravy over the warm chicken and mushrooms.

Pot-Roast Turkey Drumsticks

Prep time: 20 minutes | Cook time: 5 to 5½ hours | Serves 3

3 medium potatoes, peeled and quartered
2 cups fresh baby carrots
2 celery ribs, cut into 2½-inch pieces
1 medium onion, peeled and quartered
3 garlic cloves, peeled and quartered
½ cup chicken broth
3 turkey drumsticks (12 ounces / 340 g each), skin removed
2 teaspoons seasoned salt
1 teaspoon dried thyme
1 teaspoon dried parsley flakes
¼ teaspoon pepper

1. In a greased slow cooker, combine the first six ingredients. Place drumsticks over vegetables. Sprinkle with the seasoned salt, thyme, parsley and pepper. Cover and cook on low for 5 to 5½ hours or until turkey is tender.

Glazed Orange-Hoisin Chicken

Prep time: 15 minutes | Cook time: 5 to 6 hours | Serves 4 to 6

2 tablespoons frozen orange juice concentrate, thawed
¼ cup honey
2 tablespoons soy sauce
2 tablespoons hoisin sauce
3 slices peeled fresh ginger, about ¼ inch thick
3 cloves garlic, minced or pressed
1 tablespoon toasted sesame oil
6 individually frozen boneless, skinless chicken breast halves (do not thaw)
2 teaspoons cornstarch
2 teaspoons cold water
1 tablespoon sesame seeds (optional), toasted in a dry skillet over medium heat until fragrant

1. In a zipper-top plastic bag, combine the orange juice concentrate, honey, soy sauce, hoisin sauce, ginger, garlic, and sesame oil. One at a time, put the chicken pieces in the bag, seal, and gently shake to coat with the sauce. Transfer the coated chicken to the slow cooker, then pour the remaining sauce over the chicken. Cover and cook on low until the chicken is tender and cooked through, 5 to 6 hours.
2. Transfer the chicken to a warm platter. Strain the sauce through a fine-mesh strainer into a small saucepan. In a cup or small bowl, stir together the cornstarch and cold water. Bring the sauce to a boil over high heat, add the slurry, and cook, stirring a few times, until thickened, 1 or 2 minutes. Pour some of the sauce over the chicken and pass the rest on the side. If desired, sprinkle the sesame seeds over the top.

Filipino Chicken Adobo

Prep time: 15 minutes | Cook time: 3 to 3½ hours | Serves 6

¾ cup plain rice vinegar
½ cup low-sodium soy sauce
4 cloves garlic, pressed
1 (2- to 3-inch) piece fresh ginger, peeled and grated (optional)
1 tablespoon light brown sugar
1 teaspoon black peppercorns
2 bay leaves
2½ pounds (1.1 kg) bone-in, skin-on chicken thighs (about 8), trimmed of fat
1 pound (454 g) red or Yukon gold potatoes, scrubbed and cut into eights
2 medium-size carrots, sliced, or 2 cups baby carrots
4 ounces (113 g) green beans, ends trimmed
2 tablespoons olive oil
¾ cup water

1. In a shallow glass baking dish, stir together the vinegar, soy sauce, garlic, ginger (if using), brown sugar, peppercorns, and bay leaves. Add the chicken and turn to coat. Cover and marinate in the refrigerator for at least 1 hour or as long as overnight.
2. Place the potatoes, carrots, and green beans in the slow cooker. Lift the chicken out of the marinade and pat dry with paper towels. Heat the oil in a large skillet over medium-high heat and cook the chicken, skin side down, until it is a golden brown on both sides, about 2 minutes per side. Transfer the chicken thighs to the crock. Pour the marinade and water into the skillet and bring to a boil. Pour the sauce into the crock.
3. Cover and cook on high for 3 to 3½ hours, or until the juice of the chicken runs clear. Discard the bay leaves. Serve the chicken and vegetables with the sauce.

Whole Roasted Mexican Chicken

Prep time: 5 minutes | Cook time: 6 to 7 hours | Serves 4 to 6

1 (3- to 4-pound / 1.4- to 1.8-kg) broiler/fryer
¾ to 1 teaspoon salt
½ teaspoon freshly ground black pepper
Juice of 1 small or ½ large lime
½ cup fresh cilantro sprigs
2 cloves garlic, peeled

1. Remove the chicken giblets and neck and reserve for another use. Cut off any lumps of fat. Season the chicken inside and out with salt and pepper. Place in the cooker, breast side up. Squeeze the juice of the lime over the chicken and put the rind, cilantro sprigs, and garlic into the cavity. Cover and cook on low until an instant-read thermometer inserted into the thickest part of the thigh registers 180°F (82°C), 6 to 7 hours.
2. Transfer the chicken to a platter. Pour the liquid from the cooker into a separate container and refrigerate; then skim off the fat after it congeals. Or pour the cooking juices into a gravy separator and then into a container and refrigerate if not using. When the chicken is cool enough to handle, remove the skin, and cut or shred the meat from the carcass. Refrigerate the meat if not using it immediately.

Turkey with Apple-Berry Compote

Prep time: 20 minutes | Cook time: 3 to 4 hours | Serves 12

1 teaspoon salt
½ teaspoon garlic powder
½ teaspoon dried thyme
½ teaspoon pepper
2 boneless turkey breast halves (2 pounds / 907 g each)
⅓ cup water
Compote:
2 medium apples, peeled and finely chopped
2 cups fresh raspberries
2 cups fresh blueberries
1 cup white grape juice
¼ teaspoon crushed red pepper flakes
¼ teaspoon ground ginger

1. Mix salt, garlic powder, thyme and pepper; rub over turkey breasts. Place in a slow cooker. Pour water around turkey. Cook, covered, on low 3 to 4 hours. A thermometer inserted in turkey should read at least 165°F (74°C).
2. Remove turkey from slow cooker; tent with foil. Let stand 10 minutes before slicing.
3. Meanwhile, in a large saucepan, combine compote ingredients. Bring to a boil. Reduce heat to medium; cook, uncovered, 15 to 20 minutes or until slightly thickened and apples are tender, stirring occasionally. Serve turkey with compote.

Braised Turkey Thighs in Tomato Sauce

Prep time: 20 minutes | Cook time: 3 hours | Serves 8

6 strips thick-cut bacon, cut into ½-inch pieces
1 medium onion, finely chopped
1 teaspoon dried basil
1 pound (454 g) cremini mushrooms, quartered
1½ teaspoons salt
½ teaspoon freshly ground black pepper
1 (28- to 32-ounce / 794- to 907-g) can crushed tomatoes
½ cup finely chopped fresh Italian parsley
4 turkey thighs (about 3½ pounds / 1.6 kg), skin removed

1. Cook the bacon in a sauté pan over medium heat until it renders some fat and is beginning to turn crisp. Add the onion and basil and sauté until the onion is softened, about 3 minutes.
2. Add the mushrooms, salt, and pepper and sauté until the mushrooms begin to color, 7 to 10 minutes. Transfer the mixture to the insert of a slow cooker. Add the tomatoes and parsley and stir to combine. Add the thighs in the sauce.
3. Cover and cook on high for 3 hours, until the thighs are cooked through and register 175°F (79°C) on an instant-read thermometer. Skim off any fat from the top of the sauce. Remove the thighs from the sauce and discard the bones.
4. Cut the meat into serving-sized pieces and return to the sauce.
5. Serve from the cooker set on warm.

Turkey and Mushroom Egg Rolls

Prep time: 20 minutes | Cook time: 4 to 5 hours | Makes 3½ dozen

1½ pounds (680 g) ground turkey
½ pound (227 g) sliced fresh mushrooms
2 medium leeks (white portion only), thinly sliced
3 celery ribs, thinly sliced
½ cup hoisin sauce
2 tablespoons minced fresh ginger
2 tablespoons rice vinegar
2 tablespoons reduced-sodium soy sauce
1 tablespoon packed brown sugar
1 tablespoon sesame oil
2 garlic cloves, minced
½ cup sliced water chestnuts, chopped
3 green onions, thinly sliced
42 egg roll wrappers
Oil for frying
Sweet-and-sour sauce or Chinese-style mustard (optional)

1. In a large skillet, cook turkey over medium heat 8 to 10 minutes or until no longer pink, breaking into crumbles. Transfer to a slow cooker.
2. Stir in mushrooms, leeks, celery, hoisin sauce, ginger, vinegar, soy sauce, brown sugar, sesame oil and garlic. Cook, covered, on low 4 to 5 hours or until vegetables are tender. Stir water chestnuts and green onions into turkey mixture; cool slightly.
3. With one corner of an egg roll wrapper facing you, place 2 tablespoons filling just below center of wrapper. (Cover remaining wrappers with a damp paper towel until ready to use.) Fold bottom corner over filling; moisten remaining wrapper edges with water. Fold side corners toward center over filling. Roll egg roll up tightly, pressing at tip to seal. Repeat.
4. In an electric skillet, heat ¼ inch of oil to 375°F (190°C). Fry egg rolls, a few at a time, 3 to 4 minutes or until golden brown, turning occasionally. Drain on paper towels. If desired, serve with sweet-and-sour sauce.

Mojo Turkey

Prep time: 25 minutes | Cook time: 5 hours | Serves 8

1 medium green pepper, finely chopped
1 medium onion, finely chopped
2 garlic cloves, minced
2 teaspoons ground coriander
1 teaspoon ground cumin
⅛ teaspoon cayenne pepper
1 pound (454 g) uncooked chicken sausage links, casings removed
1 fresh boneless turkey breast (4 pounds / 1.8 kg)
¼ teaspoon salt
¼ teaspoon pepper

Mojo Sauce:
1 cup orange juice
½ cup fresh cilantro leaves
¼ cup minced fresh oregano or 4 teaspoons dried oregano
¼ cup lime juice
4 garlic cloves, minced
1 teaspoon ground cumin
½ teaspoon pepper
¼ teaspoon salt
⅛ teaspoon cayenne pepper
1 cup olive oil

1. In a bowl, combine the first six ingredients. Crumble sausage over mixture and mix well.
2. With skin side down, pound turkey breast with a meat mallet to ½-inch thickness. Sprinkle with salt and pepper. Spread sausage mixture over turkey to within 1 in. of edges. Roll up jelly-roll style, starting with a short side; tie at 1½-inch to 2-inch intervals with kitchen string. Place in a slow cooker.
3. In a blender, combine the first nine sauce ingredients; cover and process until blended. While processing, gradually add oil in a steady stream. Pour over turkey.
4. Cover and cook on low for 5 hours or until a thermometer inserted in center reads 165°F (74°C). Remove from slow cooker; cover and let stand for 10 minutes before slicing. Discard string.
5. Meanwhile, skim fat from cooking juices; transfer juices to a small saucepan. Bring to a boil; cook until liquid is reduced by half. Serve with turkey.

Herb-Butter Turkey

Prep time: 10 minutes | Cook time: 5 to 6 hours | Serves 12

1 bone-in turkey breast (6 to 7 pounds / 2.7 to 3.2 kg)
2 tablespoons butter, softened
½ teaspoon dried rosemary, crushed
½ teaspoon dried thyme
¼ teaspoon garlic powder
¼ teaspoon pepper
1 (14½-ounce / 411-g) can chicken broth
3 tablespoons cornstarch
2 tablespoons cold water

1. Rub turkey with butter. Combine the rosemary, thyme, garlic powder and pepper; sprinkle over turkey. Place in a slow cooker. Pour broth over top. Cover and cook on low for 5 to 6 hours or until tender.
2. Remove turkey to a serving platter; keep warm. Skim fat from cooking juices; transfer to a small saucepan. Bring to a boil.
3. Combine cornstarch and water until smooth. Gradually stir into the pan. Bring to a boil; cook and stir for 2 minutes or until thickened. Serve with the turkey.

BBQ Turkey Breast

Prep time: 15 minutes | Cook time: 3 to 4 hours | Serves 6

3 large onions, coarsely chopped
2 red bell peppers, deseeded and coarsely chopped
1 (4-pound / 1.8-kg) bone-in turkey breast, skin removed
1 cup ketchup
1 cup tomato sauce
½ cup Dijon mustard
¼ cup firmly packed light brown sugar
2 tablespoons Worcestershire sauce
½ teaspoon Tabasco sauce

1. Put the onions and bell peppers in the bottom of an insert of a slow cooker. Put the turkey breast on top of the vegetables. Stir the ketchup, tomato sauce, mustard, sugar, Worcestershire, and Tabasco in a small mixing bowl to combine.
2. Brush some of the barbecue sauce on the turkey breast, then pour the rest in the slow-cooker insert. Cover and cook on high for 3 to 4 hours, until the turkey is cooked and registers 175ºF (79ºC) on an instant-read thermometer.
3. Carefully remove the turkey from the slow cooker, cover with aluminum foil, and allow to rest for 20 minutes before carving.
4. Strain the sauce through a fine-mesh sieve into a bowl, discarding the solids. Return the sauce to the slow cooker.
5. carve the turkey and serve with the sauce or return the turkey to the slow cooker with the sauce and serve from the cooker set on warm.

Turkey Taco Salad

Prep time: 15 minutes | Cook time: 4 to 6 hours | Serves 6

Meat Sauce:
1½ pounds (680 g) ground dark turkey meat
1 (16-ounce / 454-g) jar tomato salsa
Salad:
1 medium firm-ripe avocado
6 cups thick shredded or chopped iceberg or romaine lettuce
3 cups corn chips
1 (15-ounce / 425-g) can pinto beans, rinsed, drained, and heated in a saucepan or microwave
1½ cups shredded Cheddar cheese
1 (16-ounce / 454-g) jar tomato salsa
2 medium-size ripe tomatoes, coarsely chopped
1 cup cold sour cream, stirred
1 (4-ounce / 113-g) can sliced ripe California black olives, drained

1. Coat the slow cooker with nonstick cooking spray. To make the meat sauce, put the ground turkey and salsa in the cooker. Cover and cook on low until cooked thoroughly, 4 to 6 hours. Stir the sauce.
2. To make the salad, slice the avocado and put all the salad components in separate containers. On each individual plate layer some lettuce, a handful of corn chips, some of the hot meat, a spoonful or two of hot pinto beans, shredded cheese, some salsa, diced tomatoes, sour cream, avocado, and olives.

Italian Turkey Sausage and Veggies

Prep time: 20 minutes | Cook time: 5½ to 6½ hours | Serves 6

1¼ pounds (567 g) sweet or hot Italian turkey sausage links
1 (28-ounce / 794-g) can diced tomatoes, undrained
2 medium potatoes, cut into 1-inch pieces
4 small zucchini, cut into 1-inch slices
1 medium onion, cut into wedges
½ teaspoon garlic powder
¼ teaspoon crushed red pepper flakes
¼ teaspoon dried oregano
¼ teaspoon dried basil
1 tablespoon dry bread crumbs
¾ cup shredded Pepper Jack cheese

1.In a nonstick skillet, brown sausages over medium heat. Place in a slow cooker. Add vegetables and seasonings. Cover and cook on low for 5½ to 6½ hours or until a thermometer reads 165°F (74°C).
2.Remove sausages and cut into 1-inch pieces; return to slow cooker. Stir in bread crumbs. Serve in bowls; sprinkle with cheese.

Garlicky Lemon-Thyme Turkey Legs

Prep time: 10 minutes | Cook time: 6 to 8 hours | Serves 6

8 cloves garlic, peeled
Grated zest of 4 lemons
2 teaspoons fresh thyme leaves
Salt and freshly ground black pepper, to taste
¼ cup extra-virgin olive oil
6 turkey legs, skin removed
½ cup dry white wine
1 cup chicken broth

1.Put the garlic, zest, thyme, 1½ teaspoons salt, ½ teaspoon pepper, and oil in a food processor or blender and blend to a paste. Rub the paste on the turkey and put the turkey in the slow cooker.
2.Pour the wine and chicken broth in the insert of a slow cooker.
3.Cover and cook on low for 6 to 8 hours, until the turkey is cooked through and registers 175°F (79°C) on an instant-read thermometer.
4.Remove the legs from the sauce and cover with aluminum foil. Strain the sauce through a fine-mesh sieve into a saucepan and bring to a boil.
5.Season with salt and pepper before serving.

Duck Breasts with Port and Orange Sauce

Prep time: 10 minutes | Cook time: 6 to 7 hours | Serves 4

2 tablespoons unsalted butter
4 boneless duck breast halves, with skin (about 1½ pounds / 680 g total)
⅓ cup port wine
Grated zest of 1 orange
1 teaspoon salt
⅛ teaspoon freshly ground black pepper
2 tablespoons cornstarch
¼ cup milk

1.Melt the butter in a large skillet (not a nonstick one) over medium-high heat. When it foams, add the duck, skin side down, and cook until deep golden brown on both sides, 2 to 3 minutes per side. Add the port and bring to a boil. Being careful of long sleeves and dangling hair, touch a long lit match to the liquid in the pan and turn off the heat. The liquid will catch fire and burn for about 30 seconds, then the flames will die out. With a slotted spoon, transfer the duck to the slow cooker. Return the liquid in the pan to a boil and cook briefly, scraping up any browned bits stuck to the pan. Pour over the duck, then sprinkle with the orange zest, salt, and pepper. Cover and cook on low for 6 to 7 hours.
2.Preheat the oven to 375°F (190°C). With a slotted spoon, transfer the duck to a shallow baking dish. Tent with aluminum foil and keep warm in the oven while you finish the sauce.
3.Skim and discard as much fat as possible from the liquid in the cooker, then pour into a small saucepan. In a small bowl, stir the cornstarch into the milk to make a smooth slurry. Bring the sauce to a boil, add the slurry, and cook, stirring, until it thickens, 3 to 4 minutes. Taste for salt and pepper. Serve the duck with the sauce.

Stuffed Turkey Cutlets with Artichokes

Prep time: 20 minutes | Cook time: 2 to 3 hours | Serves 6

4 tablespoons (½ stick) unsalted butter
2 cloves garlic, minced
1 (16-ounce / 454-g) package frozen artichoke hearts, thawed and coarsely chopped
½ cup pine nuts
1 cup fresh bread crumbs
⅔ cup freshly grated Parmigiano-Reggiano cheese
4 leaves fresh basil, finely chopped
8 turkey breast cutlets (¾ to 1 pound / 340 to 454 g)
1½ teaspoons salt
½ teaspoon freshly ground black pepper
½ cup finely chopped onion
1 teaspoon dried sage
2 tablespoons all-purpose flour
1 cup dry white wine or vermouth
1 cup chicken broth

1. Melt 2 tablespoons of the butter in a large skillet over medium-high heat. Add the garlic and artichoke hearts and sauté until the liquid in the pan evaporates, 5 to 7 minutes.
2. Transfer to a mixing bowl. Add the pine nuts, bread crumbs, cheese, and basil to the bowl and stir to combine. Place the cutlets on a cutting board, sprinkle evenly with the salt and pepper, and spread 2 tablespoons of the filling on each turkey breast.
3. Roll the cutlets lengthwise and place seam-side down in the insert of a slow cooker. Melt the remaining 2 tablespoons butter in the same skillet. Add the onion and sage and sauté until the onion is softened, about 3 minutes.
4. Add the flour and cook for 3 minutes, stirring constantly. Deglaze the pan with the wine and chicken broth, scraping up any browned bits, and bring to a boil, whisking constantly. Pour the sauce over the turkey rolls.
5. Cover and cook on high for 2 to 3 hours, until the turkey is tender.
6. Serve from the cooker set on warm.

Apricot Glazed Turkey with Herbs

Prep time: 20 minutes | Cook time: 3 to 3½ hours | Serves 4

4 turkey legs or thighs, skinned (see headnote)
1 teaspoon paprika
1 teaspoon salt
¼ teaspoon freshly ground black pepper
½ teaspoon dried rosemary, crushed, or 1½ tablespoons chopped fresh rosemary
½ teaspoon dried thyme, or 1½ tablespoons chopped fresh thyme
¼ cup apricot jam
2 tablespoons honey
1 tablespoon fresh lemon juice
1 tablespoon barbecue sauce
1 tablespoon soy sauce
1 teaspoon cornstarch
1 teaspoon cold water

1. In a small bowl, combine the paprika, salt, pepper, rosemary, and thyme. Rub all over the turkey legs. Set aside for 15 minutes or refrigerate, covered, for 2 to 3 hours.
2. Coat the slow cooker with nonstick cooking spray. Put the turkey in the cooker. In a small bowl, combine the jam, honey, lemon juice, barbecue sauce, and soy sauce. Pour over the turkey; stir if necessary to coat the turkey. Cover and cook on high until the turkey is tender, 3 to 3½ hours.
3. Preheat the oven to 375ºF (190ºC). Transfer the turkey to a baking dish, tent with aluminum foil, and keep warm in the oven while you finish the sauce.
4. Pour the sauce from the cooker into a small saucepan. Combine the cornstarch and cold water in a small bowl, stirring to remove any lumps. Bring the sauce to a boil and continue boiling for 2 to 3 minutes to reduce the sauce and concentrate the flavors. Add the slurry and cook for 2 or 3 minutes more, until thickened.
5. Remove the turkey from the oven, pour the glaze over the turkey, and serve.

Turkey Teriyaki Thighs

Prep time: 10 minutes | Cook time: 3 to 4 hours | Serves 6

½ cup soy sauce
2 tablespoons hoisin sauce
2 cloves garlic, minced
1 teaspoon freshly grated ginger
2 tablespoons rice wine (mirin) or dry sherry
¼ firmly packed light brown sugar
4 turkey thighs, skin removed

1. Blend the soy sauce, hoisin, garlic, ginger, rice wine, and brown sugar in a mixing bowl and stir to combine.
2. Pour the marinade in a zipper-top plastic bag. Add the turkey thighs to the bag. Seal the bag and refrigerate for at least 8 hours or overnight. Pour the contents of the bag in the insert of a slow cooker.
3. Cover and cook on high for 3 to 4 hours, until the turkey is cooked through and registers 175ºF (79ºC) on an instant-read thermometer.
4. Remove the turkey from the slow cooker, cover with aluminum foil, and allow to rest for 20 minutes before serving.

Tea Smoked Turkey Legs

Prep time: 10 minutes | Cook time: 5 hours | Serves 6

2 cups chicken broth
8 bags Lapsang Souchong or black tea
4 slices fresh ginger
1 cinnamon stick
½ cup soy sauce
¼ cup hoisin sauce
6 turkey legs, skin removed

1. Bring the broth to a boil in a saucepan and add the tea bags, ginger, and cinnamon. Allow the broth to cool, about 45 minutes. Strain the broth through a fine-mesh sieve into a bowl and whisk in the soy sauce and hoisin.
2. Brush some of the sauce on the turkey legs with a silicone pastry brush. Pour the remaining sauce in the insert of a slow cooker. Fit the rack in the slow cooker and place the turkey legs on the rack.
3. Cover and cook on high for 5 hours, basting the turkey a few times during cooking.
4. Slice the turkey legs into serving-size pieces and serve.

Mexican Turkey

Prep time: 15 minutes | Cook time: 3 to 3½ hours | Serves 6 to 8

2 pounds (907 g) turkey thighs, skinned
1 (8-ounce / 227-g) can tomato sauce
1 (4-ounce / 113-g) can chopped roasted green chiles, with their juice
2 medium-size or 3 small white onions, chopped
2 tablespoons Worcestershire sauce
2 tablespoons chili powder
Pinch of ground cumin
1 clove garlic, crushed
For Serving:
8 large flour tortillas, at room temperature
¾ cup shredded Cheddar cheese
⅔ cup sour cream
Diced fresh tomatoes
Shredded iceberg lettuce

1. Put the turkey thighs in the slow cooker. Add the tomato sauce, chiles, onions, Worcestershire, chili powder, cumin, and garlic and stir to coat the thighs with the mixture. Cover and cook on high until the turkey is tender, 3 to 3½ hours.
2. Remove the turkey from the cooker and, once it cools a bit, pick the meat off the bones. Shred the meat, return it to the cooker, and stir to combine well with the sauce. Spoon the meat and sauce onto a tortilla and roll up. Top with cheese, sour cream, tomatoes, and lettuce. Repeat with the remaining tortillas and toppings and serve immediately.

Chapter 10 Red Meat

Basil Beef Steak with Mushrooms

Prep time: 15 minutes | Cook time: 6 to 8 hours | Serves 4

1¼ pounds (567 g) boneless beef shoulder top blade or flat iron steaks
½ pound (227 g) whole fresh mushrooms, quartered
1 medium sweet yellow pepper, julienned
1 (14½-ounce / 411-g) can stewed tomatoes, undrained
1 (8-ounce / 227-g) can tomato sauce
1 envelope onion soup mix
2 tablespoons minced fresh basil
Hot cooked rice, for serving

1. Place steaks in a slow cooker. Add mushrooms and pepper. In a bowl, mix tomatoes, tomato sauce, soup mix and basil; pour over top.
2. Cook, covered, on low 6-8 hours or until beef and vegetables are tender. Serve with rice.

Braised Shepherd's Pie

Prep time: 25 minutes | Cook time: 5¼ to 6¼ hours | Serves 5

2 pounds (907 g) medium Yukon Gold potatoes, peeled and quartered
2 tablespoons butter
¼ to ⅓ cup 2% milk
¾ teaspoon salt, divided
½ teaspoon pepper, divided
1 pound (454 g) ground beef
1 large onion, chopped
2 garlic cloves, minced
3 tablespoons tomato paste
1¾ cups sliced fresh mushrooms
2 medium carrots, chopped
1 cup beef broth
¼ cup dry white wine
2 teaspoons Worcestershire sauce
½ teaspoon dried thyme
⅓ cup frozen peas
½ cup shredded Monterey Jack cheese

1 tablespoon minced fresh parsley

1. Place potatoes in a large saucepan and cover with water. Bring to a boil. Reduce heat; cover and cook for 10 to 15 minutes or until tender. Drain, then shake potatoes over low heat for 1 minute to dry. Mash the potatoes, gradually adding butter and enough milk to reach desired consistency. Stir in ½ teaspoon salt and ¼ teaspoon pepper.
2. Meanwhile, in a large skillet, cook the beef, onion and garlic over medium heat until meat is no longer pink; drain.
3. Add the tomato paste; cook for 2 minutes. Add the mushrooms, carrots, broth, wine, Worcestershire sauce and thyme. Bring to a boil. Reduce heat; simmer, uncovered, until most of the liquid is evaporated. Stir in peas. Season with remaining salt and pepper.
4. Transfer beef mixture to a greased slow cooker. Spread mashed potatoes over top. Cover and cook on low for 5 to 6 hours or until bubbly. Sprinkle with cheese. Cover and cook 10 minutes longer or until cheese is melted. Just before serving, sprinkle with parsley.

BBQ Beef Sandwiches

Prep time: 5 minutes | Cook time: 8 to 10 hours | Serves 8

1 boneless beef chuck roast (3 pounds / 1.4 kg)
1 envelope chili seasoning
½ cup barbecue sauce
8 onion rolls, split
8 slices Cheddar cheese

1. Cut roast in half; place in a slow cooker. Sprinkle with chili seasoning. Pour barbecue sauce over top. Cover and cook on low for 8 to 10 hours or until meat is tender.
2. Remove roast; cool slightly. Shred meat with two forks. Skim fat from cooking juices. Return meat to slow cooker; heat through. Using a slotted spoon, place ½ cup meat mixture on each roll bottom; top with cheese. Replace tops.

Garlicky Beef with Sesame

Prep time: 15 minutes | Cook time: 5 to 7 hours | Serves 6

6 green onions, sliced
½ cup sugar
½ cup water
½ cup reduced-sodium soy sauce
¼ cup sesame oil
3 tablespoons toasted sesame seeds
2 tablespoons all-purpose flour
4 garlic cloves, minced
1 beef sirloin tip roast (3 pounds / 1.4 kg), thinly sliced
Additional sliced green onions and toasted sesame seeds
Hot cooked rice, for serving

1. In a large resealable plastic bag, mix the first eight ingredients. Add beef; seal bag and turn to coat. Refrigerate 8 hours or overnight.
2. Pour beef and marinade into a slow cooker. Cook, covered, on low 5 to 7 hours or until meat is tender.
3. Using a slotted spoon, remove beef to a serving platter; sprinkle with additional green onions and sesame seeds. Serve with rice.

Beef and Baby Carrot Stew

Prep time: 20 minutes | Cook time: 6½ to 8½ hours | Serves 8

1½ pounds (680 g) boneless beef chuck roast, cut into 1-inch cubes
3 medium potatoes, peeled and cubed
3 cups hot water
1½ cups fresh baby carrots
1 (10¾-ounce / 305-g) can condensed tomato soup, undiluted
1 medium onion, chopped
1 celery rib, chopped
2 tablespoons Worcestershire sauce
1 tablespoon browning sauce (optional)
2 teaspoons beef bouillon granules
1 garlic clove, minced
1 teaspoon sugar
¾ teaspoon salt
¼ teaspoon pepper
¼ cup cornstarch
¾ cup cold water

2 cups frozen peas, thawed

1. Place the beef, potatoes, hot water, carrots, soup, onion, celery, Worcestershire sauce, browning sauce if desired, bouillon granules, garlic, sugar, salt and pepper in a slow cooker. Cover and cook on low for 6 to 8 hours or until meat is tender.
2. Combine cornstarch and cold water in a small bowl until smooth; gradually stir into stew. Stir in peas. Cover and cook on high 30 minutes or until thickened.

Coffee-Braised Beef Short Ribs

Prep time: 25 minutes | Cook time: 6 to 8 hours | Serves 8

4 pounds (1.8 kg) bone-in beef short ribs
1½ teaspoons salt, divided
1 teaspoon ground coriander
½ teaspoon pepper
2 tablespoons olive oil
1½ pounds (680 g) small red potatoes, cut in half
1 medium onion, chopped
1 cup reduced-sodium beef broth
1 whole garlic bulb, cloves separated, peeled and slightly crushed
4 cups strong brewed coffee
2 teaspoons red wine vinegar
3 tablespoons butter

1. Sprinkle ribs with 1 teaspoon salt, coriander and pepper. In a large skillet, brown ribs in oil in batches. Using tongs, transfer ribs to a slow cooker. Add potatoes and onion.
2. Add broth to the skillet, stirring to loosen browned bits. Bring to a boil; cook until liquid is reduced by half. Stir in garlic and remaining salt; add to slow cooker. Pour coffee over top. Cover and cook on low for 6 to 8 hours or until meat is tender.
3. Remove ribs and potatoes to a serving platter; keep warm. Strain cooking juices into a small saucepan; skim fat. Bring to a boil; cook until liquid is reduced by half. Stir in vinegar. Remove from the heat; whisk in butter. Serve with ribs and potatoes.

Cheesy Beef-Stuffed Peppers

Prep time: 15 minutes | Cook time: 5 to 6 hours | Serves 4

4 medium green or sweet red peppers
1 pound (454 g) ground beef
1 (8.8-ounce / 249-g) package ready-to-serve Spanish rice
2 cups shredded Colby-Monterey Jack cheese, divided
1½ cups salsa
1 tablespoon hot pepper sauce
1 cup water
2 tablespoons minced fresh cilantro

1. Cut tops off peppers and remove seeds; set aside. In a large skillet, cook beef over medium heat until no longer pink; drain.
2. Stir in the rice, 1½ cups cheese, salsa and pepper sauce. Spoon into peppers. Transfer to a slow cooker. Pour water around peppers.
3. Cover and cook on low for 5 to 6 hours or until peppers are tender and filling is heated through. Top with remaining cheese; sprinkle with cilantro.

Simple Beef-Stuffed Cabbage Rolls

Prep time: 20 minutes | Cook time: 6 to 8 hours | Serves 6

12 cabbage leaves
1 cup cooked brown rice
¼ cup finely chopped onion
1 egg, lightly beaten
¼ cup fat-free milk
½ teaspoon salt
¼ teaspoon pepper
1 pound (454 g) 90% lean ground beef
Sauce:
1 (8-ounce / 227-g) can tomato sauce
1 tablespoon brown sugar
1 tablespoon lemon juice
1 teaspoon Worcestershire sauce

1. In batches, cook cabbage in boiling water 3 to 5 minutes or until it is crisp-tender. Drain; cool slightly. Trim the thick vein from the bottom of each cabbage leaf, making a V-shaped cut.
2. In a large bowl, combine rice, onion, egg, milk, salt and pepper. Add beef; mix lightly but thoroughly. Place about ¼ cup beef mixture on each cabbage leaf. Pull together cut edges of leaf to overlap; fold over filling. Fold in sides and roll up.
3. Place six rolls in a slow cooker, seam side down. In a bowl, mix sauce ingredients; pour half of the sauce over cabbage rolls. Top with remaining rolls and sauce. Cook, covered, on low 6 to 8 hours or until a thermometer inserted in beef reads 160°F (71°C) and cabbage is tender.

Beef Roast with Root Vegetables

Prep time: 30 minutes | Cook time: 8 to 10 hours | Serves 6

2 tablespoons olive oil
1 boneless beef chuck or venison roast (3 to 3½ pounds / 1.4 to 1.6 kg), trimmed
2 large onions, sliced
3 celery ribs, cut into 1-inch pieces
3 medium carrots, cut into 1-inch pieces
1 medium sweet potato, peeled and cut into 1-inch cubes
½ pound (227 g) fresh whole mushrooms, quartered
1 (12-ounce / 340-g) bottle dark beer or 1½ cups beef broth
4 tablespoons minced fresh parsley, divided
3 tablespoons Worcestershire sauce
3 tablespoons seedless blackberry spreadable fruit
1 teaspoon salt
1 teaspoon pepper
2 tablespoons cornstarch
½ cup cold water

1. In a large skillet, heat oil over medium heat. Brown roast on all sides. Place vegetables in a slow cooker. Place roast over vegetables. In a bowl, combine beer, 2 tablespoons parsley, Worcestershire sauce, spreadable fruit, salt and pepper; pour over meat. Cook, covered, on low 8 to 10 hours or until meat and vegetables are tender.
2. Using a slotted spoon, remove roast and vegetables to a serving platter; keep warm. Pour cooking juices into a small saucepan; skim fat and bring to a boil. Mix cornstarch and cold water until smooth; stir into cooking juices. Return to a boil; cook and stir 1 to 2 minutes or until thickened. Serve with roast and vegetables; sprinkle with remaining parsley.

Cabbage and Beef Stew

Prep time: 20 minutes | Cook time: 6 to 8 hours | Serves 6

½ pound (227 g) 90% lean ground beef
3 cups shredded cabbage or angel hair coleslaw mix
1 (16-ounce / 454-g) can red beans, rinsed and drained
1 (14½-ounce / 411-g) can diced tomatoes, undrained
1 (8-ounce / 227-g) can tomato sauce
¾ cup salsa or picante sauce
1 medium green pepper, chopped
1 small onion, chopped
3 garlic cloves, minced
1 teaspoon ground cumin
½ teaspoon pepper

1. In a large skillet, cook beef over medium heat 4 to 6 minutes or until no longer pink, breaking into crumbles; drain.
2. Transfer meat to a slow cooker. Stir in remaining ingredients. Cook, covered, on low 6 to 8 hours or until cabbage is tender.

Beef Vindaloo with Snap Peas

Prep time: 20 minutes | Cook time: 8¼ to 10¼ hours | Serves 4

1 tablespoon cumin seeds
2 teaspoons coriander seeds
1 tablespoon butter
1 medium onion, finely chopped
8 garlic cloves, minced
1 tablespoon minced fresh ginger
2 teaspoons mustard seed
½ teaspoon ground cloves
¼ teaspoon kosher salt
¼ teaspoon ground cinnamon
¼ teaspoon cayenne pepper
½ cup red wine vinegar
4 bay leaves
2 pounds (907 g) bone-in beef short ribs
1 cup halved fresh sugar snap peas
Hot cooked rice and plain yogurt, for serving

1. In a dry small skillet over medium heat, toast cumin and coriander seeds until aromatic, stirring frequently. Cool. Coarsely crush seeds in a spice grinder or with a mortar and pestle.
2. In a large saucepan, heat butter over medium heat. Add onion, garlic and ginger; cook and stir for 1 minute. Add the mustard seed, cloves, salt, cinnamon, cayenne pepper and crushed seeds; cook and stir 1 minute longer. Cool completely.
3. In a large resealable plastic bag, combine the vinegar, bay leaves and onion mixture. Add ribs; seal bag and turn to coat. Refrigerate overnight.
4. Transfer rib mixture to a slow cooker. Cover and cook on low for 8 to 10 hours or until meat is tender. Stir in peas; cook 8 to 10 minutes longer or until peas are crisp-tender. Skim fat; discard bay leaves. Serve rib mixture with rice and yogurt.

Mexican Beef Enchilada

Prep time: 10 minutes | Cook time: 6 to 7 hours | Serves 10

1½ pounds (680 g) 90% lean ground beef
1 small onion, chopped
1 garlic clove, minced
1 envelope taco seasoning
½ teaspoon salt
½ teaspoon pepper
9 corn tortillas (6 inches)
½ cup chicken broth
½ cup tomato sauce
1 (10-ounce / 283-g) can enchilada sauce
1½ cups shredded Cheddar cheese
2 (15-ounce / 425-g) cans pinto beans, rinsed and drained
1 (11-ounce / 312-g) can Mexicorn, drained
1 (4-ounce / 113-g) can chopped green chilies, drained
1 (2¼-ounce / 64-g) can chopped ripe olives, drained
Sour cream and avocado slices, for serving

1. In a large skillet, cook the beef, onion and garlic over medium heat until meat is no longer pink; drain. Stir in the taco seasoning, salt and pepper.
2. In a greased slow cooker, layer three tortillas, beef mixture, broth, tomato sauce and enchilada sauce; sprinkle with ½ cup cheese. Add three tortillas, beans, Mexicorn, green chilies, half of the olives and ½ cup cheese. Top with remaining tortillas, cheese and olives.
3. Cover and cook on low for 6 to 7 hours. Serve with sour cream and avocado if desired.

Vinegary Steak with Green Chilies

Prep time: 20 minutes | Cook time: 6 to 8 hours | Serves 4

1 tablespoon canola oil
1 beef flank steak (1½ pounds / 680 g)
1 large onion, sliced
⅓ cup water
1 (4-ounce / 113-g) can chopped green chilies
2 tablespoons cider vinegar
2 to 3 teaspoons chili powder
1 teaspoon garlic powder
1 teaspoon sugar
½ teaspoon salt
⅛ teaspoon pepper

1. In a large skillet, heat oil over medium-high heat; brown steak on both sides. Transfer to a slow cooker.
2. Add onion to same skillet; cook and stir 1 to 2 minutes or until crisp-tender. Add water to pan; cook 30 seconds, stirring to loosen browned bits from pan. Stir in remaining ingredients; return to a boil. Pour over steak.
3. Cook, covered, on low 6 to 8 hours or until meat is tender. Slice steak across the grain; serve with onion mixture.

Thyme Short Ribs in Red Wine

Prep time: 25 minutes | Cook time: 6¼ to 8¼ hours | Serves 6

3 pounds (1.4 kg) bone-in beef short ribs
½ teaspoon salt
½ teaspoon pepper
1 tablespoon canola oil
4 medium carrots, cut into 1-inch pieces
1 cup beef broth
4 fresh thyme sprigs
1 bay leaf
2 large onions, cut into ½-inch wedges
6 garlic cloves, minced
1 tablespoon tomato paste
2 cups dry red wine or beef broth
4 teaspoons cornstarch
3 tablespoons cold water
Salt and pepper, to taste

1. Sprinkle ribs with ½ teaspoon each salt and pepper. In a large skillet, heat oil over medium heat. In batches, brown ribs on all sides; transfer to a slow cooker. Add carrots, broth, thyme and bay leaf to ribs.
2. Add onions to the same skillet; cook and stir over medium heat 8 to 9 minutes or until tender. Add garlic and tomato paste; cook and stir 1 minute longer. Stir in the wine. Bring to a boil; cook 8 to 10 minutes or until liquid is reduced by half. Add to the slow cooker. Cook, covered, on low 6 to 8 hours or until meat is tender.
3. Remove ribs and vegetables; keep warm. Transfer cooking juices to a small saucepan; skim fat. Discard thyme and bay leaf. Bring juices to a boil. In a small bowl, mix cornstarch and water until smooth; stir into cooking juices. Return to a boil; cook and stir 1 to 2 minutes or until thickened. Season with salt and pepper to taste. Serve with ribs and vegetables.

Pork and Apple Stew in Cider

Prep time: 25 minutes | Cook time: 7 to 9 hours | Serves 6

1 large yellow onion, coarsely chopped
1 large tart cooking apple, such as Granny Smith or pippin, peeled, cored, and roughly cut into 1-inch cubes
1 (8-ounce / 227-g) can water chestnuts (optional), drained and cut in half
1½ pounds (680 g) boneless pork shoulder, cut into ½-inch cubes
½ teaspoon salt
7 grinds of black pepper
1½ tablespoons rubbed sage
2 cups dry hard cider
Long-grain rice or egg noodles, for serving

1. Coat the slow cooker with nonstick cooking spray. Layer the onion, apple, water chestnuts, and pork in the cooker; sprinkle with the salt, pepper, and sage. Pour the cider over all. Turn to high for 20 minutes, if you have time, to heat through.
2. Cover and cook on low for 7 to 9 hours.
3. Serve in shallow soup bowls with long-grain white rice or egg noodles.

Braised Beef Brisket in Beer

Prep time: 20 minutes | Cook time: 6 to 9 hours | Serves 8 to 10

1 (4- to 5-pound / 1.8- to 2.3-kg) brisket or boneless chuck roast, trimmed off as much fat as possible and blotted dry
3 medium-size yellow onions, cut in half and thinly sliced into half-moons
2 ribs celery, chopped
1 cup prepared chili sauce
1 (12-ounce / 340-g) bottle beer (not dark)
½ cup water
1 package dried onion soup mix
1 teaspoon salt
¼ teaspoon freshly ground black pepper

1. Put the roast in the slow cooker. If the meat is too big to lie flat in your cooker, cut it in half and stack the pieces one atop the other. Add the sliced onions and the celery.
2. In a medium-size bowl, combine the chili sauce, beer, water, onion soup mix, salt, and pepper; pour it over the meat and vegetables. Cover and cook on low for 6 to 9 hours.
3. Skim off as much fat as possible from the sauce, slice the meat, and serve with the sauce.

Round Steak with Sweet Potatoes

Prep time: 20 minutes | Cook time: 7 to 9 hours | Serves 6

2 pounds (907 g) sweet potatoes, peeled and cut into 1-inch pieces
1 large onion, chopped
1 medium green pepper, sliced
2 beef top round steaks (¾ inch thick and 1 pound / 454 g each)
1 teaspoon salt, divided
2 tablespoons olive oil
1 garlic clove, minced
3 tablespoons all-purpose flour
1 (28-ounce / 794-g) can diced tomatoes, undrained
½ cup beef broth
1 teaspoon sugar
½ teaspoon dried thyme
½ teaspoon pepper
¼ teaspoon hot pepper sauce

1. Place the sweet potatoes, onion and green

pepper in a slow cooker. Cut each steak into three serving-size pieces; sprinkle with ½ teaspoon salt. In a large skillet over medium heat, brown steaks in oil in batches on both sides. Place steaks over vegetables, reserving drippings in a pan.
2. Add garlic to drippings; cook and stir for 1 minute. Stir in flour until blended. Stir in the remaining ingredients and remaining salt. Bring to a boil, stirring constantly. Cook and stir for 4 to 5 minutes or until thickened. Pour over meat. Cover and cook on low for 7 to 9 hours or until beef is tender.

Beef Burgundy with Portobello

Prep time: 25 minutes | Cook time: 7½ to 9½ hours | Serves 6

¼ cup all-purpose flour
½ teaspoon salt
½ teaspoon seasoned salt
1½ teaspoons minced fresh thyme or ½ teaspoon dried thyme
¾ teaspoon minced fresh marjoram or ¼ teaspoon dried thyme
½ teaspoon pepper
2 pounds (907 g) beef sirloin tip steak, cubed
2 bacon strips, diced
3 tablespoons canola oil
1 garlic clove, minced
1 cup Burgundy wine or beef broth
1 teaspoon beef bouillon granules
1 pound (454 g) sliced baby portobello mushrooms
Hot cooked noodles, for serving (optional)

1. In a large resealable plastic bag, combine the first six ingredients. Add beef, a few pieces at a time, and shake to coat.
2. In a large skillet, cook bacon over medium heat until crisp. Remove to paper towels with a slotted spoon; drain. In same skillet, brown beef in oil in batches, adding garlic to the last batch; cook 1-2 minutes longer. Drain.
3. Transfer to a slow cooker. Add wine to skillet, stirring to loosen browned bits from pan. Add bouillon; bring to a boil. Stir into a slow cooker. Stir in bacon. Cover and cook on low for 7 to 9 hours or until meat is tender.
4. Stir in mushrooms. Cover and cook on high 30 to 45 minutes longer or until mushrooms are tender and sauce is slightly thickened. Serve with noodles if desired.

Pork Ribs with Sauerkraut

Prep time: 20 minutes | Cook time: 8 to 9 hours | Serves 4

2 to 3 pounds (907 g to 1.4 kg) country-style pork ribs
Salt and freshly ground black pepper, to taste
2 medium-size white onions, sliced ¼ inch thick
2 medium-size tart cooking apples, peeled, cored, and sliced ¼ inch thick
2 pounds (907 g) fresh sauerkraut, rinsed and drained
½ teaspoon caraway seeds
½ cup apple juice or dry white wine
¼ cup beef or vegetable broth

1.Grease the bottom of the slow cooker with some butter or oil. Season the ribs with salt and pepper. Layer in the onions, apples, ribs, and sauerkraut. Sprinkle with the caraway seeds and pour the juice and broth over everything. Cover and cook on low until tender and the meat starts to separate from the bone, 8 to 9 hours. Serve immediately.

Mediterranean Beef Roast

Prep time: 30 minutes | Cook time: 8 to 10 hours | Serves 8

2 pounds (907 g) potatoes (about 6 medium), peeled and cut into 2-inch pieces
5 medium carrots (about ¾ pound / 340 g), cut into 1-inch pieces
2 tablespoons all-purpose flour
1 boneless beef chuck roast (3 to 4 pounds / 1.4 to 1.8 kg)
1 tablespoon olive oil
8 large fresh mushrooms, quartered
2 celery ribs, chopped
1 medium onion, thinly sliced
¼ cup sliced Greek olives
½ cup minced fresh parsley, divided
1 (14½-ounce / 411-g) can fire-roasted diced tomatoes, undrained
1 tablespoon minced fresh oregano or 1 teaspoon dried oregano
1 tablespoon lemon juice
2 teaspoons minced fresh rosemary or ½ teaspoon dried rosemary, crushed
2 garlic cloves, minced

¾ teaspoon salt
¼ teaspoon pepper
¼ teaspoon crushed red pepper flakes (optional)

1.Place potatoes and carrots in a slow cooker. Sprinkle flour over all surfaces of roast. In a large skillet, heat oil over medium-high heat. Brown roast on all sides. Place over vegetables.
2.Add mushrooms, celery, onion, olives and ¼ cup parsley to slow cooker. In a small bowl, mix remaining ingredients; pour over top.
3.Cook, covered, on low 8 to 10 hours or until the meat and vegetables are tender. Remove beef. Stir remaining parsley into vegetables. Serve beef with vegetables.

Pork Spareribs with Sauerkraut

Prep time: 30 minutes | Cook time: 6 to 7 hours | Serves 4

1 pound (454 g) fingerling potatoes
1 medium onion, chopped
1 medium Granny Smith apple, peeled and chopped
3 slices thick-sliced bacon strips, cooked and crumbled
1 (16-ounce / 454-g) jar sauerkraut, undrained
2 pounds (907 g) pork spareribs
½ teaspoon salt
¼ teaspoon pepper
1 tablespoon vegetable oil
3 tablespoons brown sugar
¼ teaspoon caraway seeds
½ pound (227 g) smoked Polish sausage, cut into 1-inch slices
1 cup beer

1.In a slow cooker, place the potatoes, onion, apple and bacon. Drain sauerkraut, reserving ⅓ cup of the liquid; add sauerkraut and reserved liquid to slow cooker.
2.Cut spareribs into serving-size portions; sprinkle with salt and pepper. In a large skillet, heat oil over medium-high heat; brown ribs in batches. Transfer to slow cooker; sprinkle with brown sugar and caraway seeds.
3.Add sausage; pour in beer. Cover and cook on low for 6 to 7 hours or until ribs are tender.

Braised Mahogany Glazed Pork

Prep time: 15 minutes | Cook time: 8 to 10 hours | Serves 6 to 8

⅓ cup soy sauce
½ cup orange marmalade
1 to 2 cloves garlic, to your taste, pressed
1 to 1½ teaspoons red pepper flakes, to your taste
3 tablespoons ketchup
1 (3½-pound / 1.6-kg) boneless Boston pork butt, cut into large pieces, or 3½ pounds (1.6 kg) country-style pork spareribs
8 ounces (227 g) sugar snap peas
½ cup julienned red bell pepper

1.Coat the slow cooker with nonstick cooking spray.
2.Combine the soy sauce, marmalade, garlic, red pepper flakes, and ketchup in a small bowl and mix until smooth; brush over both sides of the meat. Arrange the pork butt or ribs in the cooker. (If you have a round cooker, stack the ribs.) Pour over any extra sauce. Cover and cook on low until fork-tender and the meat starts to separate from the bone, 8 to 10 hours.
3.Stir in the sugar snap peas and bell pepper; cover and let stand a few minutes to warm. Serve immediately.

Balsamic Beef with Cranberry Gravy

Prep time: 20 minutes | Cook time: 7 to 9 hours | Serves 6

1 boneless beef chuck roast (3 to 4 pounds / 1.4 to 1.8 kg)
2 teaspoons salt
1 teaspoon pepper
2 tablespoons canola oil
2 medium carrots, finely chopped
1 medium onion, chopped
2 garlic cloves, minced
1 cup cranberry juice
¾ cup water
½ cup fresh or frozen cranberries
½ cup balsamic vinegar
2 fresh thyme sprigs
1 bay leaf
3 tablespoons cornstarch
3 tablespoons cold water

1.Sprinkle beef with salt and pepper. In a large skillet, heat oil over medium heat. Brown roast on all sides. Transfer to a slow cooker.
2.Add carrots and onion to drippings; cook and stir over medium heat 4 to 5 minutes or until tender. Add garlic; cook 1 minute longer. Spoon vegetables around roast; add cranberry juice, ¾ cup water, cranberries, vinegar, thyme and bay leaf. Cook, covered, on low 7 to 9 hours or until meat is tender.
3.Using a slotted spoon, remove roast and vegetables to a serving platter; keep warm. Pour cooking juices into a small saucepan; skim fat. Discard thyme and bay leaf. Bring cooking juices to a boil. Mix cornstarch and water until smooth; gradually stir into pan. Return to a boil, stirring constantly; cook and stir 1 to 2 minutes or until thickened. Serve with roast.

Maple Pork Chops in Bourbon

Prep time: 10 minutes | Cook time: 3 to 4 hours | Serves 6

2 tablespoons olive oil
1½ teaspoons salt
½ teaspoon freshly ground black pepper
6 (1-inch-thick) pork loin chops
2 tablespoons unsalted butter
2 medium onions, finely chopped
½ cup ketchup
½ cup bourbon
¼ cup pure maple syrup
1 teaspoon Tabasco sauce
1 teaspoon dry mustard
½ cup beef broth

1.Heat the oil in a large skillet over high heat. Sprinkle the salt and pepper evenly over the pork chops and add to the skillet.
2.Brown the chops on both sides, adding a few at a time, being careful not to crowd the pan, and transfer to the insert of a slow cooker.
3.Melt the butter in the skillet over medium-high heat. Add the onions and sauté until they begin to soften, about 5 minutes. Add the remaining ingredients and scrape up any browned bits from the bottom of the pan. Transfer the contents of the skillet to the slow-cooker insert.
4.Cover and cook on high for 3 to 4 hours or on low for 6 to 8 hours. Skim off any fat from the top of the sauce.
5.Serve from the cooker set on warm.

Sweet and Sour Tomato Brisket

Prep time: 25 minutes | Cook time: 5 to 7 hours | Serves 6 to 8

3 ounces (85 g) tomato paste (half of a 6-ounce / 170-g can)
¼ cup firmly packed light brown sugar
2 tablespoons cider vinegar
½ teaspoon Worcestershire sauce
⅛ teaspoon dry mustard
2 to 3 large cloves garlic, pressed
1 (3- to 4-pound / 1.4- to 1.8-kg) brisket, trimmed off as much fat as possible and blotted dry
Salt and freshly ground black pepper, to taste
Paprika, to taste
1 tablespoon oil of your choice
2 large or 3 small yellow onions, cut in half and thinly sliced into half-moons

1. In a small bowl, stir together the tomato paste, brown sugar, vinegar, Worcestershire, mustard, and garlic.
2. If the meat is too big to lie flat in your slow cooker, cut it in half. Season the meat generously with salt, pepper, and paprika.
3. In a large, heavy skillet, preferably one without a nonstick coating, heat the oil over high heat. When hot, brown the brisket very well, about 3 minutes per side. Transfer to a plate. Add the onions to the pan and cook, stirring a few times, until browned or even a bit blackened on the edges, 5 to 7 minutes.
4. Put half the onions in the cooker. (If you have cut your brisket into 2 pieces, place one-third of the onions in the cooker.) Smear the tomato paste mixture thickly on both sides of the brisket and place in the cooker, with the fattier side facing up. Top with the remaining onions. (If you have cut your brisket into 2 pieces, place one-third of the onions between the two pieces of brisket, and the remaining onions on top of the second piece.) Pour any meat juices from the plate over the brisket. Cover and cook on low until the brisket is tender when pierced with a fork, 5 to 7 hours.
5. Transfer to a cutting board and cut on the diagonal, against the grain, into thin slices. Pour the sauce into a bowl and allow to settle so that you can skim the fat. Serve the meat with the sauce and sliced onions.

Beef Ragoût with Veggies

Prep time: 25 minutes | Cook time: 7 to 8 hours | Serves 4 to 5

2 tablespoons olive oil
2 pounds (907 g) lean beef stew meat or beef cross rib roast, trimmed of fat, cut into 1½-inch chunks, and blotted dry
2 medium-size onions, coarsely chopped
2 large tomatoes, peeled, deseeded, and chopped, or 1 (14½-ounce / 411-g) can diced tomatoes, with their juice
1 cup dry red wine
1 cup baby carrots
2 cloves garlic, minced
2 tablespoons quick-cooking tapioca
1 teaspoon dried Italian herb seasoning
½ teaspoon salt
¼ teaspoon freshly ground black pepper
2 medium-size zucchini, ends trimmed, cut in half lengthwise and sliced crosswise into ¼-inch-thick half-moons
8 ounces (227 g) fresh mushrooms, thickly sliced

1. In a large skillet over medium-high heat, heat 1 tablespoon of the oil until very hot. Add half of the beef and brown on all sides, 3 to 4 minutes total. Transfer to the slow cooker. Add the remaining 1 tablespoon of oil and brown the remaining beef.
2. Add the onions to the skillet and brown slightly over medium-high heat. Add the tomatoes and wine and bring to a boil, scraping up any browned bits stuck to the pan; pour into the cooker. Add the carrots, garlic, tapioca, and Italian herbs to the cooker. Cover and cook on low for 6 to 7 hours.
3. Add the salt, pepper, zucchini, and mushrooms, cover, turn the cooker to high, and cook for about 45 minutes, until the meat, mushrooms, and zucchini are tender. Serve in shallow bowls or on rimmed dinner plates.

Lamb Cassoulet with White Beans

Prep time: 25 minutes | Cook time: 6½ to 8½ hours | Serves 6

1 pound (454 g) dried white beans, soaked overnight and drained
½ cup extra-virgin olive oil
6 meaty lamb shanks, fat trimmed
1½ teaspoons salt
½ teaspoon freshly ground black pepper
3 medium onions, coarsely chopped
4 cloves garlic, minced
4 medium carrots, coarsely chopped
4 stalks celery, coarsely chopped
1 tablespoon fresh rosemary leaves, finely chopped
1 (28- to 32-ounce / 794- to 907-g) can crushed tomatoes, with their juice
5 cups chicken broth
3 cups beef broth
1 bay leaf
Topping:
1½ cups fresh bread crumbs
½ cup freshly grated Parmigiano-Reggiano cheese
4 cloves garlic, minced
½ cup finely chopped fresh Italian parsley

1. Place the beans in the insert of a slow cooker. Heat the oil in a large skillet over medium-high heat. Sprinkle the meat evenly with the salt and pepper. Add as many lamb shanks as will fit in a single layer and brown on all sides. Transfer the browned shanks to the slow-cooker insert. Brown any remaining shanks and transfer them to the slow cooker insert.
2. Add the onions, garlic, carrots, celery, and rosemary to the same skillet and sauté until the vegetables are softened, 5 to 7 minutes. Add the tomatoes and 1 cup of the chicken broth to the skillet and heat, scraping up any browned bits from the bottom of the pan. Transfer the tomato mixture to the slow cooker insert and stir in the remaining broths, and the bay leaf. Cover and cook on high for 6 to 8 hours or low for 10 to 12 hours, until the beans and lamb are tender.
3. Combine all the ingredients for the topping in a small bowl while the lamb is cooking. Cover and refrigerate.
4. Uncover the cooker and spoon off any fat on the surface. Taste and adjust with the seasoning. Sprinkle the topping over the cassoulet, cover, and cook on high another 30 minutes.
5. Serve the cassoulet from the cooker set on warm.

Tangy Flank Steak Fajitas

Prep time: 25 minutes | Cook time: 6 to 8 hours | Serves 6

¾ cup prepared chunky salsa, such as a fire-roasted one
1 tablespoon tomato paste
1 tablespoon olive oil
1 clove garlic, minced
3 tablespoons fresh lime juice
1 teaspoon freshly ground black pepper
½ teaspoon salt
1 (1½-pound / 680-g) flank steak, trimmed of excess fat and silver skin
1 large white onion, cut in half and thinly sliced into half-moons
3 red bell peppers, deseeded and cut into ¼-inch-wide strips
For Serving:
Warm flour tortillas (the small ones, not the grandes for burritos)
1 cup guacamole
1 cup chopped plum tomatoes
½ bunch fresh cilantro, chopped

1. In a small bowl, combine salsa, tomato paste, olive oil, garlic, lime juice, pepper, and salt. Lay the flank steak in the slow cooker and pour the mixture over it, making sure to coat all exposed surfaces well. Lay the onion and bell peppers on top. Cover and cook on low for 6 to 8 hours, until the meat is tender.
2. Remove the steak and vegetables from the juice and transfer to a serving platter. Cover with aluminum foil and let stand 10 minutes. Cut the meat across the grain into ½-inch-thick slices. Serve it heaped over warm tortillas, with the peppers and onions on top. Garnish with a dab of guacamole, some chopped tomatoes, and the cilantro on top.

Teriyaki Pork with Peanut Sauce

Prep time: 20 minutes | Cook time: 8 to 9 hours | Serves 4

1 (2-pound / 907-g) boneless pork loin, trimmed of fat and cut into 4 pieces
2 large red bell peppers, deseeded and cut into strips
⅓ cup prepared teriyaki sauce
2 tablespoons rice vinegar
1 teaspoon red pepper flakes
2 cloves garlic, minced
¼ cup creamy peanut butter
For Serving:
½ cup chopped green onions (white part and some of the green)
¼ cup chopped dry-roasted peanuts
2 limes, cut to make 8 to 12 wedges

1.Coat the slow cooker with nonstick cooking spray. Put the pork, bell peppers, teriyaki sauce, rice vinegar, red pepper flakes, and garlic in the cooker. Cover and cook on low until the pork is fork-tender, 8 to 9 hours.
2.Remove the pork from the cooker and coarsely chop. Add the peanut butter to the liquid in the cooker; stir well to dissolve the peanut butter and blend with the liquid to make the sauce. Return the pork to the sauce and toss to coat the meat evenly.
3.Serve in shallow bowls over hot jasmine rice, and sprinkle each serving with some of the green onions and peanuts. Pass the lime wedges.

Honey Mustard Pork Roast

Prep time: 20 minutes | Cook time: 6 to 7 hours | Serves 8

1 boneless pork shoulder butt roast (3 to 4 pounds / 1.4 to 1.8 kg)
¾ teaspoon salt
¼ teaspoon pepper
1 tablespoon canola oil
1 (14½-ounce / 411-g) can diced tomatoes, drained
1 medium onion, chopped
1 (14½-ounce / 411-g) can beef broth
½ cup dry red wine
¾ cup stone-ground mustard
6 garlic cloves, minced
2 tablespoons honey
2 tablespoons molasses
1 teaspoon dried thyme
2 tablespoons cornstarch
2 tablespoons cold water

1.Sprinkle roast with salt and pepper; brown in oil in a large skillet on all sides. Transfer to a slow cooker. Add tomatoes and onion; pour broth and wine around meat. Combine the mustard, garlic, honey, molasses and thyme; pour over pork. Cover and cook on low for 6 to 7 hours or until meat is tender.
2.Remove roast; cover and let stand for 15 minutes before slicing. Meanwhile, skim fat from cooking juices; transfer juices to a small saucepan. Bring to a boil. Combine cornstarch and water until smooth; gradually stir into the pan. Bring to a boil; cook and stir for 2 minutes or until thickened. Slice pork and serve with sauce.

Slow Cooker Pork Verde

Prep time: 15 minutes | Cook time: 4½ to 5 hours | Serves 8

3 medium carrots, sliced
1 boneless pork shoulder butt roast (3 to 4 pounds / 1.4 to 1.8 kg)
1 (15-ounce / 425-g) can black beans, rinsed and drained
1 (10-ounce / 283-g) can green enchilada sauce
¼ cup minced fresh cilantro
1 tablespoon cornstarch
¼ cup cold water
Hot cooked rice, for serving

1.Place carrots in a slow cooker. Cut roast in half; place in slow cooker. Add the beans, enchilada sauce and cilantro. Cover and cook on low for 4½ to 5 hours or until a meat thermometer reads 160°F (71°C). Remove roast to a serving platter; keep warm.
2.Skim fat from cooking juices. Transfer the cooking liquid, carrots and beans to a small saucepan. Bring to a boil. Combine cornstarch and water until smooth. Gradually stir into the pan. Bring to a boil; cook and stir for 2 minutes or until thickened. Serve with meat and rice.

Pork Chili Verde

Prep time: 10 minutes | Cook time: 5 to 6 hours | Serves 12

1 boneless pork shoulder roast (4 to 5 pounds / 1.8 to 2.3 kg), cut into 1-inch pieces
3 (10-ounce / 283-g) cans green enchilada sauce
1 cup salsa verde
1 (4-ounce / 113-g) can chopped green chilies
½ teaspoon salt
Hot cooked rice, for serving
Sour cream (optional)

1. In a slow cooker, combine pork, enchilada sauce, salsa verde, green chilies and salt. Cook, covered, on low 5 to 6 hours or until pork is tender. Serve with rice. If desired, top with sour cream.

Pork Chops and Bell Peppers

Prep time: 25 minutes | Cook time: 3½ to 4 hours | Serves 6

4 tablespoons olive oil
2 medium onions, cut into half rounds
2 medium red bell peppers, deseeded and cut into ½-inch slices
2 medium yellow bell peppers, deseeded and cut into ½-inch slices
1 teaspoon ground cumin
1 teaspoon sugar
1 teaspoon salt
½ teaspoon freshly ground black pepper
1 (28- to 32-ounce / 794- to 907-g) can crushed tomatoes, with their juice
1 teaspoon ancho chile powder
6 (1-inch-thick) pork loin chops

1. Heat 2 tablespoons of the oil in a large skillet over medium-high heat. Add the onions, bell peppers, cumin, sugar, salt, and pepper and sauté until the onions begin to turn translucent, about 10 minutes. Add the tomatoes and stir to combine. Transfer the mixture to the insert of a slow cooker. Cover the cooker and set on low.
2. Heat the remaining 2 tablespoons oil in the skillet over medium-high heat. Sprinkle the chile powder evenly over the chops and add to the skillet. Brown the chops on all sides. Transfer the chops to the slow-cooker insert and spoon some of the sauce over the chops.
3. Cover the slow cooker and cook on high for 3½ to 4 hours or on low for 6 to 8 hours, until the pork is tender.
4. Serve the pork chops with the sauce.

Braised Pork Loin in Cider

Prep time: 20 minutes | Cook time: 4 hours | Serves 6 to 8

2 tablespoons olive oil
½ cup Dijon mustard
½ cup firmly packed light brown sugar
1 (2½- to 3-pound / 1.1- to 1.4-kg) pork loin roast, rolled and tied
1 large onion, finely sliced
2 teaspoons dried thyme
½ cup apple cider
1 cup beef stock
4 large Gala or Braeburn apples, peeled, cored, and cut into 8 wedges each
¾ cup heavy cream
Salt and freshly ground black pepper, to taste
1 pound (454 g) buttered cooked wide egg noodles, for serving

1. Heat the oil in a large sauté pan over medium-high heat. Make a paste of the mustard and sugar and spread over the roast on all sides. Add the roast to the pan and brown on all sides. Add the onion and thyme to the sauté pan and cook until the onion is softened, 3 to 5 minutes.
2. Transfer the roast, onion, and any bits from the bottom of the pan to the insert of a slow cooker. Add the cider and beef stock. Cover the slow cooker and cook on high for 3 hours. Remove the cover and add the apples and cream. Cover and cook on high for an additional 1 hour.
3. Remove the pork from the slow-cooker insert, cover with aluminum foil, and allow to rest for 15 minutes. Season the sauce with salt and pepper. Remove the strings from the roast, cut into thin slices, and serve the pork on the buttered noodles, napping both with some of the sauce.

Balsamic Pork Chops with Figs

Prep time: 10 minutes | Cook time: 3½ to 4 hours | Serves 6

¼ cup olive oil
1 teaspoon salt
½ teaspoon freshly ground black pepper
6 (1-inch-thick) pork loin chops
12 dried figs, cut in half
2 medium onions, cut into half rounds
2 teaspoons finely chopped fresh sage leaves
½ cup balsamic vinegar
¼ cup chicken broth
2 tablespoons unsalted butter

1.Heat the oil in a large skillet over high heat. Sprinkle the salt and pepper evenly over the pork chops and add the pork to the skillet.
2.Brown the pork on all sides. Transfer to the insert of a slow cooker. Add the figs to the slow-cooker insert. Add the onions and sage to the same skillet and sauté until the onions are softened, about 5 minutes. Deglaze the skillet with the vinegar and scrape up any browned bits from the bottom of the pan. Transfer the contents of the skillet to the slow-cooker insert and pour in the broth.
3.Cover and cook on high for 3½ to 4 hours or on low for 6 to 8 hours. Carefully remove the pork from the pot and cover with aluminum foil. Using an immersion blender, purée the sauce and whisk in the butter.
4.Return the pork to the slow cooker and set on warm to serve.

Tangy Pork Chop with Sweet Potato

Prep time: 15 minutes | Cook time: 3 hours | Serves 6 to 8

2 teaspoons dried thyme
2 teaspoons salt
1 teaspoon freshly ground black pepper
8 center-cut 1-inch-thick boneless pork loin chops
2 tablespoons vegetable oil
½ cup (1 stick) unsalted butter
1 large sweet onion, such as Vidalia, thinly sliced into half rounds
4 medium sweet potatoes, peeled and cut into ½-inch slices
1 cup orange juice

1.Combine the thyme, salt, and pepper in a small bowl. Sprinkle half the mixture over both sides of the pork chops. Heat the oil in a large skillet over medium-high heat.
2.Add the pork chops and brown on both sides. Transfer the pork to the insert of a slow cooker. Melt the butter in the same skillet over medium-high heat. Add the remaining thyme mixture and sauté for 1 minute.
3.Add the onion and sauté until the onion is beginning to soften, about 3 minutes. Transfer the onion to the slow-cooker insert, leaving some of the butter in the skillet. Cover the onion with the sweet potato slices and pour the orange juice over all.
4.Drizzle the potatoes with the butter remaining in the skillet. Cover the slow cooker and cook on high for 3 hours or on low for 6 hours, until the sweet potatoes and pork chops are tender.
5.Serve the pork chops with the sweet potatoes and some of the sauce.

Pork Chops with Plum Sauce

Prep time: 10 minutes | Cook time: 3½ to 4 hours | Serves 6

¼ cup olive oil
1 teaspoon salt
½ teaspoon freshly ground black pepper
6 (1-inch-thick) pork loin chops
2 medium onions, finely chopped
1 cup plum preserves
2 tablespoons Dijon mustard
2 tablespoons fresh lemon juice
Grated zest of 1 lemon
½ cup ketchup

1.Heat the oil in a large skillet over high heat. Sprinkle the salt and pepper evenly over the pork chops and add to the skillet. Brown the pork on all sides.
2.Transfer to the insert of a slow cooker. lower heat to medium-high. Add the onions to the skillet and sauté until the onions are softened, about 3 to 5 minutes. Add the preserves to the skillet and scrape up any browned bits from the bottom of the pan. Transfer the contents of the skillet to the slow-cooker insert.
3.Add the mustard, lemon juice and zest, and ketchup and stir to combine. Cover and cook on high for 3½ to 4 hours or on low for 6 to 8 hours. Skim off any fat from the surface of the sauce.
4.Serve the pork chops from the slow cooker set on warm.

Pork Ribs with Peach Sauce

Prep time: 20 minutes | Cook time: 5½ to 6½ hours | Serves 4

2 pounds (907 g) boneless country-style pork ribs
2 tablespoons taco seasoning
½ cup mild salsa
¼ cup peach preserves
¼ cup barbecue sauce
2 cups chopped fresh peeled peaches or frozen unsweetened sliced peaches, thawed and chopped

1. In a large bowl, toss pork ribs with taco seasoning. Cover and refrigerate overnight.
2. Place pork in a slow cooker. In a small bowl, combine the salsa, preserves and barbecue sauce. Pour over ribs. Cover and cook on low for 5 to 6 hours or until meat is tender.
3. Add peaches; cover and cook 30 minutes longer or until peaches are tender.

Pork Loin with Cran-Orange Sauce

Prep time: 20 minutes | Cook time: 4 hours | Serves 6 to 8

2 tablespoons olive oil
1 (3- to 4-pound / 1.4- to 1.8-kg) pork loin roast, tied
Salt and freshly ground black pepper, to taste
1 large sweet onion, such as Vidalia, coarsely chopped
2 (16-ounce / 454-g) cans whole-berry cranberry sauce
Grated zest of 2 oranges
Juice of 2 oranges (about 1 cup)
2 teaspoons dried thyme leaves
½ cup beef broth

1. Spray the insert of a slow cooker with nonstick cooking spray or line it with a slow-cooker liner according to the manufacturer's directions.
2. Heat the oil in a large sauté pan over high heat. Sprinkle the roast with 1½ teaspoons salt and 1 teaspoon pepper and add to the pan.
3. Sauté the pork on all sides until browned. Transfer the roast to the slow-cooker insert. Add the remaining ingredients and stir to combine.

Cover the slow cooker and cook the roast on high for 4 hours or on low for 8 hours.
4. Remove the cover, transfer the roast to a cutting board, and cover loosely with aluminum foil. Let the meat rest for 15 minutes. Skim off any fat from the top of the sauce. Stir the sauce and season with salt and pepper.
5. Slice the roast and nap with some of the sauce. Serve the remaining sauce in a gravy boat on the side.

Sweet and Spiced Pork Loin

Prep time: 25 minutes | Cook time: 4 to 5 hours | Serves 6 to 8

2 medium sweet potatoes, peeled and cut into 1-inch chunks or wedges
2 medium Yukon gold potatoes, peeled and cut into 1-inch chunks or wedges
2 medium red onions, cut into quarters
½ cup olive oil
1 teaspoon ground cumin
1½ teaspoons fennel seeds
½ teaspoon ground cinnamon
½ teaspoon ground ginger
¼ cup firmly packed light brown sugar
2 teaspoons salt
1 teaspoon freshly ground black pepper
1 (4-pound / 1.8-kg) pork loin roast, rolled and tied
½ cup chicken broth

1. Arrange the vegetables in the insert of a slow cooker. Drizzle ¼ cup of the oil over the vegetables and toss to coat. Combine the cumin, fennel seeds, cinnamon, ginger, sugar, salt, and pepper in a small bowl. Sprinkle 1 tablespoon of the rub over the vegetables and toss again.
2. Pat the rest of the rub over the meat, place the meat on the vegetables, and drizzle with the remaining ¼ cup olive oil. Pour in the chicken broth. Cover and cook on high for 4 to 5 hours or on low for 8 to 10 hours, until the pork and vegetables are tender. The roast should register 175ºF (79ºC) on an instant-read thermometer.
3. Transfer the pork to a cutting board, cover with aluminum foil, and let rest for 20 minutes. Cut the meat into ½-inch-thick slices and arrange on the center of a platter. Spoon the vegetables around the meat and serve.

Pork Tenderloin with Mango Sauce

Prep time: 20 minutes | Cook time: 3 hours | Serves 6

4 tablespoons (½ stick) unsalted butter, melted
2 large mangoes, peeled, pitted, and coarsely chopped
2 navel oranges, peeled and sectioned
2 tablespoons soy sauce
½ cup dark rum
½ cup beef broth
2 (1-pound / 454-g) pork tenderloins
2 tablespoons Jamaican jerk seasoning
6 green onions, finely chopped, using the white and tender green parts for garnish

1. Stir the butter, mangoes, oranges, soy sauce, rum, and broth together in the insert of a slow cooker. Remove the silver skin from the outside of the pork with a boning knife and discard.
2. Rub the jerk seasoning on the pork and arrange it in the slow cooker. Cover and cook on high for 3 hours, until the pork is tender and cooked through. (The pork should register 175°F (79°C) on an instant-read thermometer.)
3. Remove the pork from the sauce, cover with aluminum foil, and allow to rest for 20 minutes. Skim off any fat from the top of the sauce.
4. Slice the meat and garnish with the green onions. Serve the sauce on the side.

Teriyaki Pork Tenderloin

Prep time: 5 minutes | Cook time: 3 hours | Serves 6

2 tablespoons vegetable oil
2 cloves garlic, minced
1 teaspoon grated fresh ginger
1 cup soy sauce
¼ cup rice vinegar
3 tablespoons light brown sugar
2 (1-pound / 454-g) pork tenderloins

1. Whisk the oil, garlic, ginger, soy sauce, vinegar, and sugar together in a bowl until blended. Remove the silver skin from the outside of the pork with a boning knife and discard.
2. Place the tenderloins in a 1-gallon zipper-top plastic bag or 13-by-9-inch baking dish. Pour the marinade over the tenderloins and seal the bag or cover the dish with plastic wrap.
3. Marinate for at least 4 hours or overnight, turning the meat once or twice during that time. Place the marinade and pork in the insert of a slow cooker. Cover and cook on high for 3 hours.
4. Remove the meat from the sauce, cover loosely with aluminum foil, and allow the meat to rest for about 10 minutes. Skim off any fat from the top of the sauce.
5. Cut the meat diagonally in ½-inch-thick slices. Nap each serving of pork with some of the sauce.

Leg of Lamb with Mint Pesto

Prep time: 20 minutes | Cook time: 8 to 10 hours | Serves 8

2 large onions, cut into half rounds
1 cup dry white wine
1 cup beef broth
1 (3- to 4-pound / 1.4- to 1.8-kg) leg of lamb, boned and butterflied
Mint Pesto:
1 cup packed fresh mint leaves
4 cloves garlic
1 tablespoon rice vinegar or white vinegar
¼ cup olive oil
6 or 7 leaves fresh oregano
1 teaspoon salt
⅛ teaspoon cayenne pepper

1. Put all the pesto ingredients in a food processor or blender and process until the ingredients are a paste. Cover and refrigerate for up to 4 days.
2. Spread the onions over the bottom of the insert of a slow cooker. Pour in the wine and beef broth. Lay the lamb, fat-side down, boned-side up on a cutting board or flat surface and spread all the pesto over the surface of the lamb.
3. Roll up the meat, starting from the short end, and tie with kitchen string or silicone loops. Arrange on top of the onions in the slow-cooker insert. Cover and cook on low for 8 to 10 hours, until the lamb is tender. Remove the lamb from the slow-cooker insert, cover with aluminum foil, and allow to rest for 20 minutes.
4. Strain the sauce through a fine-mesh sieve into a saucepan and remove any fat from the surface. Boil the sauce until it is reduced by about one quarter, 10 to 15 minutes.
5. Remove the strings from the lamb, cut into ½-inch-thick slices, and serve with the sauce on the side.

Asian BBQ Baby Back Ribs

Prep time: 10 minutes | Cook time: 7½ to 8½ hours | Serves 6

½ cup soy sauce
¼ cup hoisin sauce
2 teaspoons grated fresh ginger
2 cloves garlic, minced
¼ cup firmly packed light brown sugar
1 tablespoon toasted sesame oil
½ cup chicken broth
4 green onions, finely chopped, using the white and tender green parts
4 pounds (1.8 kg) baby back ribs (about 3 slabs), cut to fit the slow cooker

1. Stir the soy sauce, hoisin, ginger, garlic, sugar, sesame oil, broth, and green onions together in the insert of a slow cooker. Add the ribs and push them down into the sauce.
2. Cover and cook on low for 7 to 8 hours, until the meat is tender. Remove cover and cook for an additional 30 to 35 minutes.
3. Serve the ribs with the remaining sauce on the side.

Asian-Flavored Braised Spareribs

Prep time: 5 minutes | Cook time: 8 to 10 hours | Serves 6

2 cups soy sauce
1 cup rice wine (mirin)
1 teaspoons freshly grated ginger
¼ cup hoisin sauce
¼ cup rice vinegar
2 tablespoons sugar
3 pounds (1.4 kg) country-style spareribs

1. Stir the soy sauce, rice wine, ginger, hoisin, rice vinegar, and sugar together in the insert of a slow cooker.
2. Add the ribs to the pot and spoon the liquid over the ribs. Cover and cook on low for 8 to 10 hours, until the ribs are tender. Skim off any fat from the sauce.
3. Serve the ribs from the cooker set on warm.

Guinness-Glazed Lamb Shanks

Prep time: 25 minutes | Cook time: 6 to 8 hours | Serves 4

4 lamb shanks (about 20 ounces / 567 g each)
4 garlic cloves, thinly sliced
1 cup lemon juice
4 tablespoons olive oil, divided
1 tablespoon each minced fresh thyme, rosemary and parsley
1 teaspoon salt
½ teaspoon pepper
Sauce:
1 cup Guinness (dark beer)
¼ cup honey
3 fresh thyme sprigs
2 bay leaves
1 tablespoon Dijon mustard
2 garlic cloves, minced
½ teaspoon salt
¼ teaspoon pepper
⅛ teaspoon crushed red pepper flakes
2 pounds (907 g) Yukon Gold potatoes, peeled and cut into chunks

1. Cut slits into each lamb shank; insert garlic slices. In a large resealable plastic bag, combine the lemon juice, 2 tablespoons oil, thyme, rosemary, parsley, salt and pepper. Add the lamb; seal bag and turn to coat. Refrigerate overnight.
2. Drain and discard marinade. In a large skillet, brown shanks in remaining oil on all sides in batches. Place shanks in a slow cooker.
3. In the same skillet, combine the beer, honey, thyme, bay leaves, Dijon, garlic, salt, pepper and pepper flakes. Bring to a boil, stirring constantly. Pour over meat. Cover and cook on low for 6-8 hours or until meat and potatoes are tender, adding the potatoes during the last 2 hours of cooking.
4. Remove lamb and potatoes from the slow cooker. Strain sauce and discard bay leaves. If desired, thicken sauce. Serve with lamb and potatoes.

Sausage and Peppers in Wine

Prep time: 15 minutes | Cook time: 6 to 8 hours | Serves 4 to 6

3 large assorted colored bell peppers, such as red, yellow, and orange, deseeded and cut into chunks
1 large yellow onion, cut into wedges
3 cloves garlic, peeled
Salt and freshly ground black pepper, to taste
1 tablespoon minced fresh thyme
2 tablespoons olive oil
2 pounds (907 g) assorted sausages, such as hot and sweet Italian and chicken basil
⅓ cup dry red wine

1.Put the peppers in the slow cooker. Add the onion and garlic and toss to combine. Sprinkle with a small amount of salt and pepper and all the thyme.
2.In a large skillet, heat the olive oil over medium-high heat and brown the sausages all over, 3 to 5 minutes, pricking them with a fork. Place them on top of the vegetables in the cooker. Add the wine to the skillet and bring to a boil, scraping up any browned bits stuck to the pan. Pour into the cooker. Cover and cook on low for 6 to 8 hours. Serve the sausage and peppers hot.

Leg of Lamb with Pinto Beans

Prep time: 20 minutes | Cook time: 8 to 10 hours | Serves 8

2 cups pinto beans, soaked overnight and drained
¼ cup olive oil
3 pounds (1.4 kg) leg of lamb, cut into 1-inch chunks
½ teaspoon chili powder
2 medium onions, coarsely chopped
2 Anaheim chiles, deseeded and coarsely chopped
1 teaspoon ground cumin
½ teaspoon dried oregano
1 (14- to 15-ounce / 397- to 425-g) can chopped tomatoes, with their juice
1½ cups beef broth

1.Put the beans in the bottom of the insert of a slow cooker. Heat the oil in a large skillet over medium-high heat.

2.Sprinkle the meat with the chili powder. Add the meat a few pieces at a time to the skillet and brown on all sides. Transfer the browned meat to the slow-cooker insert. Add the onions, chiles, cumin, and oregano to the same skillet and cook until the onions are softened, about 5 minutes.
3.Add the tomatoes to the skillet and heat, stirring up any browned bits from the bottom of the pan.
4.Transfer the contents of the skillet to the cooker and stir in the broth. Cover and cook on low for 8 to 10 hours, until the meat and beans are tender.
5.Remove any fat from the top of the stew and serve from the cooker set on warm.

Dijon Lemony Leg of Lamb

Prep time: 10 minutes | Cook time: 3 to 4 hours | Serves 8

½ cup Dijon mustard
¼ cup fresh lemon juice
Grated zest of 2 lemons
6 garlic cloves, minced
¼ cup extra-virgin olive oil
1 teaspoon dried oregano
1 teaspoon salt
½ teaspoon freshly ground black pepper
1 (3- to 4-pound / 1.4- to 1.8-kg) boneless leg of lamb, butterflied, fat trimmed
1 cup dry white wine
½ cup finely chopped fresh Italian parsley

1.Combine the mustard, lemon juice, zest, garlic, oil, oregano, salt, and pepper in a mixing bowl. Pour the marinade into a zipper-top plastic bag, add the lamb to the bag, and turn it to coat. Seal the bag and refrigerate for at least 8 hours or up to 24 hours.
2.Drain the marinade, and roll the meat into a compact cylinder, tying the meat at 1-inch intervals with kitchen string or silicone loops, and put the lamb in insert of a slow cooker. Add the wine. Cover and cook on high for 3 to 4 hours, until the meat is tender. Remove the meat from the slow cooker, cover with aluminum foil, and allow to rest for 20 minutes.
3.Strain the sauce through a fine-mesh sieve into a saucepan and remove any fat from the surface. Boil until the sauce is reduced by half. Taste and adjust the seasonings, adding the parsley to the sauce.
4.Cut the meat into ½-inch-thick slices and serve with the sauce on the side.

Smoked Sausages with BBQ Sauce

Prep time: 10 minutes | Cook time: 4 hours | Serves 6 to 8

2 cups yellow mustard
1 cup apple cider
¾ cup firmly packed light brown sugar
¼ cup molasses
1 tablespoon sweet paprika
1 teaspoon Worcestershire sauce
½ teaspoon cayenne pepper
½ teaspoon ground white pepper
3 pounds (1.4 kg) smoked sausages, such as kielbasa, cut into 3-inch lengths
6 to 8 hot dog rolls

1. Mix the mustard, cider, sugar, molasses, paprika, Worcestershire, cayenne, and white pepper in the insert of a slow cooker.
2. Add the sausages, pushing them into the sauce, cover, and cook on high for 4 hours, until the sausages are heated through and the sauce is thickened.
3. Serve the sausage in hot dog rolls with some of the sauce.

Moroccan Lamb Tagine

Prep time: 15 minutes | Cook time: 6 to 7 hours | Serves 8

½ cup all-purpose flour
1 teaspoon salt
½ teaspoon freshly ground black pepper
3 pounds (1.4 kg) lamb shoulder meat, fat trimmed, cut into 1-inch pieces
½ cup olive oil
3 large onions, coarsely chopped
2 cloves garlic, chopped
1 teaspoon ground cumin
½ teaspoon ground cinnamon
½ teaspoon ground ginger
Pinch of saffron threads
1 cup chicken broth
1 cup beef broth
1 cup pitted dates, quartered
¼ cup finely chopped fresh cilantro

1. Mix the flour, salt, and pepper in a large zipper-top plastic bag. Add the meat, toss to coat, and shake off any excess flour. Heat ¼ cup of the oil in a large skillet over high heat.
2. Add the meat a few pieces at a time and brown on all sides. Transfer the browned meat to the insert of a slow cooker. Add the remaining oil to the same skillet and heat over medium-high heat. Add the onions, garlic, cumin, cinnamon, ginger, and saffron and sauté until the onions begin to soften, about 5 minutes.
3. Pour the chicken broth into the skillet and heat, scraping up any browned bits from the bottom of the pan.
4. Transfer the contents of the skillet to the slow cooker and stir in the beef broth and dates. Cover and cook on low for 6 to 7 hours, until the lamb is tender. Skim off any fat from the top of the sauce and stir in the cilantro.
5. Serve from the cooker set on warm.

Country-Style Spareribs

Prep time: 10 minutes | Cook time: 8 to 10 hours | Serves 6

3 pounds (1.4 kg) country-style spareribs
1½ teaspoons salt
2 tablespoons extra-virgin olive oil
3 medium onions, finely chopped
⅛ teaspoon red pepper flakes
3 cloves garlic, minced
1 teaspoon dried oregano
½ cup red wine, such as Chianti or Barolo
1 (28- to 32-ounce / 794- to 907-g) can crushed tomatoes, with their juice

1. Sprinkle the ribs with the salt and arrange in the insert of a slow cooker. Heat the oil in a large skillet over medium-high heat. Add the onions, red pepper flakes, garlic, and oregano and sauté until the onions are softened, about 5 minutes.
2. Add the wine to the skillet and stir up any browned bits from the bottom of the pan. Transfer the contents of the skillet to the slow-cooker insert and stir in the tomatoes. Cover and cook on low for 8 to 10 hours, until the meat is tender. Skim off any fat from the surface of the sauce.
3. Serve the ribs from the cooker set on warm.

Classic Lamb Curry

Prep time: 25 minutes | Cook time: 6 to 8 hours | Serves 8

4 tablespoons olive oil
3 pounds (1.4 kg) lamb shoulder meat, fat trimmed and cut into 2-inch cubes
1½ teaspoons salt
½ teaspoon freshly ground black pepper
2 medium onions, coarsely chopped
4 garlic cloves, minced
2 tablespoons grated fresh ginger
2 tablespoons sweet curry powder
Pinch of red pepper flakes
1 (14-ounce / 397-g) can coconut milk
1 (15-ounce / 425-g) can diced tomatoes, drained
1 cup chicken broth
8 medium Yukon gold potatoes, quartered
8 ounces (227 g) green beans, ends snipped and cut into 1-inch pieces
2 bay leaves
Condiments:
Major Grey's chutney
Chopped green onions
Raisins (dark or golden)
Toasted unsweetened coconut
Chopped roasted peanuts or cashews
Dried banana chips
Lime pickle

1.Heat 2 tablespoons of the oil in a large skillet over high heat. Sprinkle the meat evenly with the salt and pepper. Add the meat to the skillet and brown on all sides. Transfer the meat to the insert of a slow cooker.
2.Add the remaining 2 tablespoons oil to the same skillet and heat over medium-high heat. Add the onions, garlic, ginger, curry powder, and red pepper flakes and sauté to release the oils in the spices and to soften the onions, 2 to 3 minutes. Add the coconut milk to the skillet and heat, scraping up any browned bits from the bottom of the pan.
3.Transfer the contents of the skillet to the slow-cooker insert and stir in the tomatoes, broth, potatoes, beans, and bay leaves. Cover and cook on low for 6 to 8 hours, until the lamb is tender. Remove any fat from the top of the sauce, discard the bay leaves.
4.Serve the lamb with the condiments.

Lemony Lamb with Artichokes

Prep time: 20 minutes | Cook time: 8 hours | Serves 6 to 8

½ cup olive oil
1½ teaspoons salt
1 teaspoon ground cumin
Pinch of cayenne pepper
1 teaspoon sweet paprika
3 pounds (1.4 kg) lamb shoulder meat, fat trimmed and cut into 1-inch chunks
4 leeks, cut into ½-inch pieces, using the white and tender green parts
4 garlic cloves, minced
1 cup dry white wine
½ cup chicken broth
Grated zest of 2 lemons
1 (16-ounce / 454-g) package frozen artichoke hearts, thawed and drained

1.Mix ¼ cup of the oil, the salt, cumin, cayenne, and paprika in a large bow. Add the meat and toss to coat with the spice mixture. Heat the remaining oil in a large skillet over medium-high heat. Add the meat a few pieces at a time and brown on all sides. Transfer the browned meat to the insert of a slow cooker.
2.Add the leeks and garlic to the same skillet and sauté until the leeks are softened, 3 to 4 minutes. Add the wine, broth, and zest and heat, scraping up any browned bits from the bottom of the pan.
3.Pour the contents of the skillet over the lamb and add the artichokes, stirring to distribute the ingredients in the pot. Cover and cook on low for 8 hours, until the lamb is tender.
4.Using a slotted spoon, carefully transfer the lamb and artichokes to a serving bowl. Strain the sauce through a fine-mesh sieve into a saucepan. Skim off any fat from the top and bring to a boil. Boil until the sauce is reduced to about 1½ cups to concentrate the flavor. Taste and adjust the seasoning.
5.Spoon the sauce over the lamb and artichokes and serve.

Braised Lamb with Eggplant

Prep time: 25 minutes | Cook time: 3 to 4 hours | Serves 8

¼ cup extra-virgin olive oil
3 pounds (1.4 kg) lamb shoulder, fat trimmed and cut into 1-inch chunks
1½ teaspoons salt
½ teaspoon freshly ground black pepper
2 large onions, coarsely chopped
4 cloves garlic, sliced
4 Japanese eggplants (about 1 pound / 454 g), cut into ½-inch cubes
1 teaspoon dried oregano
½ cup dry white wine or vermouth
1 (28- to 32-ounce / 794- to 907-g) can chopped tomatoes, with their juice
½ cup finely chopped fresh Italian parsley
1 cup crumbled feta cheese, for garnish

1.Heat the oil in a large skillet over medium-high heat. Sprinkle the lamb evenly with the salt and pepper, add a few pieces at a time to the skillet, and brown on all sides. Transfer the browned meat to the insert of a slow cooker.
2.Add the onions, garlic, eggplants, and oregano to the skillet and sauté until the onions begin to soften and turn translucent, 5 to 7 minutes. Add the wine to the skillet and heat, scraping the browned bits from the bottom of the pan. Transfer the contents of the skillet to the slow-cooker insert and stir in the tomatoes.
3.Cover and cook on high 3 to 4 hours or low for 7 to 8 hours. Skim off any fat from the top of the stew and stir in the parsley. Keep the stew in the cooker set on warm until ready to serve.
4.Garnish each serving with a sprinkling of feta.

Mediterranean Lamb and Lentils

Prep time: 20 minutes | Cook time: 8 to 10 hours | Serves 6 to 8

¼ cup extra-virgin olive oil
2 pounds (907 g) lamb shoulder meat, fat trimmed and cut into 1-inch chunks
1½ teaspoons salt
½ teaspoon freshly ground black pepper
2 medium onions, coarsely chopped
3 medium carrots, cut into 1-inch lengths
3 stalks celery, coarsely chopped

2 teaspoons dried thyme
1 (14- to 15-ounce / 397- to 425-g) can crushed tomatoes, with their juice
1 cup green lentils
2 cups chicken broth

1.Heat the oil in a large skillet over medium-high heat. Sprinkle the lamb evenly with the salt and pepper. Add the meat a few pieces at a time to the skillet and brown on all sides. Transfer the meat to the insert of a slow cooker.
2.Add the onions, carrots, celery, and thyme to the same skillet and sauté until the vegetables begin to soften and the onions begin to turn translucent. Add the tomatoes and heat, scraping up any browned bits from the bottom of the pan.
3.Transfer the contents of the skillet to the slow-cooker insert and stir in the lentils and chicken broth. Cover and cook on low for 8 to 10 hours, until the meat and lentils are tender. Skim any fat from the top of the stew.
4.Serve from the cooker set on warm.

Indian Tandoori Lamb

Prep time: 20 minutes | Cook time: 3 hours | Serves 8

1½ cups plain yogurt
2 tablespoons fresh lemon juice
4 cloves garlic, minced
1½ teaspoons ground cumin
1½ teaspoons garam masala
1 teaspoon ground coriander
Pinch of cayenne pepper
1 teaspoon salt
3 pounds (1.4 kg) lamb shoulder, fat trimmed and cut into 1-inch chunks
4 medium Yukon gold potatoes, cut into quarters
3 medium carrots, cut into 1-inch lengths
½ cup chicken broth

1.Whisk together the yogurt, lemon juice, garlic, and spices in a large bowl. Add the lamb and toss to coat well with the marinade. Cover and refrigerate for at least 2 hours or overnight.
2.Drain the marinade and add the lamb to the insert of a slow cooker. Add the vegetables and broth and stir to combine. Cover and cook on high for 3 hours, until the lamb is tender and the vegetables are cooked through. Skim off any fat from the top of the sauce.
3.Serve from the cooker set on warm.

Guinness Lamb Shanks

Prep time: 20 minutes | Cook time: 10 to 12 hours | Serves 6

½ cup all-purpose flour
1½ teaspoons salt
½ teaspoon freshly ground black pepper
6 meaty lamb shanks, fat trimmed (lamb shanks range in size from 12 to 16 ounces / 340 to 454 g, depending on the size of the bone)
¼ cup olive oil
3 large onions, cut into half rounds
1 (12-ounce / 340-g) bottle Guinness or other dark ale
4 medium carrots, cut into 1-inch lengths
4 medium parsnips, cut into 1-inch lengths
2 tablespoons tomato paste
½ cup beef broth

1.Mix the flour, salt, and pepper in a large zipper-top plastic bag. Add the meat, toss to coat, and shake off any excess flour. Heat the oil in a large skillet over high heat. Add the meat a few pieces at a time and brown on all sides. Transfer the browned meat to the insert of a slow cooker.
2.Add the onions to the same skillet and sauté until they begin to soften and turn translucent, 4 to 5 minutes. Pour in the Guinness and scrape up any browned bits from the bottom of the pan.
3.Transfer the contents of the skillet to the slow-cooker insert, add the carrots and parsnips, and stir to distribute evenly. Stir the tomato paste into the broth and pour into the insert. Cover and cook on low for 10 to 12 hours, until the meat is tender. Skim off any fat from the top of the sauce.
4.Serve the lamb directly from the cooker set on warm.

Braised White Beans and Lamb Chops

Prep time: 20 minutes | Cook time: 5 to 7 hours | Serves 4

1 to 2 tablespoons olive oil
4 shoulder lamb chops
1 medium-size yellow onion, chopped
½ cup chicken broth
½ cup dry white wine
¼ cup chopped oil-packed sun-dried tomatoes, drained
½ teaspoon dried marjoram or thyme
Pinch of ground cumin

1 (15-ounce / 425-g) can small white beans, rinsed and drained
Salt and freshly ground black pepper, to taste
Hot cooked rice, for serving

1.In a large nonstick skillet, heat the oil and brown the lamb on both sides over medium-high heat; transfer to the slow cooker. Add the onion to the skillet and cook for a few minutes until limp; add to the cooker. Add the broth, wine, tomatoes, marjoram, and cumin, cover, and cook on low for 2½ to 3½ hours.
2.Add the beans, cover, and continue to cook on low until the lamb is very tender, another 2½ to 3½ hours. Season with salt and pepper and serve over rice.

Leg of Lamb and Cabbage

Prep time: 10 minutes | Cook time: 5⅓ to 6⅓ hours | Serves 4 to 6

½ teaspoon allspice berries
½ teaspoon black peppercorns
½ teaspoon whole cloves
1 small leg of lamb (about 2 pounds / 907 g), bone-in or boned and tied
2 cups hot chicken broth (optional)
½ cup dry white wine (optional)
¾ teaspoon to 1 teaspoon salt, to your taste
1 head cabbage, cored and cut into 8 wedges

1.Put the allspice berries, peppercorns, and cloves in a cheesecloth bag or tea ball and set aside.
2.Put the lamb in the slow cooker. If you are using a round cooker, put the lamb in meaty end down. Add the broth and wine, if using. Add hot water to cover the lamb by an inch. Add the salt, using the lesser amount if you used salted chicken broth. Add the spice ball. Cover and cook on high for 1 hour.
3.Turn the cooker to low and cook until the lamb is fork-tender, 4 to 5 hours. About 20 minutes before it is done, preheat the oven to 200°F (93°C).
4.Transfer the lamb to a platter, tent with aluminum foil, and place in the oven to keep warm. Put the cabbage wedges in the hot broth remaining in the cooker, cover, and turn the heat to high. Cook until tender, 20 to 30 minutes.
5.Just before cabbage is done, carve the meat. Serve the lamb in shallow bowls with 1 or 2 wedges of cabbage and some of the broth.

Chapter 11 Fish and Seafood

Citrus Sea Bass with Parsley

Prep time: 15 minutes | Cook time: 1½ hours | Serves 4

1½ pounds sea bass fillets, rinsed and blotted dry
Sea salt and white pepper, to taste
1 medium-size white onion, chopped
¼ cup minced fresh flat-leaf parsley
1 tablespoon grated lemon, lime, or orange zest or a combination
3 tablespoons dry white wine or water
1 tablespoon olive oil or toasted sesame oil
For Serving:
Lemon wedges
Lime wedges
Cold tartar sauce

1. Coat the slow cooker with nonstick cooking spray or butter and arrange the fish in the crock. Season lightly with salt and white pepper, then add the onion, parsley, and zest. Drizzle with the wine and oil. Cover and cook on high for 1½ hours.
2. Carefully lift the fish out of the cooker with a plastic spatula or pancake turner. Serve immediately with lemon and lime wedges and tartar sauce.

Wine Braised Trout with Parsley

Prep time: 10 minutes | Cook time: ¾ to 1¼ hours | Serves 6

6 boned trout (each about 1½ pounds / 680 g), head and tail left on
Salt and freshly ground black pepper, to taste
2 tablespoons unsalted butter
2 medium-size shallots, chopped
¼ cup chopped fresh flat-leaf parsley
1 lemon, sliced
1½ cups dry white wine

1. Coat the slow cooker with nonstick cooking spray. Sprinkle the inside and outside of the fish with salt and pepper and arrange the trout in the cooker; they can be lying against each other.
2. In a small skillet over medium heat, melt the butter, then cook the shallots until softened, 3 to 4 minutes; stir in the parsley and stuff some of the mixture inside each trout. Arrange the lemon slices on top.
3. Heat the wine in a saucepan or the microwave until boiling. Pour around the trout. Cover and cook on high until the fish is tender, 45 minutes to 1¼ hours.

Cheddar Tuna-Stuffed Potatoes

Prep time: 10 minutes | Cook time: 3¾ to 6 hours | Serves 4

4 medium-size Idaho or russet potatoes, scrubbed
¾ cup finely shredded Cheddar cheese
¼ cup milk
1 (6-ounce / 170-g) can water-packed tuna, drained
½ cup sour cream
1 green onion (white and some of the green), thinly sliced

1. Prick each dripping-wet potato with a fork or the tip of a sharp knife and pile them into the slow cooker; do not add water. Cover and cook until fork-tender, on high for 3 to 5 hours or on low for 6 to 8 hours.
2. Remove the potatoes from the cooker with tongs and cut in half lengthwise. Scoop out the center of each half with a large spoon, leaving enough potato to keep the shell intact. Put the potato flesh in a bowl and add ½ cup of the cheese, the milk, tuna, sour cream, and green onion. Mash the filling with a fork and spoon it back into the shells, mounding it high. Return to the slow cooker, setting down the stuffed potatoes in a single layer if possible so that they touch each other. Sprinkle with the remaining ¼ cup of cheese. Cover and cook on high for 45 minutes to 1 hour. Remove carefully from the cooker and serve immediately.

Miso-Honey Poached Salmon

Prep time: 5 minutes | Cook time: 1½ hours | Serves 8

3 pounds (1.4 kg) salmon fillets
3 tablespoons white Miso
3 tablespoons honey
¼ cup rice wine (mirin) or dry sherry
2 teaspoons freshly grated ginger

1. Place the salmon in the insert of a slow cooker.
2. Combine the miso, honey, rice wine, and ginger in a mixing bowl and stir.
3. Pour the sauce over the salmon in the slow cooker. Cover and cook on high for 1½ hours, until the salmon is cooked through and registers 165ºF (74ºC) on an instant-read thermometer inserted in the center of a thick fillet.
4. Carefully remove the salmon from the slow-cooker insert with a large spatula. Remove the skin from the underside of the salmon (if necessary) and arrange the salmon on a serving platter.
5. Strain the sauce through a fine-mesh sieve into a saucepan. Boil the sauce, reduce it to a syrupy consistency, and serve with the salmon.

Veracruz-Style Snapper

Prep time: 25 minutes | Cook time: 5½ to 6½ hours | Serves 4 to 5

1 small to medium-size yellow or white onion, finely chopped
2 cloves garlic, pressed
½ teaspoon dried oregano
Pinch of ground cinnamon
2 tablespoons olive oil
2 tablespoons minced fresh flat-leaf parsley or cilantro
1 to 2 jalapeños, to your taste, deseeded and finely chopped
1 (28-ounce / 794-g) can diced tomatoes, drained
½ cup bottled clam juice
1 pound (454 g) snapper fillets
3 tablespoons fresh lime juice
1 tablespoon large capers, rinsed and drained
2 limes, sliced, for serving

1. Combine the onion, garlic, oregano, cinnamon, olive oil, parsley, jalapeños, tomatoes, and clam juice in the slow cooker. Cover and cook until the sauce is bubbling hot and well blended, on low for 5 to 6 hours or on high for 2½ to 3 hours.
2. Lay the fish in the sauce; if the fillets are thick and you have an oval cooker, lay them flat and slightly overlapping. If you have a round cooker, roll up the fillets and set them in the sauce. Spoon some of the sauce over the fillets; drizzle with the lime juice and sprinkle with the capers. Cover and cook on high until the fish is cooked through and flakes when prodded with a fork, 20 to 30 minutes. Do not overcook.
3. Serve immediately, garnished with lime slices.

Hearty Cod Stew

Prep time: 30 minutes | Cook time: 6½ to 8½ hours | Serves 8

1 pound (454 g) potatoes (about 2 medium), peeled and finely chopped
1 (10-ounce / 283-g) package frozen corn, thawed
1½ cups frozen lima beans, thawed
1 large onion, finely chopped
1 celery rib, finely chopped
1 medium carrot, finely chopped
4 garlic cloves, minced
1 bay leaf
1 teaspoon lemon-pepper seasoning
1 teaspoon dried parsley flakes
1 teaspoon dried rosemary, crushed
½ teaspoon salt
1½ cups vegetable or chicken broth
1 (10¾-ounce / 305-g) can condensed cream of celery soup, undiluted
½ cup white wine or additional vegetable broth
1 pound (454 g) cod fillets, cut into 1-inch pieces
1 (14½-ounce / 411-g) can diced tomatoes, undrained
1 (12-ounce / 340-g) can fat-free evaporated milk

1. In a slow cooker, combine the first 15 ingredients. Cook, covered, on low 6-8 hours or until potatoes are tender.
2. Remove bay leaf. Stir in cod, tomatoes and milk; cook, covered, 30-35 minutes longer or until fish just begins to flake easily with a fork.

Cod with Olives and Raisins

Prep time: 25 minutes | Cook time: 4 to 5 hours | Serves 4 to 6

2 pounds (907 g) salt cod
Milk, as needed
¼ cup all-purpose flour or whole wheat pastry flour
Salt and freshly ground black pepper, to taste
¼ cup olive oil
16 white boiling onions, peeled and cut in half
4 medium-size ripe tomatoes, peeled, deseeded, and chopped; or 1 cup chopped canned tomatoes, drained
¾ cup pitted ripe olives of your choice, drained
½ cup golden raisins
¾ cup chicken or vegetable broth
3 tablespoons tomato paste
3 tablespoons balsamic vinegar
3 tablespoons chopped fresh flat-leaf parsley or celery leaves
2 tablespoons nonpareil capers, rinsed and drained
⅓ cup pine nuts (optional), lightly toasted

1.Wash the salt cod, place in a bowl, and cover with cold water. Cover and refrigerate for about 12 hours, pouring off the water and refilling 3 times. Drain and rinse in a colander under cold running water and pat dry with paper towels. Remove the skin and cut the fish into 2-inch chunks. Put in a bowl and cover with cold milk. Cover and refrigerate for about 2 hours. Rinse the salt cod again in a colander under cold water and pat dry. Put the flour on a plate, season with salt and pepper, and coat each chunk of fish with the flour.
2.Heat 2 tablespoons of the oil in a large, heavy skillet over medium-high heat and quickly brown the cod on both sides. Transfer to the slow cooker. Add the remaining 2 tablespoons of oil to the skillet and quickly cook the onions, stirring, for 5 minutes only, until limp. Transfer to the cooker. Add the tomatoes, olives, raisins, broth, tomato paste, vinegar, parsley, and capers to the cooker. Cover and cook on high for 1 hour.
3.Turn the cooker to low and cook until the onions are tender, 3 to 4 hours.
4.Stir in the pine nuts, if using, during the last 20 minutes of cooking. Serve hot ladled out of the crock.

Smoky Salmon Fettuccine

Prep time: 10 minutes | Cook time: 1 to 2 hours | Serves 4

2 cups heavy cream
3 to 4 ounces (85 to 113 g) top quality lox or smoked salmon, chopped or flaked into ½-inch pieces
1 pound (454 g) fresh fettuccine, regular egg or spinach flavored
2 tablespoons olive oil (optional)
Freshly ground black pepper, to taste

1.Combine the cream and the lox in the slow cooker. Cover and cook on low until very hot, 1 to 2 hours.
2.Meanwhile, cook the fettuccine in boiling water until tender to the bite, about 3 minutes. Take care not to overcook. Toss with the olive oil if the pasta is to stand for over 5 minutes. Add the fettuccine to the hot sauce and toss to coat evenly. If your cooker is large enough, just add the pasta to the cooker; if not, pour the sauce over the pasta in a shallow, heated bowl. Garnish with a few grinds of black pepper and serve immediately.

Buttery Halibut with Garlic

Prep time: 10 minutes | Cook time: 4¾ hours | Serves 6

1 cup (2 sticks) unsalted butter
½ cup olive oil
6 cloves garlic, sliced
1 teaspoon sweet paprika
½ cup lemon juice
Grated zest of 1 lemon
¼ cup finely chopped fresh chives
2 to 3 pounds (907 g to 1.4 kg) halibut fillets
½ cup finely chopped fresh Italian parsley

1.Combine the butter, oil, garlic, paprika, lemon juice, zest, and chives in the insert of a slow cooker and stir to combine. Cover and cook on low for 4 hours.
2.Add the halibut to the pot, spooning the sauce over the halibut. Cover and cook for an additional 40 minutes, until the halibut is cooked through and opaque.
3.Sprinkle the parsley evenly over the fish and serve immediately.

Super Easy Braised Tuna

Prep time: 5 minutes | Cook time: 3 to 4 hours | Serves 6

3 pounds (1.4 kg) tuna fillets
Olive oil to cover (about 3 cups)
1 teaspoon coarse sea salt

1.Place the tuna in the insert of a slow cooker and pour the oil over the tuna. The oil should cover the tuna, and depending on the shape of your slow cooker, you may need to add a bit more oil. Add the salt to the slow-cooker insert.
2.Cover and cook on low for 3 to 4 hours, until the tuna is cooked through and is white. Remove the tuna from the oil and cool completely before using.

Slow Cooker Poached Salmon Steaks

Prep time: 10 minutes | Cook time: 1½ hours | Serves 4

4 (8-ounce / 227-g) salmon steaks or fillets, rinsed and blotted dry
1 cup chicken broth or water
½ cup dry white wine
Sea salt, to taste
2 black peppercorns
1 sprig fresh dill
1 thick slice onion
3 sprigs fresh flat-leaf parsley
For Serving:
Lemon wedges
Cold tartar sauce

1.Coat the slow cooker with nonstick cooking spray and arrange the salmon in it. The steaks can be set tightly side by side; tuck the ends of fillets under themselves to even out the thickness of the fish so it can cook evenly.
2.Heat the broth and wine in a saucepan or the microwave until boiling. Pour around the salmon. Sprinkle the steaks with some salt, then add the peppercorns, dill, onion slice, and parsley to the liquid around the steaks. Cover and cook on high until the salmon is opaque and firm to the touch, about 1½ hours.
3.Carefully lift the salmon out of the cooker

with a rubber spatula or pancake turner. Serve immediately while still hot or cool until lukewarm in the poaching liquid and refrigerate until cold. Accompany with lemon wedges and tartar sauce.

Lemony Sea Bass Tagine

Prep time: 20 minutes | Cook time: 6 to 7½ hours | Serves 6

2 pounds (907 g) sea bass fillets
½ cup olive oil
Grated zest of 1 lemon
¼ cup lemon juice
1 teaspoon sweet paprika
½ cup finely chopped fresh cilantro
2 cloves garlic, chopped
1 medium onion, finely chopped
1 teaspoon ground cumin
½ teaspoon saffron threads, crushed
1 (28- to 32-ounce / 794- to 907-g) can crushed tomatoes, with their juice
6 medium Yukon gold potatoes, quartered
1 teaspoon salt
½ teaspoon freshly ground black pepper
½ cup finely chopped fresh Italian parsley

1.Place the fish in a zipper-top plastic bag.
2.Whisk ¼ cup of the oil, the zest, lemon juice, paprika, and cilantro together in a small bowl. Pour the marinade over the fish in the bag. Seal the bag and refrigerate for at least 1 hour or up to 4 hours.
3.Heat the remaining ¼ cup oil in a large skillet over medium-high heat. Add the garlic, onion, cumin, and saffron and sauté until the onion is softened, 5 to 7 minutes.
4.Add the tomatoes and stir to combine. Place the potatoes in the bottom of the insert of a slow cooker and sprinkle them evenly with the salt and pepper, tossing to coat. Add the tomato mixture to the insert. Cover and cook on low for 5 to 6 hours, until the potatoes are almost tender.
5.Pour the marinade into the insert and stir the potatoes and sauce to combine. Put the fish on top of the potatoes and spoon some of the sauce over the top. Cook for an additional 1 to 1½ hours, until the sea bass is cooked through and is opaque in the center.
6.Sprinkle the parsley evenly over the top of the sea bass and serve immediately, scooping up some potatoes and sauce with the fish.

Cheesy Halibut with Salsa

Prep time: 10 minutes | Cook time: 2½ to 2¾ hours | Serves 6

3 cups prepared medium-hot salsa
2 tablespoons fresh lime juice
1 teaspoon ground cumin
2 to 3 pounds (907 g to 1.4 kg) halibut fillets
1½ cup finely shredded Monterey Jack cheese (or Pepper Jack for a spicy topping)

1. Combine the salsa, lime juice, and cumin in the insert of a slow cooker and stir. Cover the slow cooker and cook on low for 2 hours.
2. Put the halibut in the cooker and spoon some of the sauce over the top of the fish. Sprinkle the cheese evenly over the fish. Cover and cook for an additional 30 to 45 minutes.
3. Remove the halibut from the slow cooker and serve on a bed of the sauce.

Wine-Glazed Salmon with Thyme

Prep time: 10 minutes | Cook time: 1½ hours | Serves 4

2 cups water
1 cup white wine
1 medium onion, sliced
1 celery rib, sliced
1 medium carrot, sliced
2 tablespoons lemon juice
3 fresh thyme sprigs
1 fresh rosemary sprig
1 bay leaf
½ teaspoon salt
¼ teaspoon pepper
4 salmon fillets (1¼ inches thick and 6 ounces / 170 g each)
Lemon wedges

1. In a slow cooker, combine the first 11 ingredients. Cook, covered, on low 45 minutes.
2. Carefully place fillets in liquid; add additional warm water to cover if needed. Cook, covered, 45 to 55 minutes or just until fish flakes easily with a fork. A thermometer inserted in fish should read at least 145ºF (63ºC). Remove fish from cooking liquid. Serve warm or cold with lemon wedges.

Salmon with Chili-Garlic Glaze

Prep time: 20 minutes | Cook time: 1 to 2 hours | Serves 4

1⅔ cups boiling water

1½ cups instant brown rice
3 tablespoons vegetable oil
Salt and pepper, to taste
4 scallions, white parts minced, green parts sliced on bias ½ inch thick
3 tablespoons toasted sesame oil
2 tablespoons Asian chili-garlic sauce
2 tablespoons honey
4 (6- to 8-ounce / 170- to 227-g) skin-on salmon fillets, 1 to 1½ inches thick
2 oranges
¼ cup rice vinegar
1 teaspoon grated fresh ginger

1. Lightly coat slow cooker with vegetable oil spray. Combine boiling water, rice, 1 tablespoon vegetable oil, ½ teaspoon salt, and ½ teaspoon pepper in prepared slow cooker. Gently press 16 by 12-inch sheet of parchment paper onto surface of water, folding down edges as needed.
2. Combine scallion whites, sesame oil, chili-garlic sauce, and honey in bowl; measure out and reserve half of scallion mixture in medium bowl until ready to use. Season salmon with salt and pepper, brush with remaining scallion mixture, and arrange, skin side down, in even layer on top of parchment. Cover and cook until salmon is opaque throughout when checked with tip of paring knife and registers 135ºF (57ºC) (for medium), 1 to 2 hours on low.
3. Cut away peel and pith from oranges. Cut oranges into 8 wedges, then slice wedges crosswise into ½-inch-thick pieces. Using 2 metal spatulas, transfer salmon to serving dish; discard parchment and remove any white albumin from salmon. Whisk vinegar, ginger, and remaining 2 tablespoons vegetable oil into reserved scallion mixture. Fluff rice with fork, then gently fold in oranges (adding any accumulated juices), scallion greens, and half of vinaigrette. Season with salt and pepper to taste. Serve salmon with salad, passing remaining vinaigrette separately.

Cheddar Salmon Soufflé

Prep time: 5 minutes | Cook time: 2 to 3 hours | Serves 4

1 (15-ounce / 425-g) can salmon, drained and flaked
2 eggs, beaten well
2 cups seasoned croutons
1 cup shredded Cheddar cheese
2 chicken bouillon cubes
1 cup boiling water
¼ teaspoon dry mustard (optional)

1.Grease the interior of your cooker with nonstick cooking spray.
2.Combine salmon, eggs, croutons, and cheese in the slow cooker.
3.Dissolve bouillon cubes in boiling water in a small bowl. Add mustard, if you wish, and stir. Pour over salmon mixture and stir together lightly.
4.Cover and cook on high 2 to 3 hours, or until mixture appears to be set. Allow to stand 15 minutes before serving.

Sole with Pizzaiola Sauce

Prep time: 25 minutes | Cook time: 4¾ hours | Serves 6 to 8

Pizzaiola Sauce:
2 tablespoons extra-virgin olive oil
1 medium onion, finely chopped
2 teaspoons dried oregano
2 teaspoons dried basil
Pinch red pepper flakes
3 cloves garlic, minced
1 (28- to 32-ounce / 794- to 907-g) cans crushed plum tomatoes, with their juice
1½ teaspoons salt
½ teaspoon freshly ground black pepper
½ cup olive oil
1 tablespoon Old Bay seasoning
2 pounds (907 g) sole fillets
½ cup finely shredded Mozzarella cheese
½ cup freshly grated Parmigiano-Reggiano cheese
½ cup finely chopped fresh Italian parsley

1.Heat the oil in a small saucepan over medium-high heat. Add the onion, oregano, basil, red pepper flakes, and garlic and sauté until the onion is softened, about 3 minutes.
2.Add the tomatoes, salt, and pepper and stir to combine. Transfer to the insert of a slow cooker.
3.Cover and cook on low for 4 hours.
4.Mix together the oil and seasoning in a shallow dish. Dip each fillet in the oil mixture and roll up from the narrow end.
5.Place the rolled fillets in the slow cooker, wedging the pieces to fit. Spoon the sauce over each roll and sprinkle evenly with the cheese. Cover and cook on low for 35 to 45 minutes, until the fish is cooked through and flakes easily with a fork.
6.Sprinkle the parsley over the fish and serve immediately.

Miso-Glazed Sesame Black Cod

Prep time: 10 minutes | Cook time: 5 hours | Serves 6

½ cup white miso paste
¼ cup rice wine (mirin)
¼ firmly packed light brown sugar
1 teaspoon rice vinegar
1½ cups water
2 pounds (907 g) black cod (if unavailable, use fresh cod, halibut, sea bass, or salmon)
6 green onions, finely chopped, using the white and tender green parts
¼ cup toasted sesame seeds, for garnish

1.Combine the miso, rice wine, sugar, rice vinegar, and water in the insert of a slow cooker.
2.Cover and cook on low for 4 hours. Add the cod, spooning the sauce over the top. Cover and cook for an additional 30 to 45 minutes.
3.Remove the cod from the slow-cooker insert and cover with aluminum foil to keep warm. Pour the sauce in a saucepan. Bring to a boil and reduce by half until it begins to look syrupy, about 15 to 20 minutes. Add the green onions to the sauce.
4.Serve each piece of cod in a pool of the sauce and sprinkle each serving with sesame seeds. Serve any additional sauce on the side.

Red Snapper Feast

Prep time: 15 minutes | Cook time: 2 to 3 hours | Serves 8

3 pounds (1.4 kg) red snapper fillets
1 tablespoon minced garlic
1 large onion, sliced
1 green bell pepper, cut into 1-inch pieces
2 unpeeled zucchini, sliced
1 (14-ounce / 397-g) can low-sodium diced tomatoes
½ teaspoon dried basil
½ teaspoon dried oregano
¼ teaspoon salt
¼ teaspoon black pepper
¼ cup dry white wine or white grape juice

1. Rinse snapper and pat dry. Place in a slow cooker sprayed with non-fat cooking spray.
2. Mix remaining ingredients together and pour over fish.
3. Cover. Cook on high 2 to 3 hours, being careful not to overcook the fish.

Salmon Cakes in White Wine Butter Sauce

Prep time: 15 minutes | Cook time: 5 hours | Serves 6

White Wine Butter **Sauce:**
½ cup (1 stick) unsalted butter
1 teaspoon Old Bay seasoning
2 cloves garlic, sliced
2½ cups white wine or vermouth
Salmon Cakes:
4 cups cooked salmon, flaked
1 (6-ounce / 170-g) jar marinated artichoke hearts, drained and coarsely chopped
1 cup fresh bread crumbs
½ cup freshly grated Parmigiano-Reggiano cheese
1 large egg, beaten
½ teaspoon freshly ground black pepper

1. Put all the sauce ingredients in the insert of a slow cooker and stir to combine. Cover and cook on low for 4 hours.
2. Put all the salmon cake ingredients in a large mixing bowl and stir to combine. Form the

mixture into 2-inch cakes. Place the cakes in the simmering sauce and spoon the sauce over the cakes.
3. Cover and cook for an additional 1 hour, until the cakes are tender. Carefully remove the cakes to a serving platter.
4. Strain the sauce through a fine-mesh sieve into a saucepan. Bring the sauce to a boil and reduce by half.
5. Serve the sauce over the cakes, or serve on the side.

Swordfish with Tomato and Olive Relish

Prep time: 20 minutes | Cook time: 1 to 2 hours | Serves 4

1 lemon, sliced ¼ inch thick
2 tablespoons minced fresh parsley, stems reserved
¼ cup dry white wine
4 (6- to 8-ounce / 170- to 227-g) skinless swordfish steaks, 1 to 1½ inches thick
Salt and pepper, to taste
1 pound (454 g) cherry tomatoes, halved
½ cup pitted salt-cured black olives, rinsed and halved
3 garlic cloves, minced
¼ cup extra-virgin olive oil

1. Fold sheet of aluminum foil into 12 by 9-inch sling and press widthwise into a slow cooker. Arrange lemon slices in single layer in bottom of prepared slow cooker. Scatter parsley stems over lemon slices. Add wine to slow cooker, then add water until liquid level is even with lemon slices (about ¼ cup). Season swordfish with salt and pepper and arrange in an even layer on top of parsley stems. Cover and cook until swordfish flakes apart when gently prodded with a paring knife and registers 140°F (60°C), 1 to 2 hours on low.
2. Microwave tomatoes, olives, and garlic in bowl until tomatoes begin to break down, about 4 minutes. Stir in oil and minced parsley and season with salt and pepper to taste. Using sling, transfer swordfish to baking sheet. Gently lift and tilt steaks with spatula to remove parsley stems and lemon slices; transfer to serving dish. Discard poaching liquid and remove any white albumin from swordfish. Serve with relish.

Sweet and Hot Salmon

Prep time: 5 minutes | Cook time: 1½ hours | Serves 6

3 pounds (1.4 kg) salmon fillets
½ cup Colman's English mustard
¼ cup honey
2 tablespoons finely chopped fresh dill

1. Place the salmon in the insert of a slow cooker. Put the mustard, honey, and dill in a small bowl and stir to combine.
2. Pour the mixture over the salmon, spreading evenly.
3. Cover and cook on high for 1½ hours, until the salmon is cooked through.
4. Serve the salmon from the slow cooker topped with some of the sauce.

Salmon with White Rice Salad

Prep time: 20 minutes | Cook time: 1 to 2 hours | Serves 4

1⅔ cups boiling water

1½ cups instant white rice
⅓ cup extra-virgin olive oil
Salt and pepper, to taste
4 (6- to 8-ounce / 170- to 227-g) skin-on salmon fillets, 1 to 1½ inches thick
¼ cup red wine vinegar
1 tablespoon honey
2 teaspoons minced fresh oregano
2 garlic cloves, minced
8 ounces (227 g) cherry tomatoes, quartered
½ cup fresh parsley leaves
2 ounces (57 g) feta cheese, crumbled (½ cup)
Lemon wedges, for serving

1. Lightly coat slow cooker with vegetable oil spray. Combine boiling water, rice, 1 tablespoon oil, ½ teaspoon salt, and ½ teaspoon pepper in prepared slow cooker. Gently press 16 by 12-inch sheet of parchment paper onto surface of water, folding down edges as needed.
2. Season salmon with salt and pepper and arrange, skin side down, in even layer on top of parchment. Cover and cook until salmon is opaque throughout when checked with tip of paring knife and registers 135ºF (57ºC) (for medium), 1 to 2 hours on low.
3. Using 2 metal spatulas, transfer salmon to serving dish; discard parchment and remove any white albumin from salmon. Whisk vinegar, honey, oregano, garlic, and remaining oil together in a bowl. Fluff rice with fork, then gently fold in tomatoes, parsley, feta, and ½ cup vinaigrette. Season with salt and pepper to taste. Drizzle remaining vinaigrette over salmon and serve with salad and lemon wedges.

Old Bay Lemon Sea Bass

Prep time: 15 minutes | Cook time: 2 hours | Serves 6

1 cup (2 sticks) unsalted butter, melted
½ cup fresh lemon juice
Grated zest of 1 lemon
2 cloves garlic, minced
8 tablespoons olive oil
2 tablespoons Old Bay seasoning
2 to 3 pounds (907 g to 1.4 kg) sea bass fillets, cut to fit the slow-cooker insert
6 medium Yukon gold potatoes, cut into ¼-inch-thick slices

1. Stir the butter, lemon juice, zest, garlic, and 2 tablespoons of the olive oil together in a small bowl. Combine the remaining 6 tablespoons oil and the seasoning in a large mixing bowl.
2. Paint the sea bass with some of the butter sauce and set aside. Toss the potatoes in the seasoned oil. Pour half the butter sauce in the insert of a slow cooker.
3. Place half the potatoes in the bottom of the slow cooker. Place the sea bass on top of the potatoes and pour half the remaining butter sauce over the sea bass. Place the remaining potatoes on top of the sea bass and drizzle with the remaining butter sauce.
4. Cover and cook on high for 1½ hours, until the potatoes begin to turn golden and the sea bass is cooked through and opaque in the middle. Remove the cover and cook for an additional 15 to 20 minutes.
5. Serve immediately.

Spinach-Stuffed Sole

Prep time: 25 minutes | Cook time: 1 to 2 hours | Serves 4

1 lemon, sliced ¼ inch thick, plus ½ teaspoon grated lemon zest plus 1 tablespoon juice
¼ cup chopped fresh basil, stems reserved
¼ cup dry white wine
10 ounces (283 g) frozen chopped spinach, thawed and squeezed dry
4 ounces (113 g) whole-milk ricotta cheese
Pinch of nutmeg
Salt and pepper, to taste
8 (2- to 3-ounce / 57- to 85-g) skinless sole fillets, ¼ to ½ inch thick
8 ounces (227 g) cherry tomatoes
1 shallot, peeled and quartered
2 tablespoons extra-virgin olive oil

1. Fold sheet of aluminum foil into 12 by 9-inch sling and press widthwise into a slow cooker. Arrange lemon slices in single layer in bottom of prepared slow cooker. Scatter basil stems over lemon slices. Add wine to slow cooker, then add water until liquid level is even with lemon slices (about ¼ cup).
2. Combine spinach, ricotta, lemon zest, 2 tablespoons chopped basil, nutmeg, ¼ teaspoon salt, and ¼ teaspoon pepper in a bowl. Season sole with salt and pepper and place skinned side up on the cutting board. Mound filling evenly in center of fillets, fold tapered ends tightly over filling, then fold over thicker ends to make tidy bundles. Arrange bundles seam side down in an even layer on top of basil sprigs. Cover and cook until sole flakes apart when gently prodded with a paring knife, 1 to 2 hours on low.
3. Process tomatoes, shallot, oil, and lemon juice in blender until smooth, about 2 minutes, scraping down sides of the blender jar as needed. Strain sauce through fine-mesh strainer into bowl, pressing on solids to extract as much liquid as possible; discard solids. Season with salt and pepper to taste.
4. Using sling, transfer sole bundles to a baking sheet. Gently lift and tilt bundles with spatula to remove basil stems and lemon slices; transfer to serving dish. Discard poaching liquid and remove any white albumin from bundles. Spoon sauce over bundles and sprinkle with remaining 2 tablespoons basil. Serve.

Sweet and Sour Tuna

Prep time: 15 minutes | Cook time: 1 hour | Serves 3

Half a green bell pepper, cut into ¼-inch strips
1 small onion, thinly sliced
2 teaspoons olive oil
⅓ cup unsweetened pineapple juice
1½ teaspoons cornstarch
⅔ cup canned unsweetened pineapple chunks, drained
1 tablespoon sugar (scant)
1 tablespoon vinegar
1 (6-ounce / 170-g) can solid, water-packed tuna, drained and flaked
⅛ teaspoon black pepper
Dash of Tabasco sauce

1. Cook green pepper and onion with oil in a skillet over medium heat, leaving the vegetables slightly crisp.
2. Mix pineapple juice with cornstarch. Add to green pepper mixture.
3. Cook, stirring gently until thickened.
4. Add remaining ingredients. Pour into a slow cooker.
5. Cover. Cook on low 1 hour.

Herbed Perch with Potato

Prep time: 10 minutes | Cook time: 1 to 2 hours | Serves 4

1 (10¾-ounce / 305-g) can cream of celery soup
½ cup water
1 pound (454 g) perch fillet, fresh or thawed
2 cups cooked, diced potatoes, drained
¼ cup grated Parmesan cheese
1 tablespoon chopped parsley
½ teaspoon salt
½ teaspoon dried basil
¼ teaspoon dried oregano

1. Combine soup and water. Pour half in the slow cooker. Spread fillet on top. Place potatoes on fillet. Pour remaining soup mix over top.
2. Combine cheese and herbs. Sprinkle over ingredients in a slow cooker.
3. Cover. Cook on high 1 to 2 hours, being careful not to overcook fish.

Herbed Braised Flounder

Prep time: 5 minutes | Cook time: 3 to 4 hours | Serves 6

2 pounds (907 g) flounder fillets, fresh or frozen
½ teaspoon salt
¾ cup chicken broth
2 tablespoons lemon juice
2 tablespoons dried chives
2 tablespoons dried minced onion
½ to 1 teaspoon leaf marjoram
4 tablespoons chopped fresh parsley

1. Wipe fish as dry as possible. Cut fish into portions to fit slow cooker.
2. Sprinkle with salt.
3. Combine broth and lemon juice. Stir in remaining ingredients.
4. Place a meat rack in the slow cooker. Lay fish on the rack. Pour liquid mixture over each portion.
5. Cover. Cook on high 3 to 4 hours.

Garlicky Cod with Edamame

Prep time: 15 minutes | Cook time: 1 to 2 hours | Serves 4

2 shallots, minced
4 garlic cloves, minced
1 tablespoon grated fresh ginger
1 tablespoon vegetable oil
⅛ teaspoon red pepper flakes
2 cups frozen edamame, thawed
½ cup canned coconut milk
2 tablespoons fish sauce, plus extra for seasoning
4 (6- to 8-ounce / 170- to 227-g) skinless cod fillets, 1 to 1½ inches thick
Salt and pepper, to taste
¼ cup chopped fresh cilantro
1 teaspoon rice vinegar

1. Microwave shallots, garlic, ginger, oil, and pepper flakes in bowl, stirring occasionally, until shallots are softened, about 2 minutes; transfer to a slow cooker. Stir edamame, coconut milk, and fish sauce into a slow cooker. Season cod with salt and pepper and nestle into a slow cooker.

Spoon portion of sauce over cod. Cover and cook until cod flakes apart when gently prodded with a paring knife and registers 140ºF (60ºC), 1 to 2 hours on low.
2. Using 2 metal spatulas, transfer cod to serving dish. Stir cilantro and vinegar into edamame and season with extra fish sauce to taste. Spoon edamame and sauce over cod. Serve.

Fish Tagine with Artichokes

Prep time: 25 minutes | Cook time: 7 to 8 hours | Serves 4 to 6

2 onions, finely chopped
2 tablespoons tomato paste
4 garlic cloves, minced
1 tablespoon vegetable oil
2 teaspoons garam masala
1½ teaspoons paprika
¼ teaspoon cayenne pepper
3 cups jarred whole baby artichokes packed in water, halved, rinsed, and patted dry
2 cups chicken broth
1 (14½-ounce / 411-g) can diced tomatoes, drained
¼ cup dry white wine
Salt and pepper, to taste
1½ pounds (680 g) skinless cod fillets, 1 to 1½ inches thick, cut into 2-inch pieces
½ cup pitted kalamata olives, coarsely chopped
2 tablespoons minced fresh parsley

1. Microwave onions, tomato paste, garlic, oil, garam masala, paprika, and cayenne in bowl, stirring occasionally, until onions are softened, about 5 minutes; transfer to a slow cooker. Stir in artichokes, broth, tomatoes, wine, and ½ teaspoon salt. Cover and cook until flavors meld, 7 to 8 hours on low or 4 to 5 hours on high.
2. Stir cod and olives into tagine, cover, and cook on high until cod flakes apart when gently prodded with a paring knife, 30 to 40 minutes. Gently stir in parsley and season with salt and pepper to taste. Serve.

Halibut Tacos

Prep time: 25 minutes | Cook time: 1 to 2 hours | Serves 4

1 lime, sliced ¼ inch thick, plus 3 tablespoons lime juice plus lime wedges for serving
6 tablespoons minced fresh cilantro, stems reserved
¼ cup dry white wine
2 tablespoons extra-virgin olive oil
1 tablespoon minced canned chipotle chile in adobo sauce
½ teaspoon ground coriander
¼ teaspoon ground cumin
Salt and pepper, to taste
4 (6- to 8-ounce / 170- to 227-g) skinless halibut fillets, 1 to 1½ inches thick
4 cups shredded green cabbage
3 scallions, thinly sliced
¼ cup mayonnaise
¼ cup sour cream
2 garlic cloves, minced
12 (6-inch) corn tortillas, warmed

1. Fold sheet of aluminum foil into 12 by 9-inch sling and press widthwise into a slow cooker. Arrange lime slices in single layer in bottom of prepared slow cooker. Scatter cilantro stems over lime slices. Add wine to slow cooker, then add water until liquid level is even with lime slices (about ¼ cup).
2. Microwave 1 tablespoon oil, 2 teaspoons chipotle, coriander, cumin, ½ teaspoon salt, and ¼ teaspoon pepper in bowl until fragrant, about 30 seconds; let cool slightly. Rub halibut with spice mixture, then arrange in an even layer on top of cilantro stems. Cover and cook until halibut flakes apart when gently prodded with a paring knife and registers 140°F (60°C), 1 to 2 hours on low.
3. Combine cabbage, scallions, 2 tablespoons lime juice, ¼ cup cilantro, ¼ teaspoon salt, and remaining 1 tablespoon oil in the bowl. In a separate bowl, combine mayonnaise, sour cream, garlic, remaining 1 tablespoon lime juice, remaining 2 tablespoons cilantro, and remaining 1 teaspoon chipotle. Season with salt and pepper to taste.
4. Using sling, transfer halibut to cutting board. Gently lift and tilt fillets with spatula to remove cilantro stems and lime slices; discard poaching liquid and remove any white albumin from halibut. Cut each fillet into 3 equal pieces. Spread sauce evenly onto warm tortillas, top with fish and cabbage mixture, and serve with lime wedges.

Lemon-Dijon Orange Roughy

Prep time: 5 minutes | Cook time: 3 hours | Serves 4

1½ pounds (680 g) orange roughy fillets
2 tablespoons Dijon mustard
3 tablespoons butter, melted
1 teaspoon Worcestershire sauce
1 tablespoon lemon juice

1. Cut fillets to fit in the slow cooker.
2. In a bowl, mix remaining ingredients together. Pour sauce over fish. (If you have to stack the fish, spoon a portion of the sauce over the first layer of fish before adding the second layer.)
3. Cover and cook on low 3 hours, or until fish flakes easily but is not dry or overcooked.

Barbecued Shrimp

Prep time: 20 minutes | Cook time: 4 hours | Serves 6 to 8

1 cup (2 sticks) unsalted butter
¼ cup olive oil
8 cloves garlic, sliced
2 teaspoons dried oregano
1 teaspoon dried thyme
½ teaspoon freshly ground black pepper
Pinch of cayenne pepper
2 teaspoons sweet paprika
¼ cup Worcestershire sauce
¼ cup lemon juice
3 pounds (1.4 kg) large shrimp, peeled and deveined
½ cup finely chopped fresh Italian parsley

1. Put the butter, oil, garlic, oregano, thyme, pepper, cayenne, paprika, Worcestershire, and lemon juice in the insert of a slow cooker. Cover and cook on low for 4 hours.
2. Turn the cooker up to high and add the shrimp, tossing them in the butter sauce. Cover and cook for an additional 10 to 5 minutes, until the shrimp are pink.
3. Transfer the shrimp from the slow cooker to a large serving bowl and pour the sauce over the shrimp. Sprinkle with the parsley and serve.

Cheesy Salmon Casserole

Prep time: 10 minutes | Cook time: 2½ to 3½ hours | Serves 6

1 (14¾-ounce / 418-g) can salmon with liquid
1 (4-ounce / 113-g) can mushrooms, drained
1½ cups bread crumbs
⅓ cup eggbeaters
1 cup shredded fat-free cheese
1 tablespoon lemon juice
1 tablespoon minced onion

1.Flake fish in a bowl, removing bones. Stir in remaining ingredients. Pour into lightly greased slow cooker.
2.Cover. Cook on low 2½ to 3½ hours.

Halibut with Green Bean Salad

Prep time: 20 minutes | Cook time: 1 to 2 hours | Serves 4

1 (15-ounce / 425-g) can small white beans, rinsed
1 shallot, thinly sliced
2 (2-inch) strips lemon zest, plus 1 tablespoon juice
2 bay leaves
4 (6- to 8-ounce / 170- to 227-g) skinless halibut fillets, 1 to 1½ inches thick
2 tablespoons extra-virgin olive oil
Salt and pepper, to taste
8 ounces (227 g) green beans, trimmed and cut into 1-inch lengths
2 tablespoons minced fresh tarragon
1 teaspoon Dijon mustard
1 teaspoon honey
2 tablespoons chopped pitted kalamata olives

1.Stir white beans, ½ cup water, shallot, lemon zest, and bay leaves into slow cooker. Rub halibut with 1 tablespoon oil and season with salt and pepper. Nestle halibut into a slow cooker. Cover and cook until halibut flakes apart when gently prodded with a paring knife and registers 140ºF (60ºC), 1 to 2 hours on low.
2.Microwave green beans with 1 tablespoon water in the covered bowl, stirring occasionally, until tender, 4 to 6 minutes. Drain green beans and return to now-empty bowl. Whisk remaining 1 tablespoon oil, lemon juice, tarragon, mustard, and honey together in a separate bowl.
3.Transfer halibut to serving dish; discard lemon zest and bay leaves. Drain white bean mixture and transfer to bowl with green beans. Add dressing and olives and toss to combine. Season with salt and pepper to taste. Serve.

BBQ Tuna

Prep time: 10 minutes | Cook time: 8 to 10 hours | Serves 4

1 (12-ounce / 340-g) can tuna, drained
2 cups tomato juice
1 medium green pepper, finely chopped
2 tablespoons onion flakes
2 tablespoons Worcestershire sauce
3 tablespoons vinegar
2 tablespoons sugar
1 tablespoon prepared mustard
1 rib celery, chopped
Dash chili powder
½ teaspoon cinnamon
Dash of hot sauce (optional)

1.Combine all ingredients in a slow cooker.
2.Cover. Cook on low 8 to 10 hours, or on high 4 to 5 hours. If mixture becomes too dry while cooking, add ½ cup tomato juice.
3.Serve on buns.

Tuna and Egg Casserole

Prep time: 10 minutes | Cook time: 5 to 8 hours | Serves 4

2 (7-ounce / 198-g) cans tuna
1 (10¾-ounce / 305-g) can cream of celery soup
3 hard-boiled eggs, chopped
½ to 1½ cups diced celery
½ cup diced onions
½ cup mayonnaise
¼ teaspoon ground pepper
1½ cups crushed potato chips

1.Combine all ingredients except ¼ cup potato chips in slow cooker. Top with remaining chips.
2.Cover. Cook on low 5 to 8 hours.

Tuna and Veggie Casserole with Almonds

Prep time: 15 minutes | Cook time: 7 to 9 hours | Serves 6

2 (6½-ounce / 184-g) cans water-packed tuna, drained
2 (10½-ounce / 298-g) cans cream of mushroom soup
1 cup milk
2 tablespoons dried parsley
1 (10-ounce/ 283-g) package frozen mixed vegetables, thawed
1 (10-ounce / 283-g) package noodles, cooked and drained
½ cup toasted sliced almonds

1.Combine tuna, soup, milk, parsley, and vegetables. Fold in noodles. Pour into greased slow cooker. Top with almonds.
2.Cover. Cook on low 7 to 9 hours, or on high 3 to 4 hours.

Authentic Crab Cioppino with Tomatoes

Prep time: 20 minutes | Cook time: 4 to 6 hours | Serves 6

¼ cup olive oil
1 medium-size yellow onion, finely chopped
2 cloves garlic, minced
1 (15-ounce / 425-g) can tomato sauce
2 (28-ounce / 794-g) cans whole plum tomatoes, drained a bit (if packed in purée, don't drain)
1 cup dry white wine
1 bay leaf
1 tablespoon dried basil, or 3 tablespoons chopped fresh basil
1 teaspoon red pepper flakes
½ teaspoon dried oregano
Salt and freshly ground black pepper, to taste
3 steamed whole crabs, cracked and cleaned

1.In a medium-size skillet, heat the oil over medium heat, then cook the onion, stirring, until softened, about 5 minutes. Add the garlic and cook, stirring, for 2 minutes. Transfer to the slow cooker and add the tomato sauce, tomatoes, wine, bay leaf, basil, pepper flakes, and oregano. Break up the tomatoes with the back of a spoon. Cover and simmer on low for 4 to 6 hours.
2.Season with salt and pepper. Add the crab, cover, and cook on high for 20 to 30 minutes to heat the crab through. Serve immediately.

Creole Shrimp Stew

Prep time: 25 minutes | Cook time: 5 to 6 hours | Serves 6

1 (14½-ounce / 411-g) can diced tomatoes, with their juice
1 (14½-ounce / 411-g) can chicken broth
1½ cups chopped onions
1 cup deseeded and chopped green bell pepper
1 cup thinly sliced celery
2 cloves garlic, minced
1½ teaspoons paprika
½ teaspoon freshly ground black pepper
¼ teaspoon salt
¼ teaspoon hot pepper sauce, such as Tabasco
1 bay leaf
1 (6-ounce / 170-g) can tomato paste
1½ pounds (680 g) raw medium-size shrimp (31 to 35 count), peeled and deveined
1 medium-size bunch green onions (white part and a few inches of the green), chopped
1 tablespoon filé powder
For Serving:
3 cups hot cooked white or pecan rice
Hot pepper sauce, such as Tabasco

1.Combine the tomatoes with their juice, the broth, onions, bell pepper, celery, garlic, paprika, black pepper, salt, hot pepper sauce, and bay leaf in the slow cooker; stir in the tomato paste. Cover and cook on low for 5 to 6 hours or on high for 2½ to 3 hours.
2.Discard the bay leaf. Stir the shrimp, green onions, and filé powder into the hot tomato-vegetable mixture, cover, and cook until the shrimp are cooked through, about 5 minutes. Serve immediately over hot cooked rice with a bottle of hot pepper sauce on the side.

Seafood Confetti Chowder

Prep time: 30 minutes | Cook time: 5 to 6 hours | Serves 4 to 6

1½ tablespoons unsalted butter
1 small yellow onion, finely chopped
3 ribs celery, finely chopped
1 large or 2 small red bell peppers, deseeded and finely chopped
2 medium-size russet potatoes, peeled and cut into ½-inch dice
2 cups chicken broth
½ bay leaf
⅛ teaspoon paprika
1 teaspoon dried thyme or 1 tablespoon chopped fresh thyme
¼ teaspoon freshly ground black pepper
½ teaspoon salt or to taste
2 cups whole milk
1 cup half-and-half
2 cups frozen corn kernels, thawed
1 pound (454 g) shellfish, white-fleshed fish fillets, or a combination (choose fresh or individually quick-frozen shellfish), cleaned or shelled and cut into chunks, if necessary

1. In a medium-size skillet, heat the butter over medium-high heat. Add the onion and celery and cook, stirring a few times, until the onion is transparent, 2 to 3 minutes. Add the bell pepper and cook until it begins to soften, 2 to 3 minutes longer.
2. While the vegetables are cooking, put the potatoes in the slow cooker.
3. When the vegetables are ready, scrape them into the cooker along with any remaining butter. Add the broth, bay leaf, paprika, thyme, and black pepper. If the broth is unsalted, add the ½ teaspoon salt. Stir the top layer of the ingredients very gently, trying not to disturb the potatoes, which should stay submerged. Cover and cook on low until the potatoes are fork-tender, 5 to 6 hours.
4. Add the milk, half-and-half, corn, and seafood and stir to combine. Cover and cook on high until the chowder is heated through and the seafood is just cooked through, about 1 hour longer. Taste for salt and pepper. Remove the bay leaf before serving.

Slow Cooker Bay Scallops

Prep time: 15 minutes | Cook time: ¾ to 1¼ hours | Serves 4

2 tablespoons unsalted butter
2 tablespoons minced shallots
¼ cup dry vermouth
6 slices lemon
1⅓ pounds (590 g) bay scallops (or sea scallops, halved), rinsed and blotted dry
Pinch of sea salt
Pinch of white pepper
2 tablespoons minced fresh flat-leaf parsley (optional)
¼ cup crème fraîche (optional)

1. Combine the butter, shallots, vermouth, and lemon slices in the slow cooker. Cover and turn to high until the butter is melted, 15 to 30 minutes. It is very important to heat the poaching liquid first or the scallops will not cook properly.
2. Add the scallops and salt, tossing the scallops to coat with the poaching liquid. Cover and cook on high until opaque and firm, 30 to 45 minutes. Watch carefully so they don't overcook.
3. Discard the lemon slices and add a sprinkling of white pepper. Lift the scallops out of the poaching liquid and divide among 6 scallop shells or little ramekins. Serve as is sprinkled with a bit of parsley or add ¼ cup crème fraîche to the reserved poaching liquid to make a divine and decadent sauce. Spoon over the scallops.

Garlicky Crab in White Wine

Prep time: 10 minutes | Cook time: 5½ hours | Serves 6 to 8

1 cup (2 sticks) unsalted butter
½ cup olive oil
10 cloves garlic, sliced
2 tablespoons Old Bay seasoning
2 cups dry white wine or vermouth
1 lemon, thinly sliced
3 to 4 pounds (1.4 to 1.8 kg) cooked crab legs and claws, cracked

1. Put the butter, oil, garlic, seasoning, wine, and lemon in the insert of a slow cooker.
2. Cover and cook on low for 4 hours. Add the crab, spoon the sauce over the crab, and cook for an additional 1½ hours, turning the crab in the sauce during cooking.
3. Serve the crab from the cooker set on warm.

Scallops Braised in Dry Sherry

Prep time: 10 minutes | Cook time: 4½ hours | Serves 6

1 cup (2 sticks) unsalted butter
2 tablespoons olive oil
2 cloves garlic, minced
2 teaspoons sweet paprika
¼ cup dry sherry
2 pounds (907 g) dry-pack sea scallops
½ cup finely chopped fresh Italian parsley

1. Put the butter, oil, garlic, paprika, and sherry in the insert of a slower cooker.
2. Cover and cook on low for 4 hours. Turn the cooker to high and add the scallops, tossing them in the butter sauce. Cover and cook on high for 30 to 40 minutes, until the scallops are opaque.
3. Transfer the scallops and sauce from the slow cooker to a serving platter. Sprinkle with the parsley and serve.

Five-Ingredient Tuna Loaf

Prep time: 5 minutes | Cook time: 1 hour | Serves 4

1 (10¾-ounce / 305-g) can cream of mushroom soup, divided
¾ cup milk, divided
2 eggs, beaten
2 cups dry stuffing mix
1 (12-ounce / 340-g) can tuna, drained and flaked

1. Place ⅔ of the undiluted soup and ½ cup of the milk in a small saucepan. Blend together; then set aside.
2. Grease the interior of the slow cooker with nonstick cooking spray. Mix the rest of the ingredients together in the slow cooker.
3. Cover and cook on high for 1 hour. Allow to stand for 15 minutes before serving.
4. Meanwhile, heat the reserved soup and milk in the saucepan. Serve over the cooked tuna as a sauce.

Classic Bouillabaisse

Prep time: 25 minutes | Cook time: 6 to 8 hours | Serves 6 to 8

¼ cup extra-virgin olive oil
3 leeks, cleaned and coarsely chopped, using the white and tender green parts
4 cloves garlic, sliced
1 bulb fennel, ends trimmed, coarsely chopped
Grated zest of 1 orange
1 teaspoon dried thyme
1 teaspoon saffron threads, crushed
Pinch of cayenne pepper
1 (28- to 32-ounce / 794- to 907-g) can crushed tomatoes, with their juice
½ cup white wine or dry vermouth
3 cups clam juice
1 cup chicken broth
½ pound (227 g) littleneck clams
½ pound (227 g) mussels
3 pounds (1.4 kg) thick-fleshed fish, cut into 1-inch chunks
½ cup finely chopped fresh Italian parsley

1. Heat the oil in a large skillet over medium-high heat. Add the leeks, garlic, fennel, zest, thyme, saffron, and cayenne and sauté until the vegetables are softened, about 2 minutes. Add the tomatoes and wine and cook down for 10 minutes, to concentrate the flavors. Transfer the mixture to the insert of a slow cooker.
2. Add the clam juice and broth to the slow-cooker insert and stir to combine. Cover and cook on low for 6 to 8 hours. Remove the cover and place the clams and mussels in the sauce.
3. Place the fish on top of the shellfish and spoon the sauce over the top of the fish. Cover and cook on high for 45 minutes, until the fish is cooked through and opaque and the clams and mussels have opened.
4. Discard any clams and mussels that haven't opened. Sprinkle with the parsley and serve immediately.

Monterey Jack Seafood Pasta

Prep time: 15 minutes | Cook time: 1 to 2 hours | Serves 4 to 6

2 cups sour cream
3 cups shredded Monterey Jack cheese
2 tablespoons butter, melted
½ pound (227 g) crab meat or imitation flaked crab meat
⅛ teaspoon pepper
½ pound (227 g) bay scallops, lightly cooked
1 pound (454 g) medium shrimp, cooked and peeled

1. Combine sour cream, cheese, and butter in a slow cooker.
2. Stir in remaining ingredients.
3. Cover. Cook on low 1 to 2 hours.
4. Serve immediately over linguine. Garnish with fresh parsley.

Shrimp and Ham Jambalaya

Prep time: 20 minutes | Cook time: 2¼ hours | Serves 8

2 tablespoons margarine
2 medium onions, chopped
2 green bell peppers, chopped
3 ribs celery, chopped
1 cup chopped, cooked lean ham
2 garlic cloves, chopped
1½ cups minute rice, uncooked
1½ cups fat-free low sodium beef broth
1 (28-ounce / 794-g) can low-sodium chopped tomatoes
2 tablespoons fresh chopped parsley
1 teaspoon dried basil
½ teaspoon dried thyme
¼ teaspoon black pepper
⅛ teaspoon cayenne pepper
1 pound (454 g) medium-sized shrimp, shelled and deveined
1 tablespoon chopped parsley, for garnish

1. One-half hour before assembling recipe, melt margarine in a slow cooker set on high. Add onions, peppers, celery, ham, and garlic. Cook 30 minutes.
2. Add rice. Cover and cook 15 minutes.
3. Add broth, tomatoes, 2 tablespoons parsley, and remaining seasonings. Cover and cook on high 1 hour.
4. Add shrimp. Cook on high 30 minutes, or until liquid is absorbed.
5. Garnish with 1 tablespoon parsley.

Sumptuous Seafood Stew

Prep time: 25 minutes | Cook time: 6¾ hours | Serves 6 to 8

½ cup extra-virgin olive oil
2 medium onions, finely chopped
2 medium red bell peppers, deseeded and finely chopped
6 cloves garlic, minced
1 teaspoon saffron threads, crushed
1 teaspoon hot paprika
1 cup finely chopped Spanish chorizo or sopressata salami
1 (28- to 32-ounce / 794- to 907-g) can crushed tomatoes
2 cups clam juice
1 cup chicken broth
2 pounds (907 g) firm-fleshed fish, such as halibut, monkfish, cod, or sea bass fillets, cut into 1-inch chunks
1½ pounds (680 g) littleneck clams
½ cup finely chopped fresh Italian parsley

1. Heat the oil in a large skillet over medium-high heat. Add the onions, bell peppers, garlic, saffron, paprika, and chorizo and sauté until the vegetables are softened, 5 to 7 minutes. Add the tomatoes and transfer the contents of the skillet to the insert of a slow cooker. Add the clam juice and broth and stir to combine.
2. Cover and cook on low for 6 hours. Add the fish and clams to the slow-cooker insert, spooning some of the sauce over the fish and pushing the clams under the sauce.
3. Cover and cook for an additional 45 to 50 minutes, until the clams have opened and the fish is cooked through and opaque. Discard any clams that haven't opened.
4. Sprinkle the parsley over the stew and serve immediately.

Crab Angel Hair Pasta

Prep time: 15 minutes | Cook time: 4 to 6 hours | Serves 4 to 6

1 medium onion, chopped
½ pound (227 g) fresh mushrooms, sliced
2 (12-ounce / 340-g) cans low-sodium tomato sauce, or 1 (12-ounce / 340-g) can low-sodium tomato sauce and 1 (12-ounce / 340-g) can low-sodium chopped tomatoes
1 (6-ounce / 170-g) can tomato paste
½ teaspoon garlic powder
½ teaspoon dried basil
½ teaspoon dried oregano
½ teaspoon salt
1 pound (454 g) crab meat
16 ounces (454 g) angel hair pasta, cooked

1. Sauté onions and mushrooms in nonstick skillet over low heat. When wilted, place in a slow cooker.
2. Add tomato sauce, tomato paste, and seasonings. Stir in crab.
3. Cover. Cook on low 4 to 6 hours.
4. Serve over angel-hair pasta.

Creamy Braised Scallops with Leeks

Prep time: 20 minutes | Cook time: 3 to 4 hours | Serves 4

1 pound (454 g) leeks, white and light green parts only, halved lengthwise, thinly sliced, and washed thoroughly
4 garlic cloves, minced
1 teaspoon extra-virgin olive oil
⅓ cup heavy cream
¼ cup dry white wine
1½ pounds (680 g) large sea scallops, tendons removed
Salt and pepper, to taste
¼ cup grated Pecorino Romano cheese
2 tablespoons minced fresh parsley

1. Microwave leeks, garlic, and oil in bowl, stirring occasionally, until leeks are softened, about 5 minutes; transfer to a slow cooker. Stir in cream and wine. Cover and cook until leeks are tender but not mushy, 3 to 4 hours on low or 2 to 3 hours on high.
2. Season scallops with salt and pepper and nestle into a slow cooker. Spoon portion of sauce over scallops. Cover and cook on high until sides of scallops are firm and centers are opaque, 30 to 40 minutes.
3. Transfer scallops to serving dish. Stir Pecorino into sauce and season with salt and pepper to taste. Spoon sauce over scallops and sprinkle with parsley. Serve.

Green Chile and Shrimp Tacos

Prep time: 25 minutes | Cook time: 6 to 7 hours | Serves 4 to 6

4 poblano chiles, stemmed, deseeded, and cut into ½-inch-wide strips
3 onions, halved and thinly sliced
3 tablespoons extra-virgin olive oil
4 garlic cloves, thinly sliced
½ teaspoon dried oregano
Salt and pepper, to taste
1½ pounds (680 g) extra-large shrimp (21 to 25 per pound), peeled, deveined, tails removed, and cut into 1-inch pieces
2 tablespoons minced fresh cilantro
1 teaspoon grated lime zest plus 1 teaspoon juice
12 to 18 (6-inch) corn tortillas, warmed

1. Toss poblanos and onions with 2 tablespoons oil, garlic, oregano, ½ teaspoon salt, and ½ teaspoon pepper in slow cooker. Cover and cook until vegetables are tender, 6 to 7 hours on low or 4 to 5 hours on high.
2. Season shrimp with salt and pepper and stir into a slow cooker. Cover and cook on high until shrimp pieces are opaque throughout, 30 to 40 minutes. Strain shrimp mixture, discarding cooking liquid, and return to now-empty slow cooker. Stir in cilantro, lime zest and juice, and remaining 1 tablespoon oil. Season with salt and pepper to taste. Serve with tortillas.

Shrimp Spaghetti with Marinara

Prep time: 15 minutes | Cook time: 6¼ to 7¼ hours | Serves 6

1 (16-ounce / 454-g) can low-sodium tomatoes, cut up
2 tablespoons minced parsley
1 clove garlic, minced
½ teaspoon dried basil
½ teaspoon salt
¼ teaspoon black pepper
1 teaspoon dried oregano
1 (6-ounce / 170-g) can tomato paste
½ teaspoon seasoned salt
1 pound (454 g) shrimp, cooked and shelled
3 cups spaghetti
Grated Parmesan cheese, for serving

1. Combine tomatoes, parsley, garlic, basil, salt, pepper, oregano, tomato paste, and seasoned salt in a slow cooker.
2. Cover. Cook on low 6 to 7 hours.
3. Stir shrimp into sauce.
4. Cover. Cook on low 10 to 15 minutes.
5. Serve over cooked spaghetti. Top with Parmesan cheese.

Authentic Shrimp and Crab Gumbo

Prep time: 25 minutes | Cook time: 3 to 4 hours | Serves 10

1 pound (454 g) okra, sliced
2 tablespoons butter, melted
¼ cup butter, melted
¼ cup flour
1 bunch green onions, sliced
½ cup chopped celery
2 garlic cloves, minced
1 (16-ounce / 454-g) can tomatoes and juice
1 bay leaf
1 tablespoon chopped fresh parsley
1 fresh thyme sprig
1½ teaspoons salt
½ to 1 teaspoon red pepper
3 to 5 cups water, depending upon the consistency you like
1 pound (454 g) fresh shrimp, peeled and deveined

½ pound (227 g) fresh crab meat

1. Sauté okra in 2 tablespoons butter until okra is lightly browned. Transfer to a slow cooker.
2. Combine remaining butter and flour in the skillet. Cook over medium heat, stirring constantly until roux is the color of chocolate, 20 to 25 minutes. Stir in green onions, celery, and garlic. Cook until vegetables are tender. Add to a slow cooker. Gently stir in remaining ingredients.
3. Cover. Cook on high 3 to 4 hours.
4. Serve over rice.

Thai Green Curry Shrimp

Prep time: 25 minutes | Cook time: 4½ to 5½ hours | Serves 4 to 6

2 cups chicken broth, plus extra as needed
2 tablespoons Thai green curry paste
2 tablespoons instant tapioca
2 pounds (907 g) sweet potatoes, peeled and cut into 1-inch pieces
1 (13½-ounce / 383-g) can coconut milk
1½ pounds (680 g) large shrimp, peeled, deveined, and tails removed
Salt and pepper, to taste
2 tablespoons lime juice
1 tablespoon fish sauce
8 ounces (227 g) snow peas, strings removed and cut into 1-inch pieces
1 tablespoon vegetable oil
½ cup fresh cilantro leaves

1. Whisk broth, curry paste, and tapioca together in a slow cooker, then stir in potatoes. Cover and cook until flavors meld and potatoes are tender, 4 to 5 hours on low or 3 to 4 hours on high.
2. Microwave coconut milk in bowl until hot, about 2 minutes. Season shrimp with salt and pepper. Stir shrimp, coconut milk, lime juice, and fish sauce into curry. Cover and cook on high until shrimp are opaque throughout, about 30 minutes.
3. Microwave snow peas and oil in bowl, stirring occasionally, until snow peas are tender, 3 to 5 minutes. Stir snow peas into curry. Adjust consistency with extra hot broth as needed. Stir in cilantro and season with salt and pepper to taste. Serve.

Creamy Shrimp Curry

Prep time: 5 minutes | Cook time: 2 to 3 hours | Serves 4 to 5

1 small onion, chopped
2 cups cooked shrimp
1 teaspoon curry powder
1 (10¾-ounce / 305-g) can cream of mushroom soup
1 cup sour cream

1. Combine all ingredients except sour cream in a slow cooker.
2. Cover. Cook on low 2 to 3 hours.
3. Ten minutes before serving, stir in sour cream.
4. Serve over rice or puff pastry.

Asian Shrimp and Rice Casserole

Prep time: 10 minutes | Cook time: 45 minutes | Serves 10

4 cups rice, cooked
2 cups cooked or canned shrimp
1 cup cooked or canned chicken
1 (1-pound / 454-g) can Chinese vegetables
1 (10¾-ounce / 305-g) can cream of celery soup
½ cup milk
½ cup chopped green peppers
1 tablespoon soy sauce
1 can Chinese noodles

1. Combine all ingredients except noodles in a slow cooker.
2. Cover. Cook on low 45 minutes.
3. Top with noodles just before serving.

Ritzy Seafood Medley

Prep time: 20 minutes | Cook time: 3 to 4 hours | Serves 10 to 12

1 pound (454 g) shrimp, peeled and deveined
1 pound (454 g) crab meat
1 pound (454 g) bay scallops
2 (10¾-ounce / 305-g) cans cream of celery soup
2 soup cans milk
2 tablespoons butter, melted
1 teaspoon Old Bay seasoning
¼ to ½ teaspoon salt
¼ teaspoon pepper

1. Layer shrimp, crab, and scallops in a slow cooker.
2. Combine soup and milk. Pour over seafood.
3. Mix together butter and spices and pour over top.
4. Cover. Cook on low 3 to 4 hours.
5. Serve over rice or noodles.

Chapter 12 Rice, Grains, and Beans

Creamy Saffron Rice

Prep time: 10 minutes | Cook time: 1½ to 2 hours | Serves 6

1⅓ cups basmati rice
Pinch saffron
1 tablespoon vegetable oil
1 teaspoon cumin seeds
3⅓ cups hot water
1 teaspoon salt
1 tablespoon butter
4 tablespoons cream

1. Wash the rice in two or three changes of water until the water runs clear. Then leave it to soak in warm water while you prep the rest of the dish.
2. Grind a few threads of saffron in a mortar and pestle. Add 2 tablespoons of hot water and stir. Set aside.
3. Preheat the slow cooker to high and add the oil. Add the cumin seeds and let them toast.
4. Pour the hot water, salt, butter, and cream into the slow cooker. Strain the soaked rice and add to the slow cooker.
5. Stir and cover with the lid. Cook on high for 1½ to 2 hours. Halfway through the cooking, very gently stir the rice.
6. Turn off the cooker and sprinkle in the saffron water. Let it stand, uncovered, for 5 to 10 minutes. Fluff the rice with a fork and serve.

Mushroom Risotto

Prep time: 10 minutes | Cook time: 6 to 8 hours | Serves 2

1 ounce (28 g) dried wild mushrooms
1 teaspoon extra-virgin olive oil
½ cup minced onion
1 cup diced button mushrooms
1 teaspoon fresh thyme
1 cup short-grain white rice
2 cups low-sodium chicken or vegetable broth
⅛ teaspoon sea salt
Freshly ground black pepper, to taste

2 tablespoons grated Parmesan cheese
2 tablespoons minced fresh parsley, for garnish
½ lemon, cut into wedges, for garnish

1. Soak the dried mushrooms in 1 cup of very hot water while you prepare the other ingredients.
2. While the mushrooms are soaking, grease the inside of the slow cooker with the olive oil. Add the onion, button mushrooms, thyme, rice, and broth. Season with the salt and pepper and stir everything to mix well.
3. Remove the soaked mushrooms from the hot water, roughly chop them, and add them to the slow cooker.
4. Cover and cook on low for 6 to 8 hours, until the rice is tender and all the liquid is absorbed. Just before serving, stir in the Parmesan cheese and garnish each serving with the fresh parsley and a lemon wedge.

Cranberry Sweet Potato and Wild Rice

Prep time: 10 minutes | Cook time: 6 to 8 hours | Serves 2

1 teaspoon extra-virgin olive oil
¾ cup wild rice
1 medium sweet potato, peeled and cut into 1-inch pieces
¼ cup minced celery
¼ cup minced onion
¼ cup dried cranberries
1 teaspoon minced fresh sage
1 teaspoon minced fresh thyme
2 cups low-sodium chicken broth
⅛ teaspoon sea salt

1. Grease the inside of the slow cooker with the olive oil.
2. Put the remaining ingredients in the slow cooker and stir them to mix thoroughly.
3. Cover and cook on low for 6 to 8 hours until the rice has absorbed all the liquid and is tender. Serve hot.

Parmesan and Shallot Risotto

Prep time: 10 minutes | Cook time: 2 to 2½ hours | Serves 3 to 4

¼ cup olive oil
2 medium-size shallots, minced
¼ cup dry white wine
1¼ cups Arborio, Vialone nano, or Carnaroli rice
3¾ cups chicken broth
½ teaspoon salt
¾ cup freshly grated Parmigiano-Reggiano cheese

1.In a small skillet over medium heat, warm the oil. Cook the shallots until softened, 3 to 4 minutes. Add the wine and cook, stirring, for a minute or so. Add the rice and cook, stirring, until it turns from translucent to opaque (do not brown), about 2 minutes. Scrape with a rubber spatula into the slow cooker.
2.Add the broth and salt and stir well. Cover and cook on high until all the liquid is absorbed, but the rice is still moist, 2 to 2½ hours. The risotto should be only a bit liquidy, and the rice should be al dente, tender with just a touch of firmness.
3.Stir in ½ cup of the cheese and pass the remainder for sprinkling. Serve immediately, spooned into bowls.

Creamy Risotto with Edamame

Prep time: 10 minutes | Cook time: 1¾ to 2¼ hours | Serves 3 to 4

3 cups chicken broth, or 1 (15-ounce / 425-g) can low-sodium broth plus water to equal 3 cups
1 pound (454 g) in-the-pod edamame, or 1 cup shelled edamame
1 tablespoon olive oil
2 tablespoons unsalted butter, divided
1 small yellow onion, chopped
1 cup Arborio, Vialone nano, or Carnaroli rice
⅓ cup freshly grated Parmesan cheese, plus more for serving
Salt and freshly ground black pepper, to taste

1.In a large saucepan, bring the broth to a boil. Add the edamame and cook as long as specified on the package, generally about 5 minutes.

Remove the beans from the broth with a slotted spoon and spread them out on a large plate. Reserve the broth. If you are using in-the-pod edamame, as soon as they are cool enough to handle, pinch the pods to remove the beans. Discard the pods.
2.In a small skillet over medium heat, warm the oil and 1 tablespoon of the butter, add the onion, and cook, stirring, until softened, 3 to 4 minutes. Then add the rice, stirring, until it turns from translucent to opaque (do not brown), about 2 minutes. Scrape the rice with a rubber spatula into the slow cooker.
3.Add the warm broth. Cover and cook on high for 1¾ to 2¼ hours. The risotto should be only a bit liquidy and the rice should be al dente, tender with just a touch of firmness.
4.Stir in the edamame and the remaining 1 tablespoon of butter. Cover and wait about 5 minutes for the edamame to warm up and the butter to soften. Stir in the cheese and season with salt and pepper. Serve immediately, spooned into a bowl, with more Parmesan for sprinkling.

Pumpkin Cheese Grits

Prep time: 10 minutes | Cook time: 3 to 3½ hours | Serves 4

⅔ cup coarse, stone-ground grits
1½ cups water
1 cup evaporated milk
1 teaspoon salt
1 cup mashed cooked pumpkin
A few grinds of black pepper
¼ cup (½ stick) unsalted butter
½ cup finely shredded Cheddar cheese

1.Combine the grits and some cold water in a bowl (the husks will rise to the top). Drain in a mesh strainer.
2.Combine the grits, 1½ cups of water, evaporated milk, and salt in the slow cooker. With a wooden or plastic spoon, stir for 15 seconds. Add the pumpkin and pepper, cover, and cook on high for 3 to 3½ hours or on low for 7 to 9 hours, until thick and creamy.
3.Stir in the butter and cheese, cover, turn off the cooker, and let the mixture rest for 10 minutes to melt the butter and cheese. Serve immediately.

Converted White Rice

Prep time: 5 minutes | Cook time: 1½ hours | Serves 4

1 cup converted white rice
2 cups water
½ teaspoon salt (optional)
1 tablespoon unsalted butter (optional)

1. Place the rice, water, and salt (if using) in the slow cooker and stir to combine. Use a spoon to smooth the rice into as even a layer as possible. Add the butter, if using. Cover and cook on high for 1½ hours or on low for 2½ hours.
2. Turn off the cooker. Use a fork to gently stir and fluff the rice, breaking up any clumps. Serve immediately. Or, if you are not ready to eat, cover the rice. It will stay hot for about 1 hour. (Leave the insert in the cooker to help conserve the heat.)

Kedgeree (Spiced Rice with Smoked Fish)

Prep time: 20 minutes | Cook time: 3 hours | Serves 6

2 cups basmati rice
1 tablespoon ghee
2 teaspoons mustard seeds
2 teaspoons ground cumin seeds
2-inch (5-cm) piece fresh ginger, grated
2 garlic cloves, finely chopped
2 fresh bay leaves
2 fresh red chiles, finely chopped
1 bunch scallions, finely chopped
1 teaspoon turmeric
2 tomatoes, finely chopped
Sea salt, to taste
3¾ cups hot water
10 ounces (283 g) smoked fish fillets
3 large eggs
2 handfuls fresh coriander leaves, chopped
Juice of 1 lemon

1. Wash the rice and soak for 10 minutes.
2. Heat the ghee in a frying pan (or in the slow cooker if you have a sear setting). Add the mustard seeds and cook until they pop. Then add the cumin seeds. Once fragrant (a few seconds), add the ginger, garlic, bay leaves, chiles, scallions, turmeric, tomatoes and season with salt. Cook for 5 minutes.
3. Add the rice and hot water. Place the fish on top, skin-side down, and cook on high for 3 hours.
4. Meanwhile, on the stovetop, hard boil the eggs, and set aside.
5. After cooking for 3 hours, gently lift the fish out and remove the skin and bones.
6. When you are ready to eat, flake the fish into the rice, add the coriander leaves and lemon juice, and fold through.
7. Peel the shells from the eggs, slice into quarters, and arrange on top of the rice, and serve.

Double-Corn Spoonbread with Cheese

Prep time: 10 minutes | Cook time: 3 to 3½ hours | Serves 4 to 6

3 cups milk
½ cup medium-grind yellow cornmeal
1¼ teaspoons salt
¼ cup (½ stick) unsalted butter, cut into pieces
2 cups fresh yellow or white corn kernels or thawed frozen baby corn
1 teaspoon hot pepper sauce, such as Tabasco
1 tablespoon baking powder
6 large eggs
1 cup thinly shredded Cheddar cheese
Nonstick cooking spray

1. Whisk together the milk, cornmeal, and salt in a large saucepan over high heat until the mixture comes to a boil. Reduce the heat to a simmer and cook until thickened, about 1 minute. Stir in the butter until melted, the corn, and hot pepper sauce. Sprinkle with the baking powder and whisk in the eggs until completely smooth. Fold in the cheese.
2. Coat the slow cooker with nonstick cooking spray. Pour in the batter. Cover and cook on high until the spoonbread looks set but is not quite firm, 3 to 3½ hours. Serve immediately, scooped onto plates.

Sausage Spanish Brown Rice

Prep time: 15 minutes | Cook time: 8 to 9 hours | Serves 6

½ cup diced yellow onion
1 clove garlic, minced
1 medium-size red bell pepper, deseeded, and coarsely chopped
1 (15- to 16-ounce / 425- to 454-g) can crushed tomatoes, with their juice
1½ cups water
2 teaspoons chili powder
2 teaspoons Worcestershire sauce
¾ cup short-grain brown rice
1 tablespoon chopped jalapeño
1 pound (454 g) Santa Fe-style sausage or any other fully cooked spicy sausage, diced

1. Combine all the ingredients in the slow cooker and stir to evenly distribute.
2. Cover and cook on low for 8 to 9 hours. Serve hot.

Almond-Mushroom Wild Rice

Prep time: 10 minutes | Cook time: 4½ to 6 hours | Serves 6

2 cups wild rice
1 cup slivered almonds
1 to 2 shallots, finely chopped
½ cup finely chopped celery
8 ounces (227 g) fresh mushrooms, chopped or sliced
6 cups vegetable broth
Salt and freshly ground black pepper, to taste

1. Rinse the rice under cold running water until the water runs clear, then drain.
2. Place all the ingredients except the salt and pepper in the slow cooker. Stir to combine. Cover and cook on low until the kernels are open and tender, but not mushy, 4½ to 6 hours. Do not remove the lid before the rice has cooked at least 4 hours.
3. Season with salt and pepper, and serve immediately.

Aromatic Vegetable Pulao

Prep time: 10 minutes | Cook time: 2 hours | Serves 6

1½ cups basmati rice
1 tablespoon rapeseed oil
2 bay leaves
2-inch (5-cm) piece cassia bark
1 tablespoon black peppercorns
1 tablespoon cumin seeds
1 tablespoon coriander seeds
4 green cardamom pods
2 black cardamom pods
3 cloves
2 medium onions, chopped
1 teaspoon salt
1 tablespoon freshly grated ginger
1 garlic clove, chopped
2 fresh green chiles, chopped
1 teaspoon turmeric
Handful mint leaves, chopped
Handful fresh coriander leaves, chopped
2½ cups hot water
12 ounces (340 g) frozen mixed vegetables, thawed

1. Wash the rice in a few changes of water until the water runs clear. Soak the rice in warm water for 10 minutes.
2. Heat the oil in a frying pan (or in the slow cooker if you have a sear setting). Add the bay leaves, cassia bark, peppercorns, cumin, and coriander seeds, green and black cardamom pods, and cloves. Sauté for 2 minutes until the spices become aromatic.
3. Add the chopped onions and cook for about 5 minutes until soft. Stir in the salt with the ginger, garlic, green chiles, turmeric, mint, and coriander leaves. Transfer to the slow cooker. Then add the rice and hot water. Stir through gently.
4. Cover the slow cooker and cook on high for 1½ hours or 3 hours on low. Stir the rice once during the cooking time.
5. Switch the cooker to the warming function, add the mixed vegetables, and stir through gently. Cover and leave to steam for 20 minutes.
6. Remove the lid and leave the rice to stand for about 5 minutes before fluffing it with a fork to serve.

Orange Pearl Barley with Apple

Prep time: 10 minutes | Cook time: 3 to 4 hours | Serves 4

1 cup orange juice
1 cup vegetable or chicken broth
⅓ cup pearl barley
¼ cup dried currants
¼ cup dried apricots, cut into strips
¼ cup chopped pitted dates
1 tart apple, peeled, cored, and chopped
2 tablespoons chopped pecans

1.Combine all the ingredients in the slow cooker and stir to distribute them evenly.
2.Cover and cook on low for 3 to 4 hours. Serve hot.

Mujedrah

Prep time: 15 minutes | Cook time: 1½ to 2 hours | Serves 3 to 4

¾ cup dried brown or green lentils
¾ cup converted white rice
3 cups water
¾ to 1 teaspoon salt, to your taste
Freshly ground black pepper, to taste

Onion Topping:
3 medium-size or 2 large red onions, sliced ¼ inch thick
2 tablespoons olive oil

Yogurt Sauce:
1 cup plain yogurt
½ cup finely diced or coarsely grated cucumber (peel first if skin is bitter and scoop out seeds)
1 tablespoon chopped fresh mint
¼ teaspoon salt, or more to taste

1.Pick over the lentils and discard any damaged ones. Rinse in a fine-mesh strainer under cold running water and drain. Combine them in the slow cooker with the rice and water, cover, and cook on high until the lentils and rice are tender, 1½ to 2 hours.
2.Add ¾ teaspoon of the salt and 1 grind of pepper, then stir the rice and lentils gently with a wooden or plastic spoon, taking care not to mash the lentils. Taste and adjust the seasonings if

necessary.
3.While the lentils and rice are cooking, prepare the onion topping and the yogurt sauce. To make the onion topping, in a large skillet, heat the oil over medium-high heat. Add the onions, reduce the heat to medium-low, and cook, stirring occasionally, until they are very browned but not burned (this will take at least 20 minutes).
4.To make the yogurt sauce, stir together the yogurt, cucumber, mint, and salt in a small bowl. Refrigerate and cover until ready to serve.
5.To serve, place the lentil-and-rice mixture on individual plates or a large serving platter. Top with the onions and offer the yogurt sauce alongside.

Parmesan Polenta

Prep time: 5 minutes | Cook time: 6 hours | Serves 8

7½ cups water
1½ cups coarse-ground yellow polenta
1½ teaspoons salt
½ cup (1 stick) unsalted butter
1 cup grated or shredded Parmesan or Italian fontina cheese

1.Whisk the water, polenta, and salt together in the slow cooker for a few seconds. Cover and cook on high for 30 minutes to 1 hour to heat the water.
2.Stir with a wooden spoon, cover, turn the cooker to low, and cook for about 5 hours, stirring occasionally. The polenta will thicken quite quickly after 2 hours, sort of expand magically in the cooker, and look done, but it will need the extra time to cook all the grains evenly. At 5 hours, taste and make sure the desired consistency has been reached and all the grains are tender. The longer the polenta cooks, the creamier it will become. When done, it will be smooth, very thick (yet pourable), and a wooden spoon will stand up by itself without falling over (the true test). The polenta will be fine on low for an additional hour, if necessary. Add a bit more hot water if it gets too stiff.
3.To serve as a mound of soft polenta, portion out with an oversized spoon onto plates or into shallow soup bowls. Top each serving with a pat of the butter and sprinkle with some of the cheese. Serve immediately.

Chickpea Curry

Prep time: 10 minutes | Cook time: 10 hours | Serves 6

2 cups dried chickpeas
1 tablespoon rapeseed oil
2 teaspoons cumin seeds
2 bay leaves
2¾-inch (7-cm) piece cassia bark
2 medium onions, thinly sliced
1 teaspoon salt
1 tablespoon freshly grated ginger
6 garlic cloves, finely chopped
2 fresh green chiles, chopped
2 medium tomatoes, finely chopped
1 teaspoon Kashmiri chili powder
2 teaspoons ground coriander seeds
½ teaspoon turmeric
2 teaspoons mango powder
½ teaspoon black salt
4 cups hot water
1 tablespoon lemon juice
Sliced red onions, for garnish
Fresh coriander leaves, roughly chopped, for garnish
2 fresh green chiles, sliced lengthwise
1 teaspoon chaat masala

1. Wash the chickpeas and set them aside to drain.
2. Heat the oil in a frying pan (or in the slow cooker if you have a sear setting). Add the cumin seeds, bay leaves, and cassia bark, and cook until fragrant, about 1 minute.
3. Stir in the sliced onions and salt, and cook for 5 to 6 minutes. Add the ginger, garlic, and chopped chiles and stir for 1 to 2 minutes.
4. Transfer to the slow cooker. Then add the chickpeas, tomatoes, chili powder, ground coriander seeds, turmeric, mango powder, black salt, and hot water.
5. Cover and cook for 10 hours on low, or for 8 hours on high.
6. Leave the cooker on warm until ready to serve. Then top with sliced red onions, freshly chopped coriander leaves, sliced green chiles, and a sprinkle of chaat masala.

Tex-Mex Quinoa Salad

Prep time: 10 minutes | Cook time: 8 hours | Serves 2

1 cup quinoa, rinsed
2 cups low-sodium vegetable broth
½ cup minced onion
1 teaspoon minced garlic
½ cup corn kernels
½ cup black beans, drained and rinsed
½ cup canned fire-roasted diced tomatoes, undrained
½ jalapeño pepper, deseeded and minced
1 teaspoon ground cumin
½ teaspoon smoked paprika
⅛ teaspoon sea salt

1. Put all the ingredients into the slow cooker and stir everything to mix thoroughly.
2. Cover and cook on low for 8 hours. Serve warm.

Rosemary Lentils with Ham and Carrot

Prep time: 20 minutes | Cook time: 3½ to 4 hours | Serves 8

2 medium-size yellow onions, chopped
2 cups diced cooked ham
1 cup diced carrot or parsnip
1 cup chopped celery
2 cloves garlic, chopped
¾ teaspoon dried rosemary, crushed
¾ teaspoon rubbed sage
¼ teaspoon freshly ground black pepper
1 bay leaf
1 pound (454 g) dried brown lentils, picked over and rinsed
1 (14½-ounce / 411-g) can beef broth
5 cups water, or as needed to cover everything by 3 inches
Chopped fresh flat-leaf parsley, for serving (optional)

1. Combine all the ingredients in the slow cooker, except the parsley. Cover and cook on high until the lentils are tender, 3½ to 4 hours. Add boiling water if you want soupier lentils.
2. Discard the bay leaf. Garnish with parsley, if desired, before serving.

Black Lentil and Split Chickpea Dhal

Prep time: 15 minutes | Cook time: 10 hours | Serves 6

4 cups water
¾ cup split gram, washed
¾ cup black lentils, washed and checked for stones
7 to 8 ounces (198 to 227 g) canned tomatoes
1 tablespoon vegetable oil
1 heaped teaspoon freshly grated ginger
1 teaspoon turmeric
1 teaspoon salt
2 garlic cloves, minced
2 fresh green chiles, finely chopped
1 onion, finely diced
1 teaspoon garam masala
Handful fresh coriander leaves, chopped

1.Add all the ingredients except the garam masala and coriander leaves to the slow cooker. Cover and cook on low for 10 hours, or on high for 8 hours.
2.To serve, sprinkle with garam masala and coriander leaves.

Red Lentil Dhal with Tomatoes

Prep time: 15 minutes | Cook time: 2 hours | Serves 6

2 cups red lentils, rinsed
1 small onion, chopped
1 teaspoon salt, plus more as needed
1 bay leaf
3 garlic cloves, chopped
2 tomatoes, finely chopped
1 teaspoon freshly grated ginger
1 teaspoon turmeric
1 or 2 fresh green chiles, finely chopped
4 cups hot water
1 tablespoon ghee or vegetable oil
1 teaspoon cumin seeds
1 dried red chile
1 teaspoon dried fenugreek leaves
1 teaspoon garam masala
Chopped fresh coriander leaves, for garnish

1.Place the lentils, onion, salt, bay leaf, garlic,

tomatoes, ginger, turmeric, chiles, and hot water into the slow cooker. Cover and cook on high for 2 hours, or on low for 4 hours.
2.Make the tharka to finish the dish: Heat the ghee or vegetable oil in a frying pan and add the cumin seeds. Cook until fragrant, about 1 minute. Then add the whole dried chile. Toast for a second, then pour into the cooked lentils. Stir in the fenugreek and garam masala.
3.Check the seasoning, and if required, add a little salt. Top with a pinch of coriander leaves to serve. If you prefer your dhal a little thicker, leave it to simmer with the lid off until it has thickened.

Chili Yellow Mung Beans

Prep time: 10 minutes | Cook time: 2 hours | Serves 6

2 cups yellow mung beans
2-inch (5-cm) piece fresh ginger, roughly chopped
2 fresh green chiles
1 tablespoon rapeseed oil
1 teaspoon mustard seeds
1 teaspoon cumin seeds
2 dried red chiles
1 bay leaf
1 teaspoon chili powder
1 teaspoon turmeric
1 teaspoon ground coriander seeds
1 teaspoon salt
⅓ cup water
1 lime, quartered

1.Wash the mung beans in several changes of water until the water runs clear. Drain the beans and leave them in the sieve.
2.In a mortar and pestle, pound the ginger with the green chiles to form a paste.
3.Heat the oil in a frying pan (or in the slow cooker if you have a sear setting). Add the mustard and cumin seeds. When they begin to crackle, add the dried red chiles, bay leaf, and ginger paste. Cook for a few seconds.
4.Transfer everything to the slow cooker. Add the yellow mung beans and mix.
5.Add the chili powder, turmeric, coriander seeds, salt, and water, then stir.
6.Cover and cook on low for 2 hours, or on high for 1 hour. Serve with a squeeze of lime juice.

Barley Risotto Primavera

Prep time: 20 minutes | Cook time: 8 hours | Serves 2

1 teaspoon extra-virgin olive oil
½ cup minced onion
½ cup diced carrot
1 cup diced zucchini
1 cup diced red bell pepper
1 teaspoon minced garlic
1 (15-ounce / 425-g) can whole plum tomatoes, undrained, hand-crushed
2 tablespoons tomato paste
1 tablespoon Italian herbs
¾ cup pearl barley
1½ cups low-sodium chicken or vegetable broth
⅛ teaspoon sea salt
½ cup roughly chopped fresh basil, for garnish

1.Grease the inside of the slow cooker with the olive oil.
2.Put the onion, carrot, zucchini, bell pepper, garlic, tomatoes, tomato paste, Italian herbs, barley, broth, and salt in the slow cooker, and mix thoroughly.
3.Cover and cook on low for 8 hours, until the barley is tender and all the liquid is absorbed.
4.Garnish each serving with the fresh basil.

Cuban Black Beans

Prep time: 15 minutes | Cook time: 8 to 9 hours | Serves 6

6 cups water, plus extra as needed
1 pound (454 g) dried black beans (2½ cups), picked over and rinsed
1 (12-ounce / 340-g) smoked ham hock, rinsed
2 bay leaves
1 onion, finely chopped
1 green bell pepper, stemmed, deseeded, and minced
6 garlic cloves, minced
2 tablespoons extra-virgin olive oil
2 tablespoons minced fresh oregano or 2 teaspoons dried
1½ teaspoons ground cumin
½ cup minced fresh cilantro
1 tablespoon lime juice, plus extra for seasoning
Salt and pepper, to taste

1.Combine water, beans, ham hock, and bay leaves in a slow cooker. Cover and cook until beans are tender, 8 to 9 hours on high.
2.Transfer ham hock to a cutting board, let cool slightly, then shred into bite-size pieces using 2 forks, discarding fat, skin, and bones. Discard bay leaves.
3.Microwave onion, bell pepper, garlic, oil, oregano, and cumin in a bowl, stirring occasionally, until vegetables are tender, 8 to 10 minutes.
4.Drain beans, reserving 1½ cups cooking liquid. Add vegetable mixture, one-third of beans, and reserved cooking liquid to the slow cooker and mash with potato masher until mostly smooth. Stir in remaining beans, ham, cilantro, and lime juice. Season with salt, pepper, and extra lime juice to taste. Serve. (Beans can be held on warm or low setting for up to 2 hours; adjust consistency with extra hot water as needed before serving.)

Ratatouille Quinoa Casserole

Prep time: 20 minutes | Cook time: 8 hours | Serves 2

1 teaspoon extra-virgin olive oil
1 cup diced eggplant
1 cup diced zucchini
½ teaspoon sea salt
1 (15-ounce / 425-g) can whole plum tomatoes, undrained, hand-crushed
1 teaspoon minced garlic
½ cup minced onion
1 cup quinoa
1 teaspoon herbes de Provence
1½ cups low-sodium chicken or vegetable broth

1.Grease the inside of the slow cooker with the olive oil.
2.Put the eggplant and zucchini in a colander in the sink. Season them liberally with the salt and allow it to rest for 10 minutes, or up to 30 minutes if you have the time.
3.Put the tomatoes, garlic, onion, quinoa, herbes de Provence, and broth in the slow cooker.
4.Rinse the eggplant and zucchini under cool water and gently press any excess moisture from the salted vegetables before adding to them to the slow cooker. Mix everything thoroughly.
5.Cover and cook on low for 8 hours. Serve warm.

Red Kidney Bean Curry

Prep time: 15 minutes | Cook time: 8 hours | Serves 6

1½ cups red kidney beans
4 cups hot water
7 to 8 ounces (198 to 227 g) canned plum tomatoes
2 teaspoons freshly grated ginger
1 teaspoon salt, plus more for seasoning
1 teaspoon turmeric
4 garlic cloves, finely chopped
1 or 2 fresh green chiles, sliced
1 onion, finely diced
1 teaspoon garam masala
Handful fresh coriander leaves, chopped
1 teaspoon butter (optional)

1. Soak the kidney beans overnight, then rinse. If you have a boil function on your slow cooker, cover the beans with water and boil for 10 minutes. If not, do this in a large pot. Drain and put the beans back into the slow cooker.
2. Add the remaining ingredients except the garam masala, coriander leaves, and butter. Cover and cook on low for 8 hours, or on high for 6 hours.
3. Add the garam masala, chopped coriander leaves, and butter (if using). Season with salt and serve.

Braised Lentils with Escarole and Cheese

Prep time: 10 minutes | Cook time: 3 to 4 hours | Serves 6 to 8

1 onion, finely chopped
3 tablespoons extra-virgin olive oil, divided
3 garlic cloves, minced
½ teaspoon red pepper flakes
2½ cups vegetable or chicken broth
1 cup French green lentils, picked over and rinsed
1 head escarole (1 pound / 454 g), trimmed and sliced 1 inch thick
1 ounce (28 g) Parmesan cheese, grated (½ cup)
1 tablespoon lemon juice, plus extra for seasoning
Salt and pepper, to taste

1. Microwave onion, 1 tablespoon oil, garlic, and pepper flakes in a bowl, stirring occasionally, until onion is softened, about 5 minutes. Transfer to a slow cooker. Stir in broth and lentils, cover, and cook until lentils are tender, 3 to 4 hours on low or 2 to 3 hours on high.
2. Stir in escarole, 1 handful at a time, until slightly wilted. Cover and cook on high until escarole is completely wilted, about 10 minutes. Stir in Parmesan, lemon juice, and remaining 2 tablespoons oil. Season with salt, pepper, and extra lemon juice to taste. Serve.

Mexican Pinto Beans

Prep time: 20 minutes | Cook time: 8 to 9 hours | Serves 6

1 onion, finely chopped
2 tablespoons extra-virgin olive oil, divided
4 garlic cloves, minced
1 tablespoon minced fresh oregano or 1 teaspoon dried
1 tablespoon chili powder
2 teaspoons minced canned chipotle chile in adobo sauce
Salt and pepper, to taste
5 cups water, plus extra as needed
1 pound (454 g) dried pinto beans, picked over and rinsed
1 cup mild lager, such as Budweiser
2 tablespoons minced fresh cilantro
1 tablespoon packed brown sugar
1 tablespoon lime juice, plus extra for seasoning

1. Microwave onion, 1 tablespoon oil, garlic, oregano, chili powder, chipotle, and 1 teaspoon salt in a bowl, stirring occasionally, until onion is softened, about 5 minutes. Transfer to a slow cooker. Stir in water, beans, and beer. Cover and cook until beans are tender, 8 to 9 hours on high.
2. Drain beans, reserving 1 cup cooking liquid. Return beans and reserved cooking liquid to the slow cooker. Stir in cilantro, sugar, lime juice, and remaining 1 tablespoon oil. Season with salt, pepper, and extra lime juice to taste. Serve. (Beans can be held on warm or low setting for up to 2 hours; adjust consistency with extra hot water as needed before serving.)

Lemon-Herb Pearl Barley Risotto

Prep time: 10 minutes | Cook time: 6 to 8 hours | Serves 2

1 teaspoon extra-virgin olive oil
½ cup minced onion
2 tablespoons minced preserved lemon
1 teaspoon fresh thyme leaves
¼ cup roughly chopped fresh parsley, divided
¾ cup pearl barley
2 cups low-sodium vegetable broth
⅛ teaspoon sea salt
Freshly ground black pepper, to taste
½ lemon, cut into wedges, for garnish

1. Grease the inside of the slow cooker with olive oil. Add the onion, preserved lemon, thyme, 2 tablespoons of the parsley, barley, and vegetable broth. Season with the salt and pepper, and stir thoroughly.
2. Cover and cook on low for 6 to 8 hours, until the barley is tender and all the liquid is absorbed. Garnish each serving with the remaining parsley and a lemon wedge.

White Beans with Pancetta and Carrot

Prep time: 15 minutes | Cook time: 3½ to 4½ hours | Serves 4

1 heaping cup dried cannellini beans
A few slices of pancetta or prosciutto, chopped
¼ cup olive oil
3 shallots, halved
1 medium-size carrot, quartered
2 ribs celery, halved
1 bay leaf
Sprig of fresh thyme or savory
1 (15-ounce / 425-g) can chicken broth
Fine sea salt and freshly ground black pepper, to taste
4 ounces (113 g) fresh goat cheese, such as Chabis or Montrachet, crumbled
½ cup sliced pitted black olives, or your choice, drained

1. Put the beans in a colander and rinse under cold running water, picking over for damaged beans and small stones. Transfer to the slow cooker and cover by 3 inches with cold water. Soak for 6 to 12 hours, drain, and add back to the cooker.
2. In a medium-size skillet over medium-high heat, cook the pancetta in the olive oil, stirring, for 8 minutes. Add the shallots, carrot, and celery and cook, stirring, until just softened. Transfer the mixture to the beans in the cooker along with the bay leaf and herb sprig. Add the broth and enough water to cover the beans by 2 inches.
3. Cover and cook on high for 3½ to 4½ hours. The beans need to be covered with liquid at all times to cook properly. Toward the end of cooking, season with salt and pepper. When done, the beans will be tender and hold their shape, rather than fall apart. Remove the bay leaf and herb sprig and discard.
4. Serve the beans in soup bowls, topped with the crumbled goat cheese and sliced olives.

Braised Chickpeas with Cilantro

Prep time: 10 minutes | Cook time: 8 to 9 hours | Serves 6

1 red onion, halved and thinly sliced
1 tablespoon extra-virgin olive oil
1 tablespoon smoked paprika
Salt and pepper, to taste
3 cups vegetable or chicken broth, plus extra as needed
3 cups water
1 pound (454 g) dried chickpeas, picked over and rinsed
¼ cup minced fresh cilantro

1. Microwave onion, oil, paprika, and 1 teaspoon salt in bowl, stirring occasionally, until onion is softened, about 5 minutes. Transfer to a slow cooker. Stir in broth, water, and chickpeas. Cover and cook until chickpeas are tender, 8 to 9 hours on high.
2. Drain chickpeas, reserving 1 cup cooking liquid. Return one-third of chickpeas and reserved cooking liquid to the slow cooker and mash with potato masher until smooth. Stir in remaining chickpeas and cilantro. Season with salt and pepper to taste. Serve. (Chickpeas can be held on warm or low setting for up to 2 hours; adjust consistency with extra hot broth as needed before serving.)

Garlicky White Beans with Sage

Prep time: 10 minutes | Cook time: 8 to 9 hours | Serves 6

1 onion, finely chopped
5 garlic cloves, minced
3 tablespoons extra-virgin olive oil, divided
2 teaspoons minced fresh sage, divided
Salt and pepper, to taste
3 cups vegetable or chicken broth, plus extra as needed
3 cups water
1 pound (454 g) dried small white beans, picked over and rinsed

1.Microwave onion, garlic, 1 tablespoon oil, 1 teaspoon sage, and 1 teaspoon salt in a bowl, stirring occasionally, until onion is softened, about 5 minutes. Transfer to a slow cooker. Stir in broth, water, and beans. Cover and cook until beans are tender, 8 to 9 hours on high.
2.Drain beans, reserving 1 cup cooking liquid. Return one-third of beans and reserved cooking liquid to the slow cooker and mash with potato masher until smooth. Stir in remaining beans, remaining 2 tablespoons oil, and remaining 1 teaspoon sage. Season with salt and pepper to taste. Serve. (Beans can be held on warm or low setting for up to 2 hours; adjust consistency with extra hot broth as needed before serving.)

Slow Cooker Refried Beans

Prep time: 15 minutes | Cook time: 8 to 9 hours | Serves 6

1 onion, finely chopped
1 poblano chile, stemmed, deseeded, and minced
2 slices bacon
3 garlic cloves, minced
1 tablespoon ground cumin
1 pound (454 g) dried pinto beans, picked over and rinsed
6 cups chicken broth, plus extra as needed
3 tablespoons minced fresh cilantro
1 tablespoon lime juice, plus extra as needed
Salt and pepper, to taste

1.Microwave onion, poblano, bacon, garlic, and cumin in a bowl, stirring occasionally, until vegetables are softened, about 5 minutes. Transfer to a slow cooker. Stir in beans and broth, cover, and cook until beans are tender, 8 to 9 hours on high.

2.Discard bacon. Drain beans, reserving 1 cup cooking liquid. Return beans and reserved cooking liquid to the slow cooker and mash with potato masher until smooth. Stir in cilantro, lime juice, and ½ teaspoon salt. Season with salt, pepper, and extra lime juice to taste. Serve. (Beans can be held on warm or low setting for up to 2 hours; adjust consistency with extra hot broth as needed before serving.)

Traditional Boston Baked Beans

Prep time: 10 minutes | Cook time: 11½ to 13½ hours | Serves 6 to 8

1 pound (454 g) dried small white navy or pea beans
½ teaspoon baking soda
1 (8-ounce / 227-g) piece salt pork
½ cup dark molasses
½ cup firmly packed light or dark brown sugar
1½ teaspoons dry mustard
1½ teaspoons salt
¼ teaspoon freshly ground black pepper
1 medium-size white onion, peeled, left whole, and scored with a crisscross through the root end
6 cups boiling water

1.Rinse the beans in a colander under cold running water and pick over for damaged beans and small stones. Transfer to the slow cooker. Cover with cold water by 2 inches, soak overnight, and then drain.
2.Cover the beans with fresh water by 3 inches. Add the baking soda, cover, and cook on high until still undercooked, about 1½ hours. Drain.
3.Meanwhile, simmer the salt pork in boiling water for 10 minutes to remove excess salt. Drain and rinse under cold running water. Pat dry and dice.
4.Combine the drained beans, salt pork, molasses, brown sugar, mustard, salt, and pepper in the cooker, stirring to mix well. Push the onion into the center of the beans and add the boiling water (it will cover everything by ½ inch). Cover and cook on high to bring to a boil, then reduce the heat to low and cook until the beans are soft, thick, and bubbling, 10 to 12 hours. Do not stir, but you can add more boiling water to keep the beans moist if you need to. Traditionally, the beans are cooked with the cover off for the last 30 minutes to thicken them to the desired consistency. Serve.

Tuscan-Style White Beans with Herbs

Prep time: 10 minutes | Cook time: 2½ to 3½ hours | Serves 6

2½ cups dried white beans, such as great northern or navy
2 sprigs fresh sage
1 bay leaf
1 head garlic, left whole and unpeeled
10 cups water
1 tablespoon coarse sea salt, or more to taste
A few grinds of black pepper
Extra-virgin olive oil, for serving

1. Put the beans in a colander and rinse under cold running water, picking over for damaged beans and small stones. Transfer to the slow cooker and cover by 3 inches with cold water. Soak for 6 to 12 hours and then drain.
2. Add the sage, bay leaf, garlic, and 10 cups of water. Cover and cook on high for 2½ to 3½ hours. The beans need to be covered with liquid at all times to cook properly. When done, they will be tender and hold their shape, rather than fall apart. Toward the end of the cooking time, add the sea salt and remove the bay leaf and head of garlic (you can squeeze the cooked garlic back into the beans if you like or discard).
3. Let the beans cool in the cooker for 1 hour, uncovered, then drain off all but ½ cup of the liquid. Serve, seasoned with more salt and several grinds of black pepper, and drizzled with olive oil.

Mexican Black Bean and Pork Stew

Prep time: 15 minutes | Cook time: 8 to 9 hours | Serves 4 to 6

1 pound (454 g) boneless pork loin, trimmed of any fat and cut into 1-inch cubes
1 teaspoon chili powder
1 teaspoon ground coriander
Salt, to taste
1 medium-size yellow onion, chopped
1 garlic clove, minced
2 (15-ounce / 425-g) cans black beans, rinsed and drained
1 (16-ounce / 454-g) can stewed tomatoes, coarsely chopped, with their juice

2 cups water
Freshly ground black pepper, to taste
For Serving:
Hot cooked white rice
¼ cup chopped fresh cilantro, for garnish

1. Toss the pork with the chili powder, coriander, and salt until coated evenly. Heat a large ungreased skillet over medium-high heat, then lightly brown the pork with the onion and garlic, stirring.
2. Transfer the pork mixture to the slow cooker, stir in the beans, tomatoes with their juice, and water. Season with pepper, cover, and cook on low for 8 to 9 hours.
3. Serve the beans and pork ladled over steamed white rice and garnished with cilantro.

Molasses Baked Soybeans

Prep time: 10 minutes | Cook time: 9 to 10 hours | Serves 4 to 5

1 cup dried soybeans
4 cups water, or more to cover
½ medium-size yellow onion, sliced into half-moons
¼ cup firmly packed light or dark brown sugar
¼ cup molasses
1 teaspoon salt
½ teaspoon dry mustard
2 tablespoons toasted or black sesame oil

1. Rinse the beans in a colander under cold running water and pick over for damaged beans and small stones. Transfer to the slow cooker. Cover with cold water by 2 inches, soak 6 to 12 hours, and drain.
2. Cover with the 4 cups water. Cover and cook on high until tender, about 4 hours. The beans need to be covered with liquid at all times to cook properly.
3. Drain the cooked beans and return them to the cooker. Add the onion, brown sugar, molasses, salt, mustard, and sesame oil, stirring to combine. Cover and cook on low for 5 to 6 hours, until the soybeans are flavorful but still moist and the onion is soft. Stir gently so as not to mash the beans and serve hot.

Appendix 1: Measurement Conversion Chart

VOLUME EQUIVALENTS(DRY)

US STANDARD	METRIC (APPROXIMATE)
1/8 teaspoon	0.5 mL
1/4 teaspoon	1 mL
1/2 teaspoon	2 mL
3/4 teaspoon	4 mL
1 teaspoon	5 mL
1 tablespoon	15 mL
1/4 cup	59 mL
1/2 cup	118 mL
3/4 cup	177 mL
1 cup	235 mL
2 cups	475 mL
3 cups	700 mL
4 cups	1 L

VOLUME EQUIVALENTS(LIQUID)

US STANDARD	US STANDARD (OUNCES)	METRIC (APPROXIMATE)
2 tablespoons	1 fl.oz.	30 mL
1/4 cup	2 fl.oz.	60 mL
1/2 cup	4 fl.oz.	120 mL
1 cup	8 fl.oz.	240 mL
1 1/2 cup	12 fl.oz.	355 mL
2 cups or 1 pint	16 fl.oz.	475 mL
4 cups or 1 quart	32 fl.oz.	1 L
1 gallon	128 fl.oz.	4 L

TEMPERATURES EQUIVALENTS

FAHRENHEIT(F)	CELSIUS(C) (APPROXIMATE)
225 °F	107 °C
250 °F	120 °C
275 °F	135 °C
300 °F	150 °C
325 °F	160 °C
350 °F	180 °C
375 °F	190 °C
400 °F	205 °C
425 °F	220 °C
450 °F	235 °C
475 °F	245 °C
500 °F	260 °C

WEIGHT EQUIVALENTS

US STANDARD	METRIC (APPROXIMATE)
1 ounce	28 g
2 ounces	57 g
5 ounces	142 g
10 ounces	284 g
15 ounces	425 g
16 ounces (1 pound)	455 g
1.5 pounds	680 g
2 pounds	907 g

Reference

Aprons at the ready, let's go! Make some time to try out these recipes this weekend. Sit down, open the book, and find one that really sparks your imagination. It's good to kick off with a dish that you know and love, because you will have a good idea of how it should look and taste. Leave the experiments until you have got the hang of your slow cooker, if this is the first time you have used one. But, even if you are a slow cooker afficionado, it's good to try out something familiar when you are working with a new book. As you cook your way through the recipes (there are five hundred, this might take a while!) it might be fun to make some notes, so that you can tweak and personalize the dishes, or simply rate your results.

The most important aspect of preparing these recipes in your slow cooker is the fun! Cooking is meant to be relaxing and creative, whatever method you use, whatever style of food you enjoy most. So, dust off your chef's hat, sharpen your knives, tie on that apron, and go for it. Just remember: take it slow!

Printed in Great Britain
by Amazon

52081686R00102